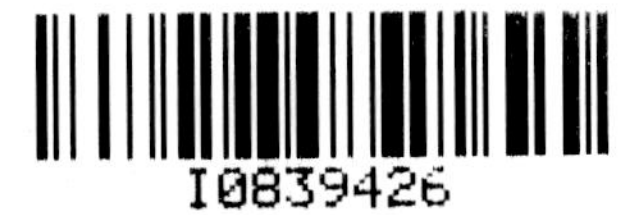

Adult Coloring Book

100 Mandalas

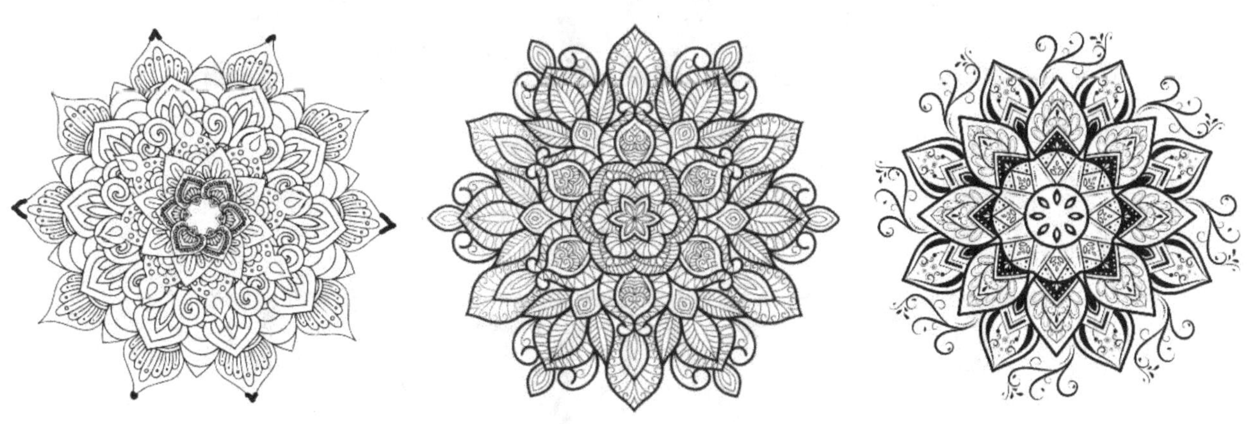

Featuring 100 Of The Most Beautiful Mandalas
For Stress Relief And Relaxation

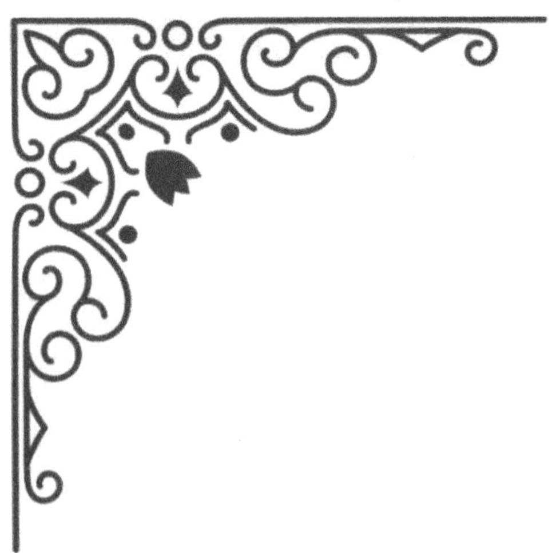
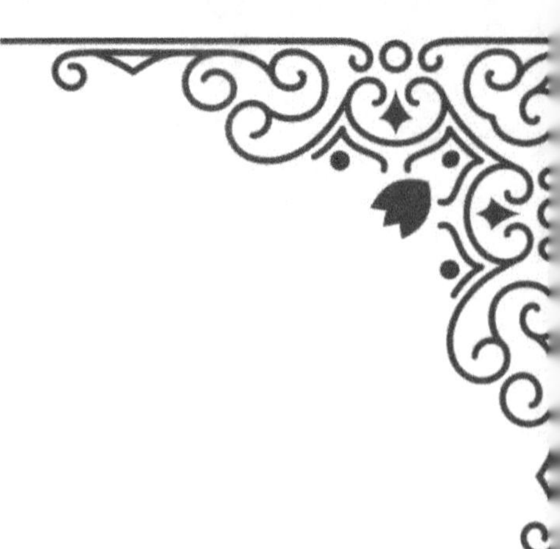

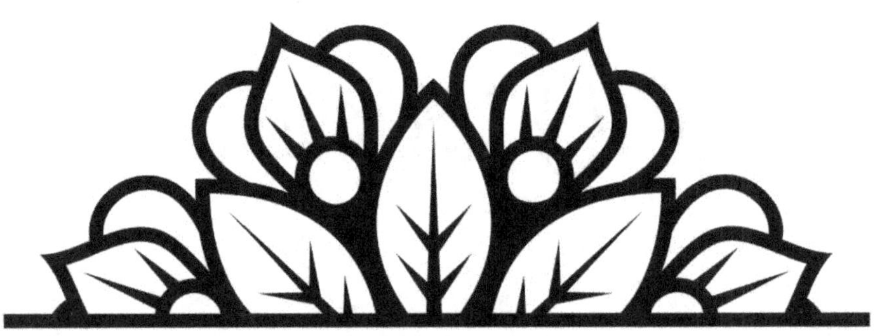

This Book Belongs To

....

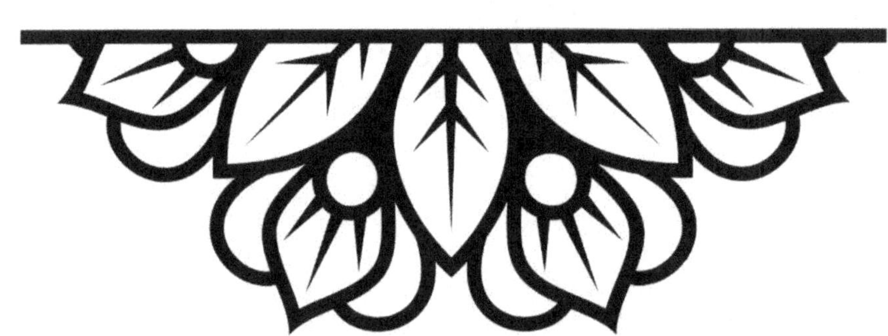

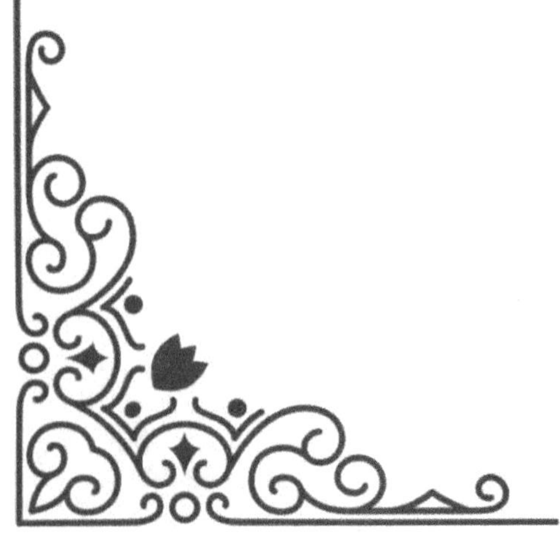
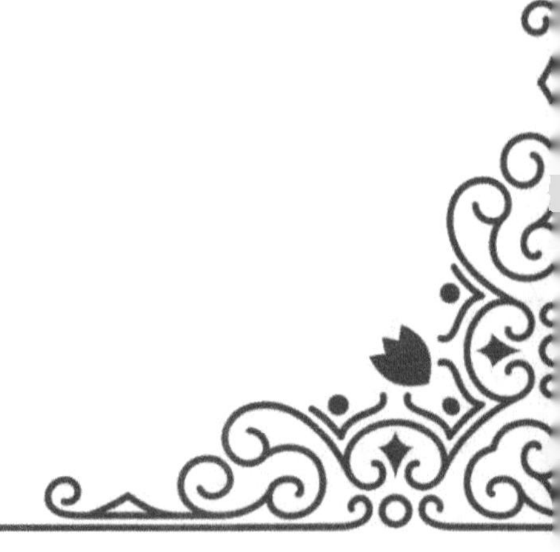

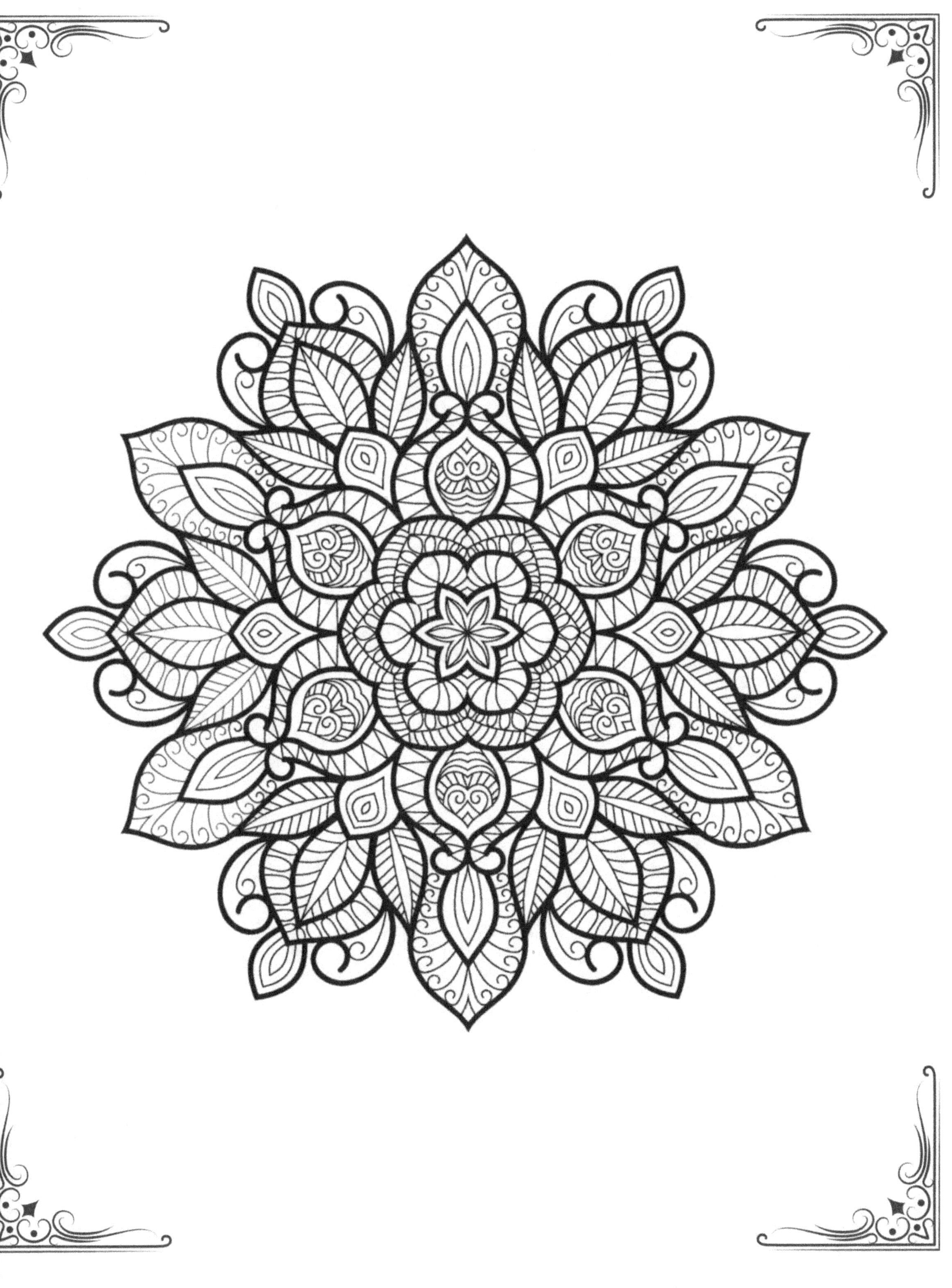

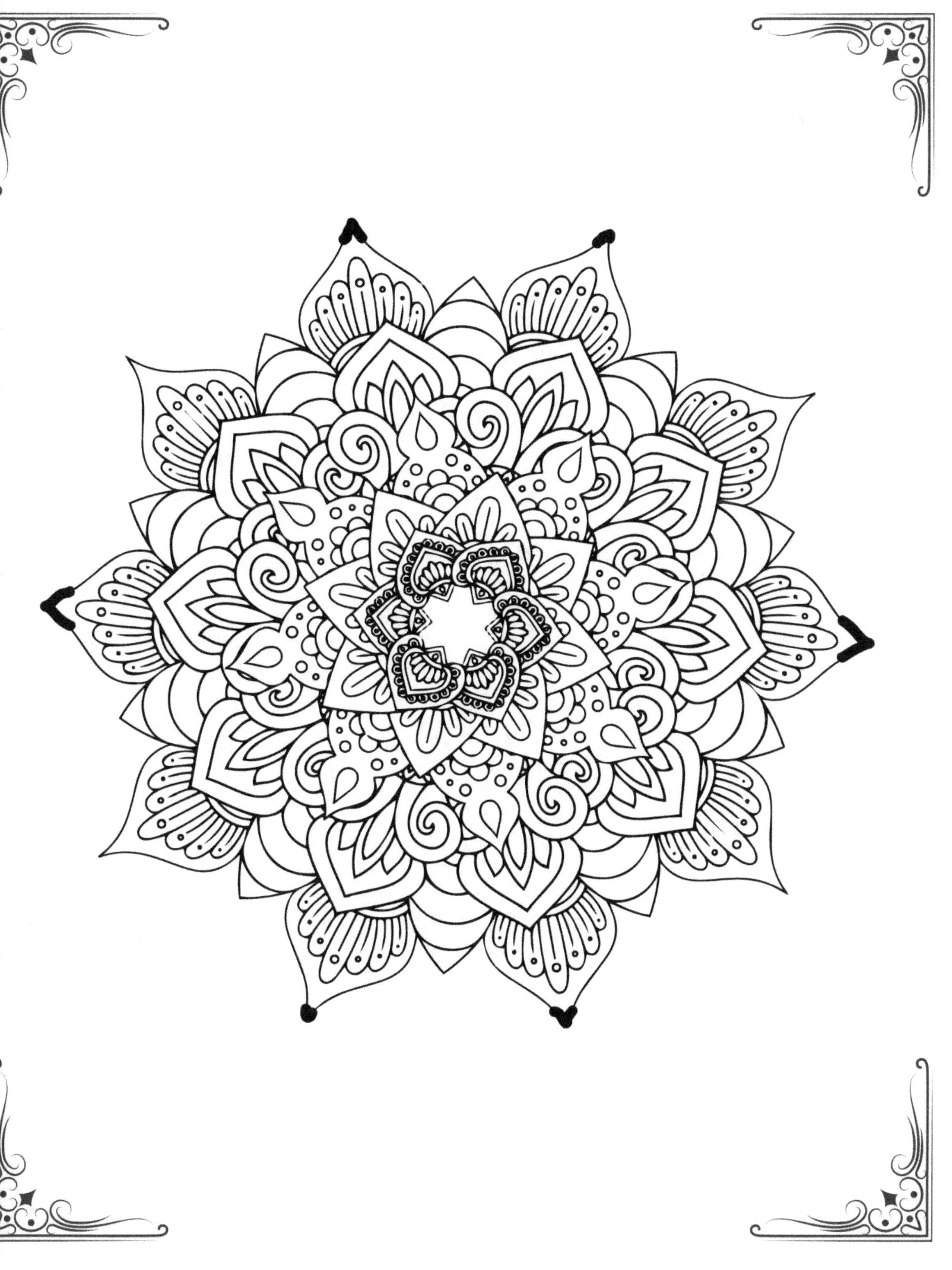

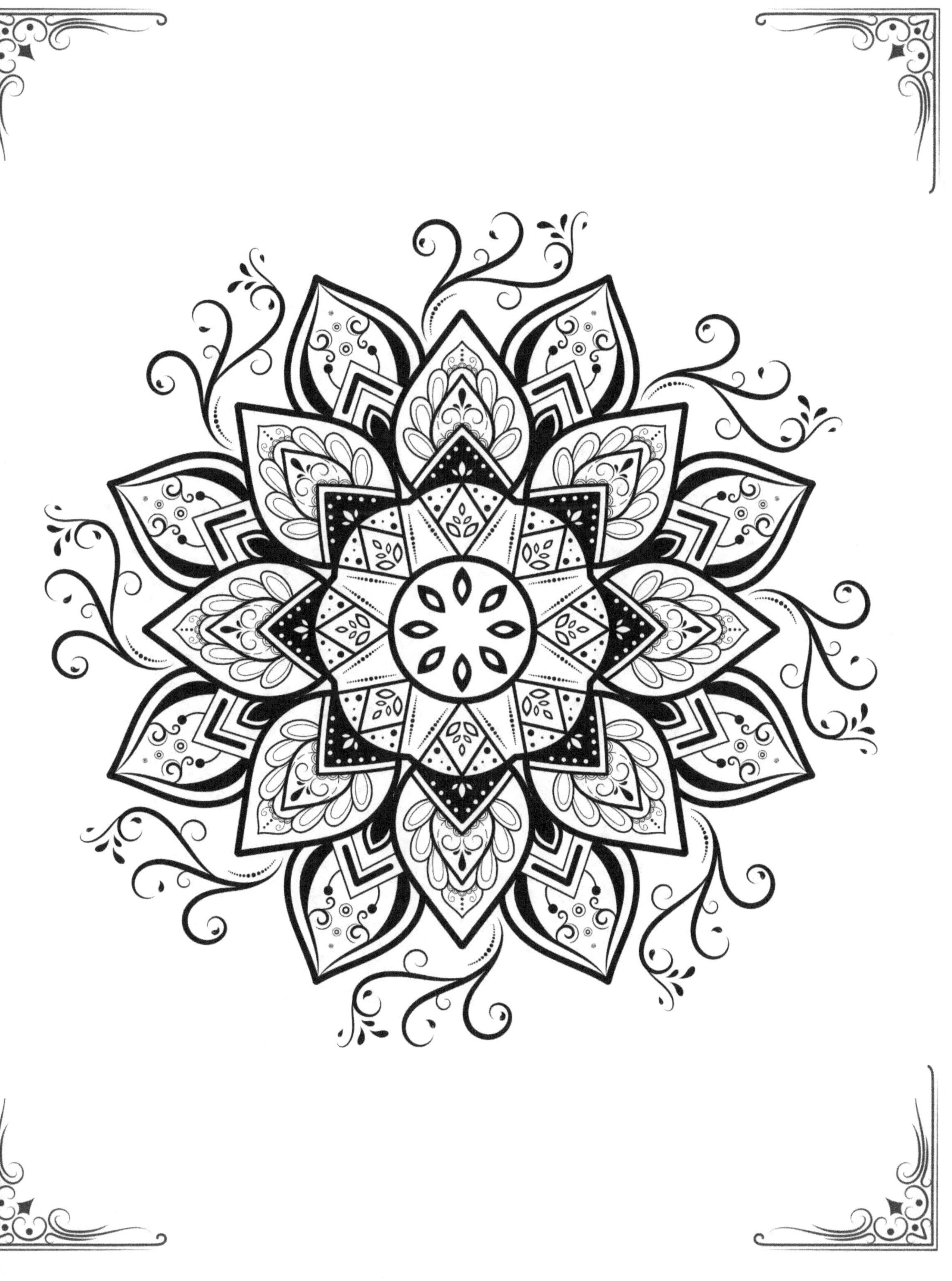

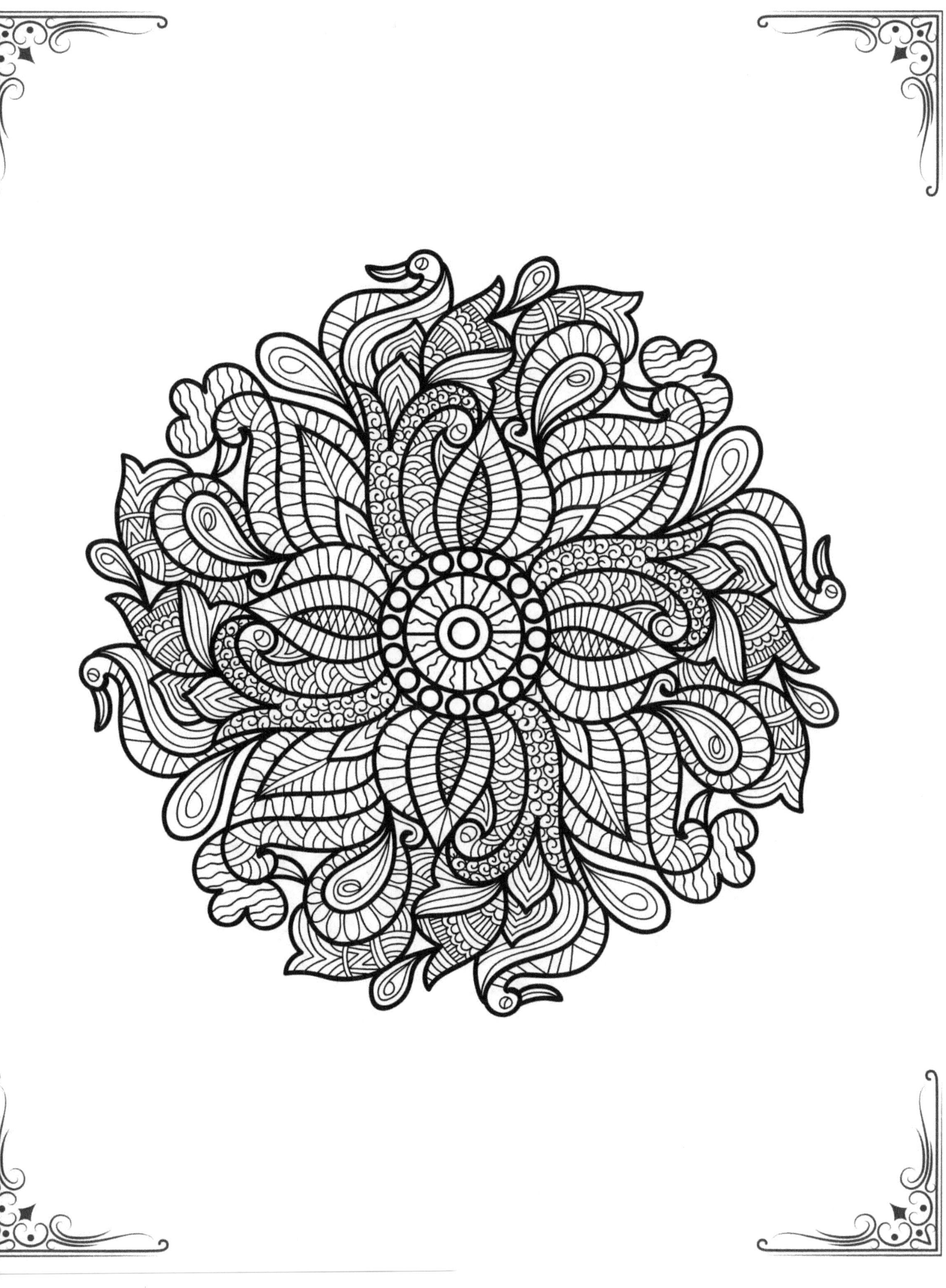

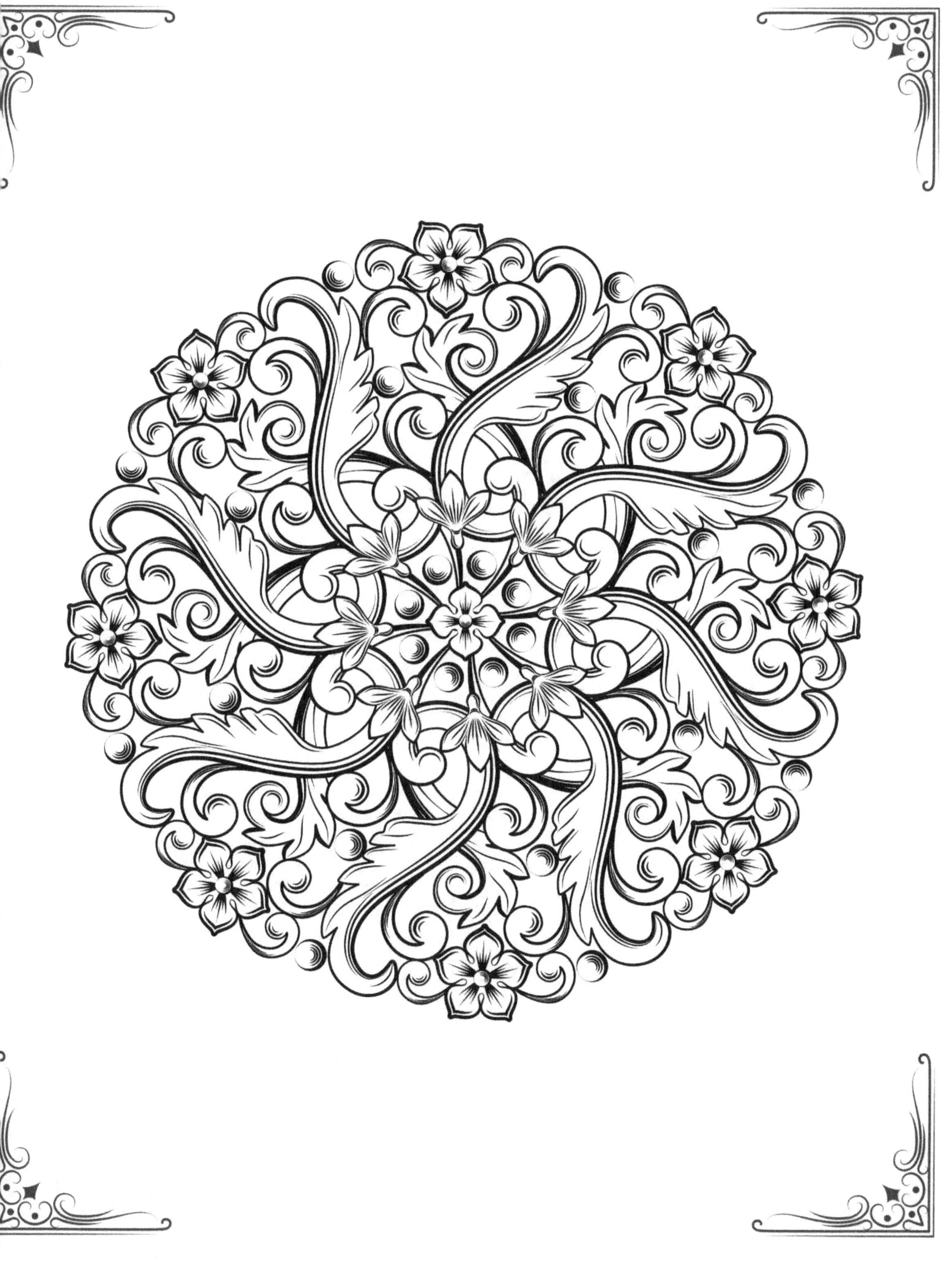

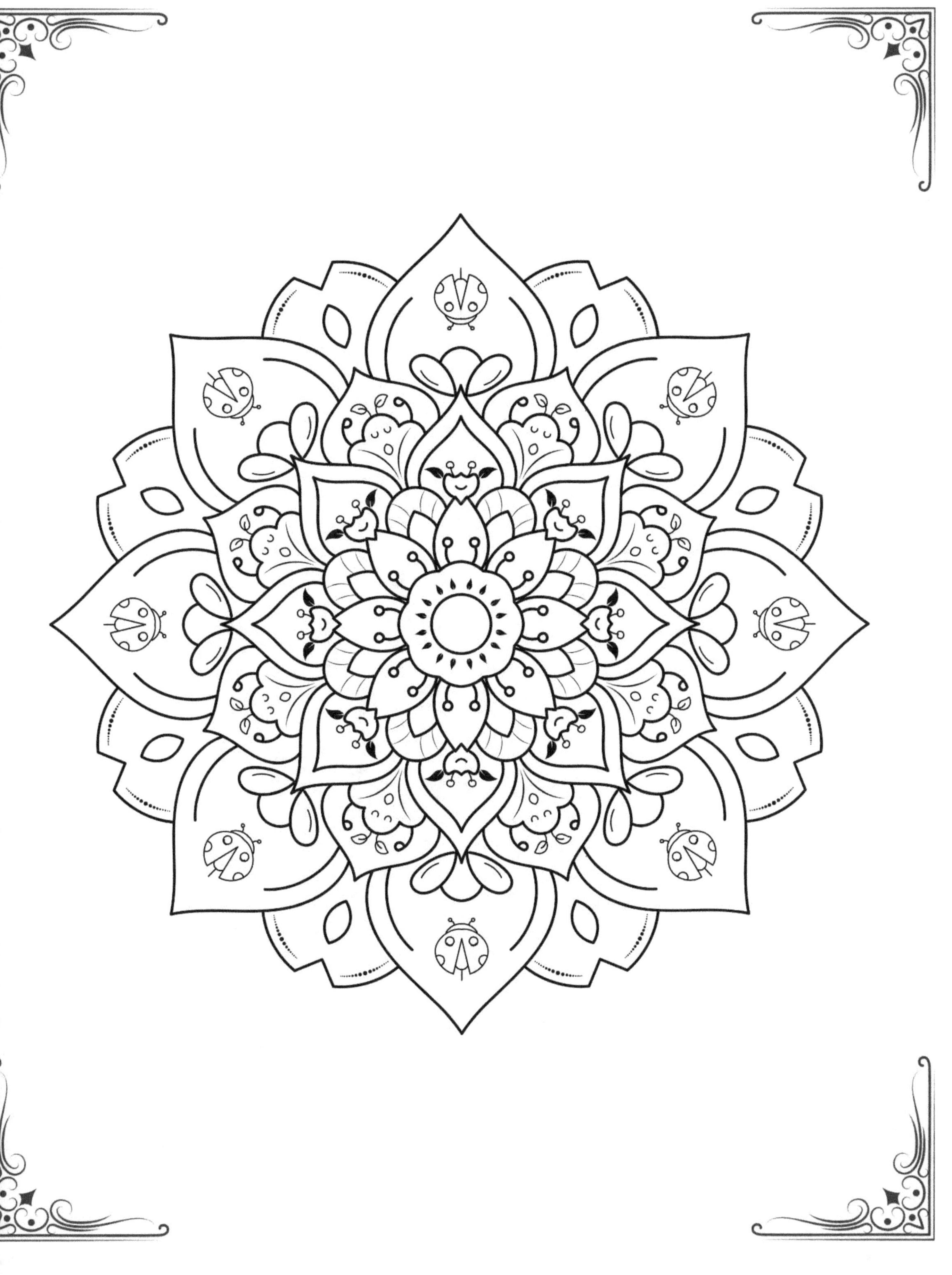

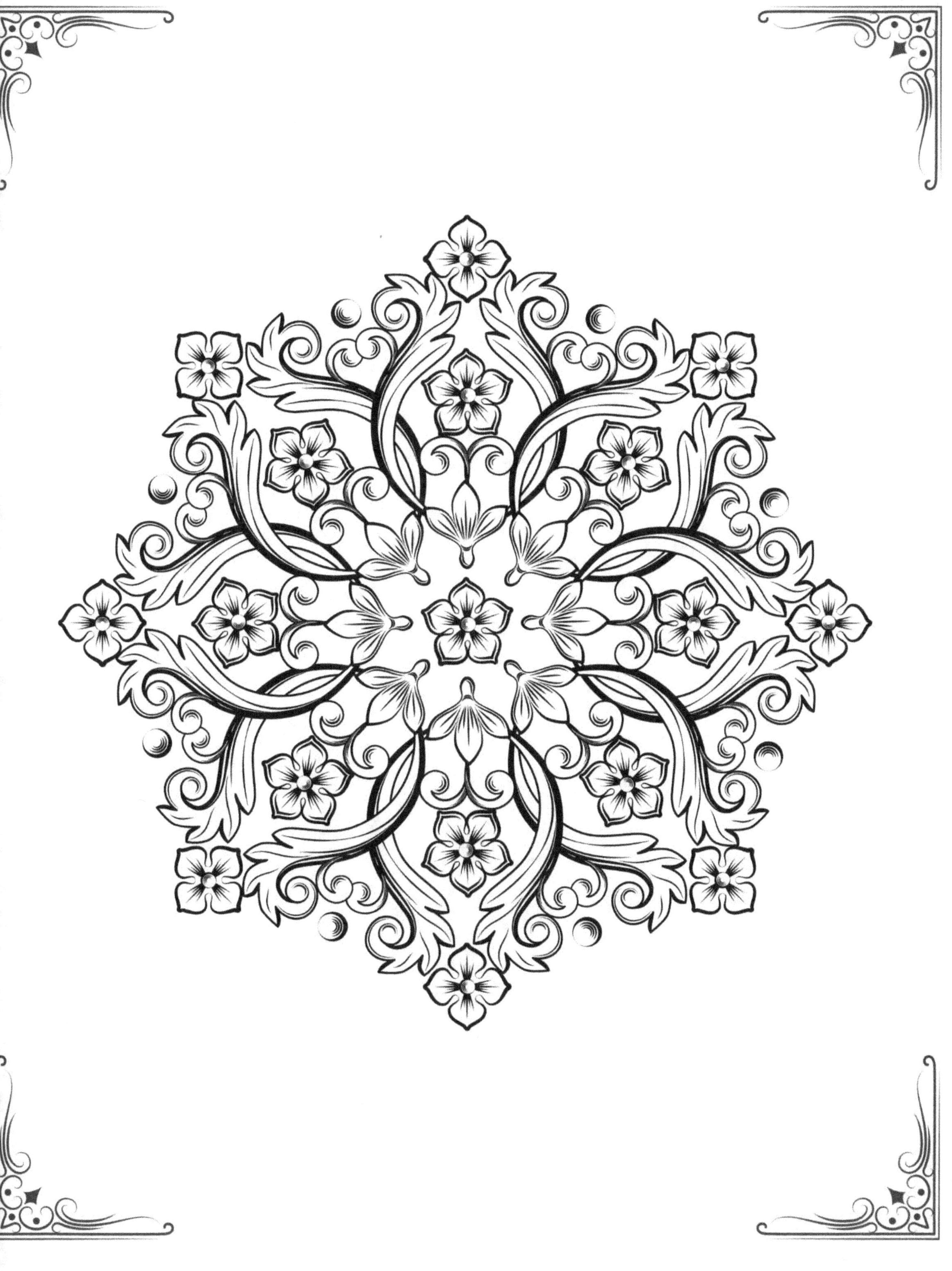

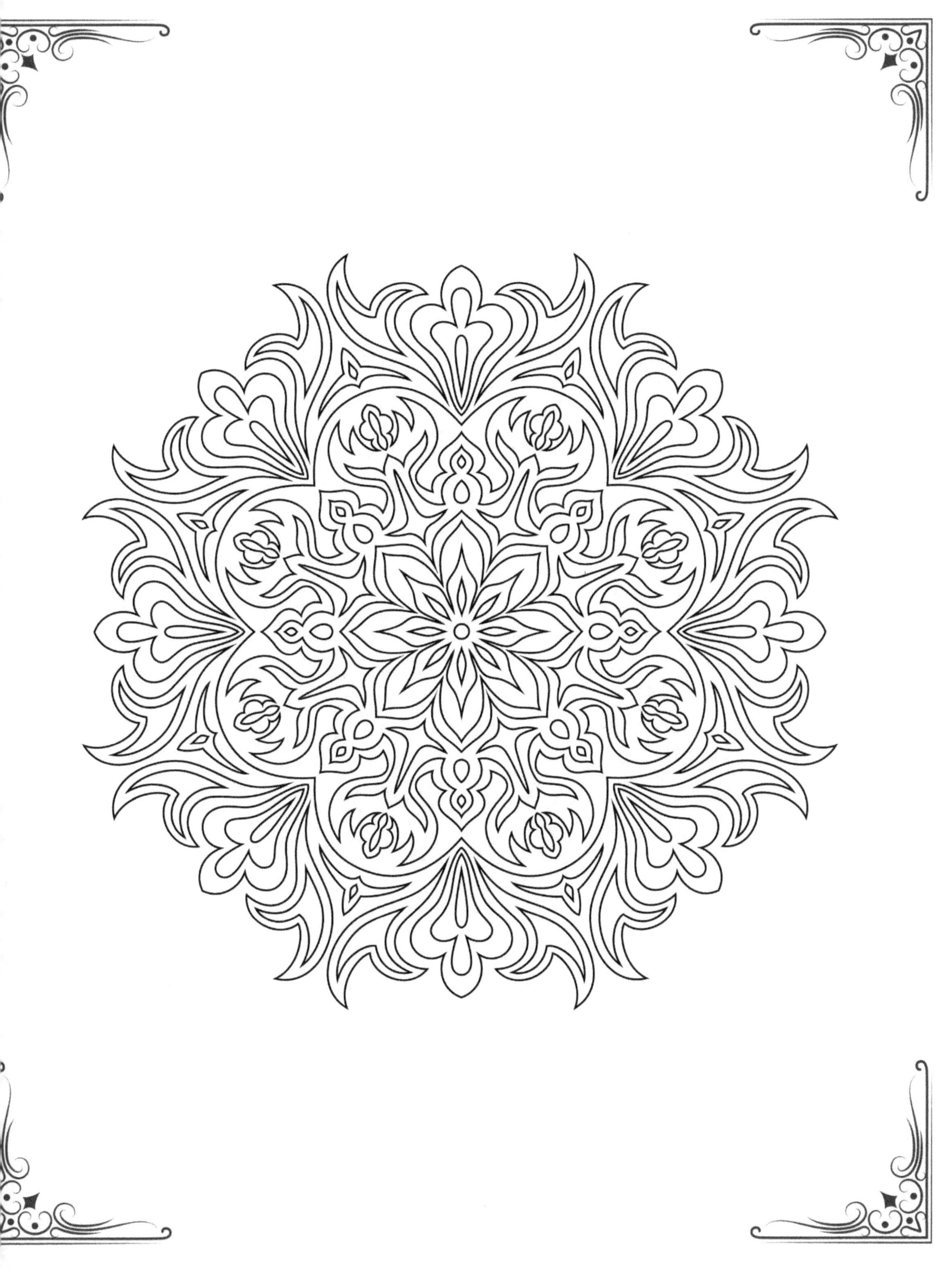

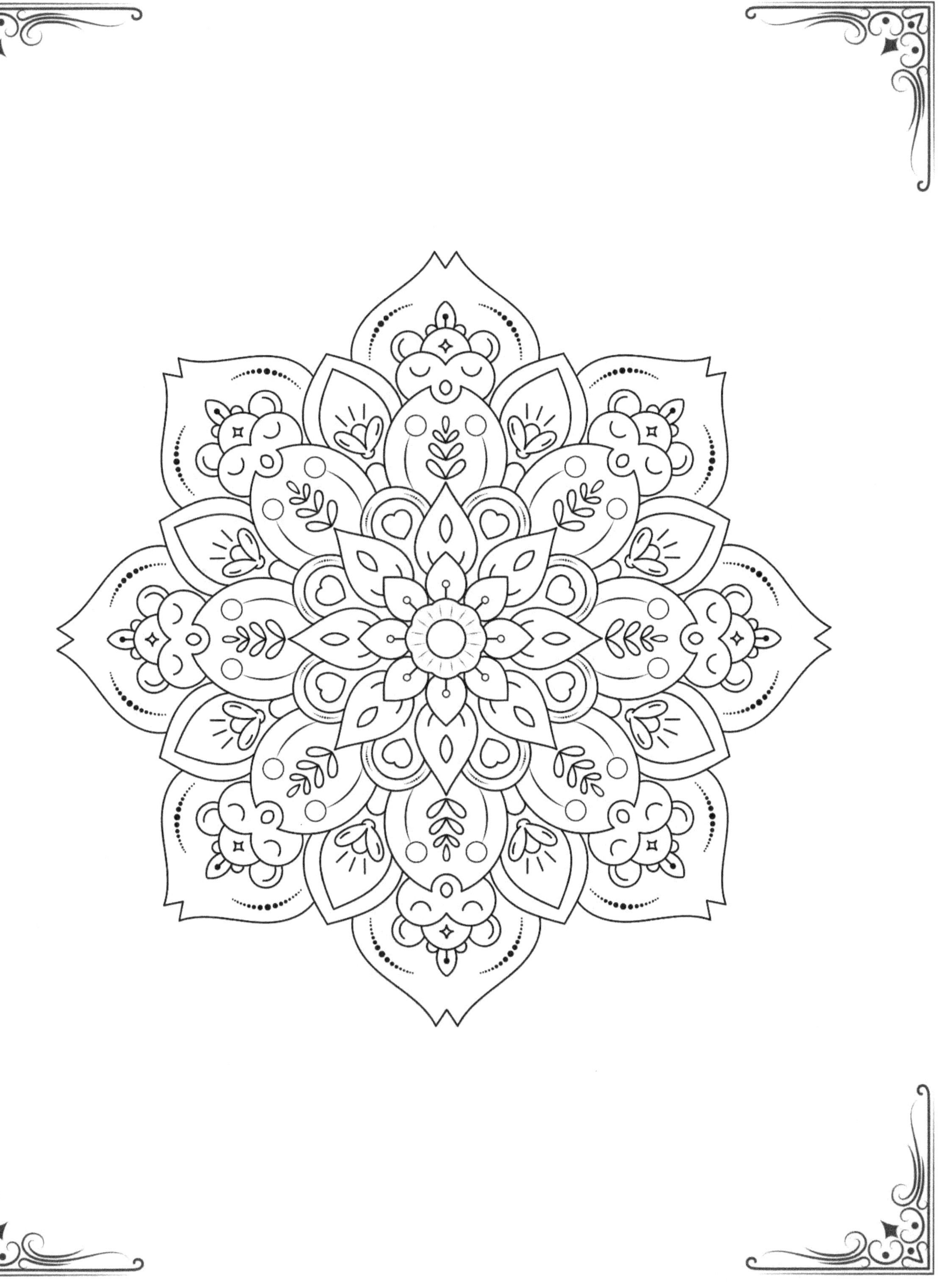

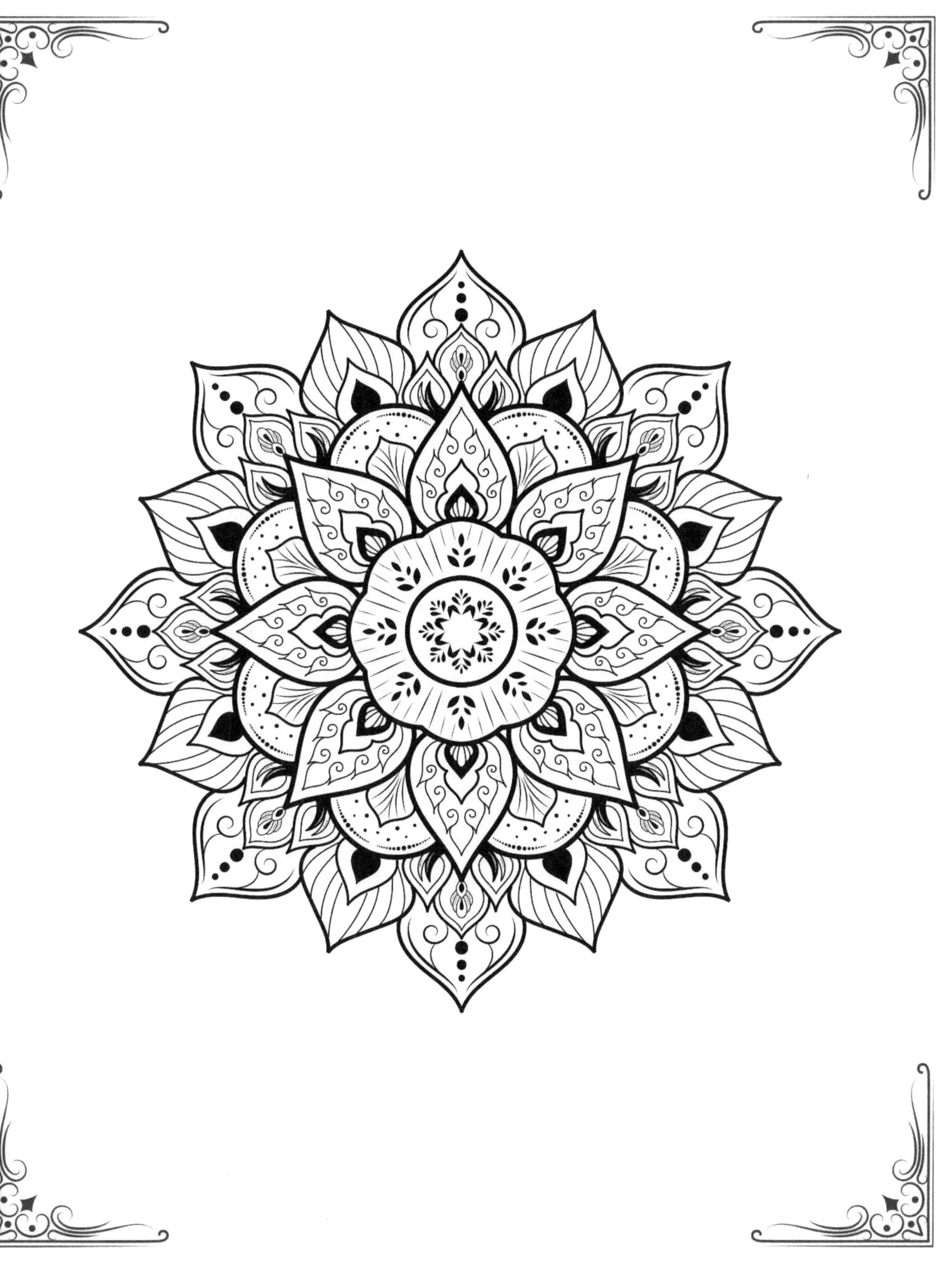

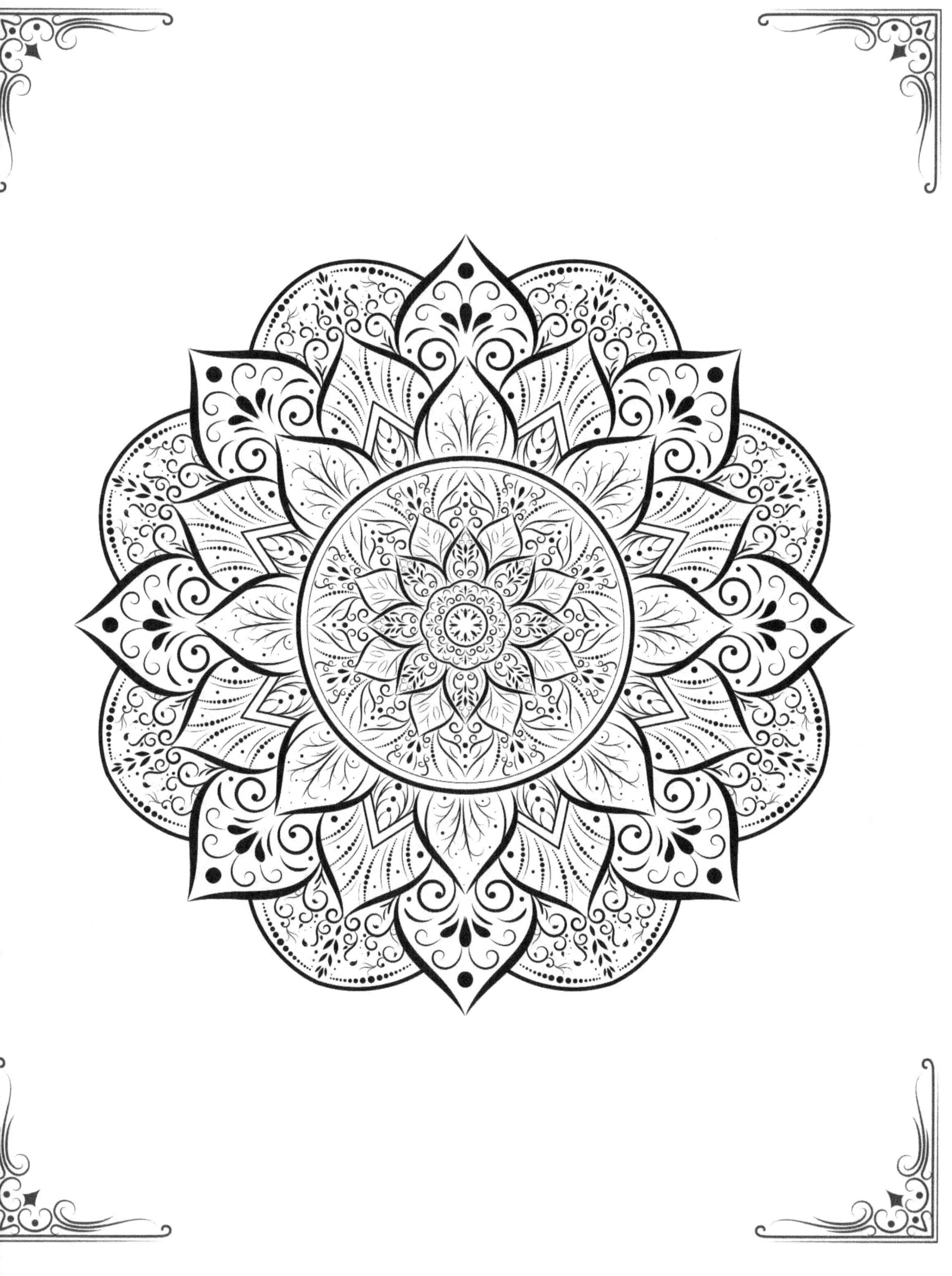

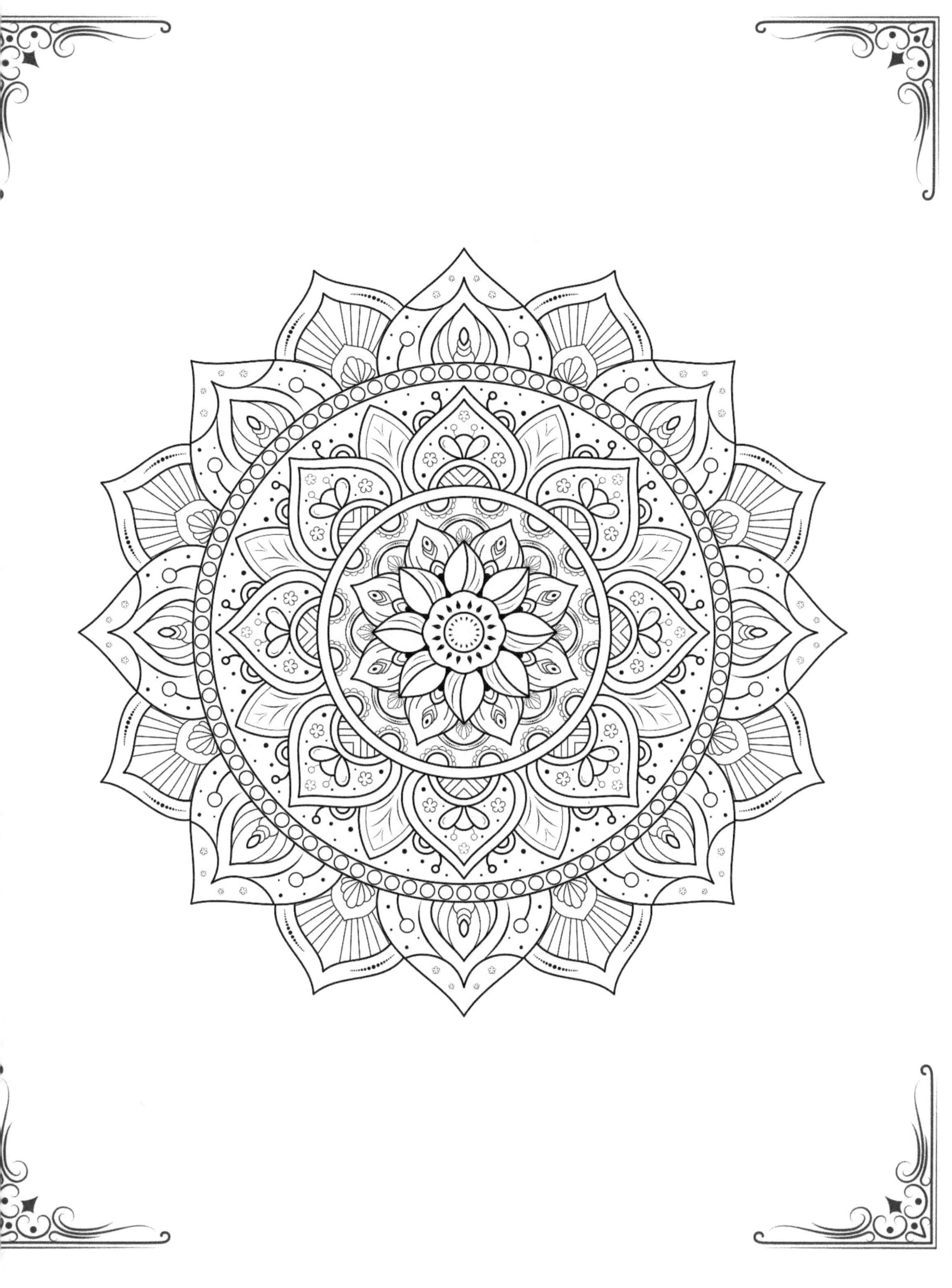

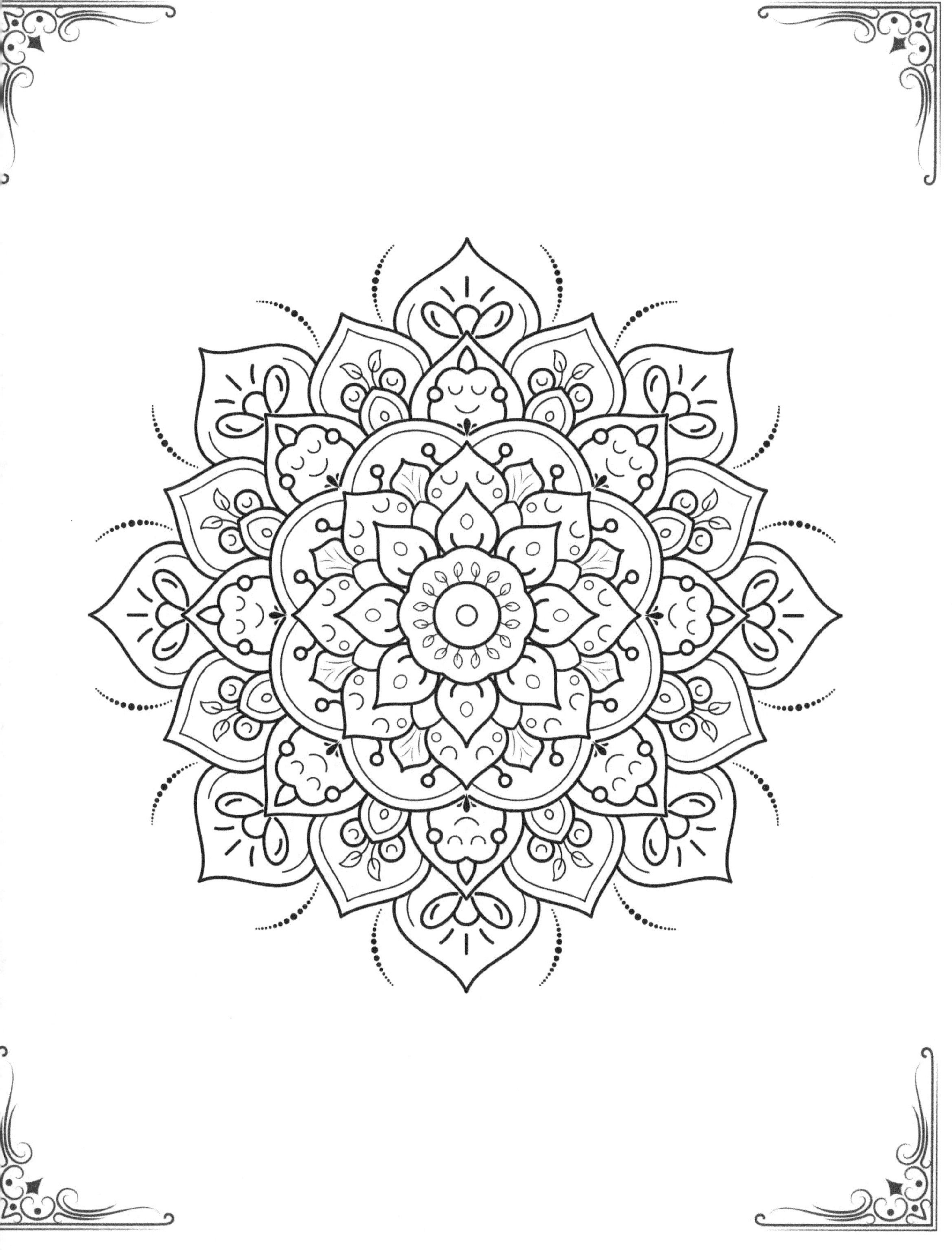

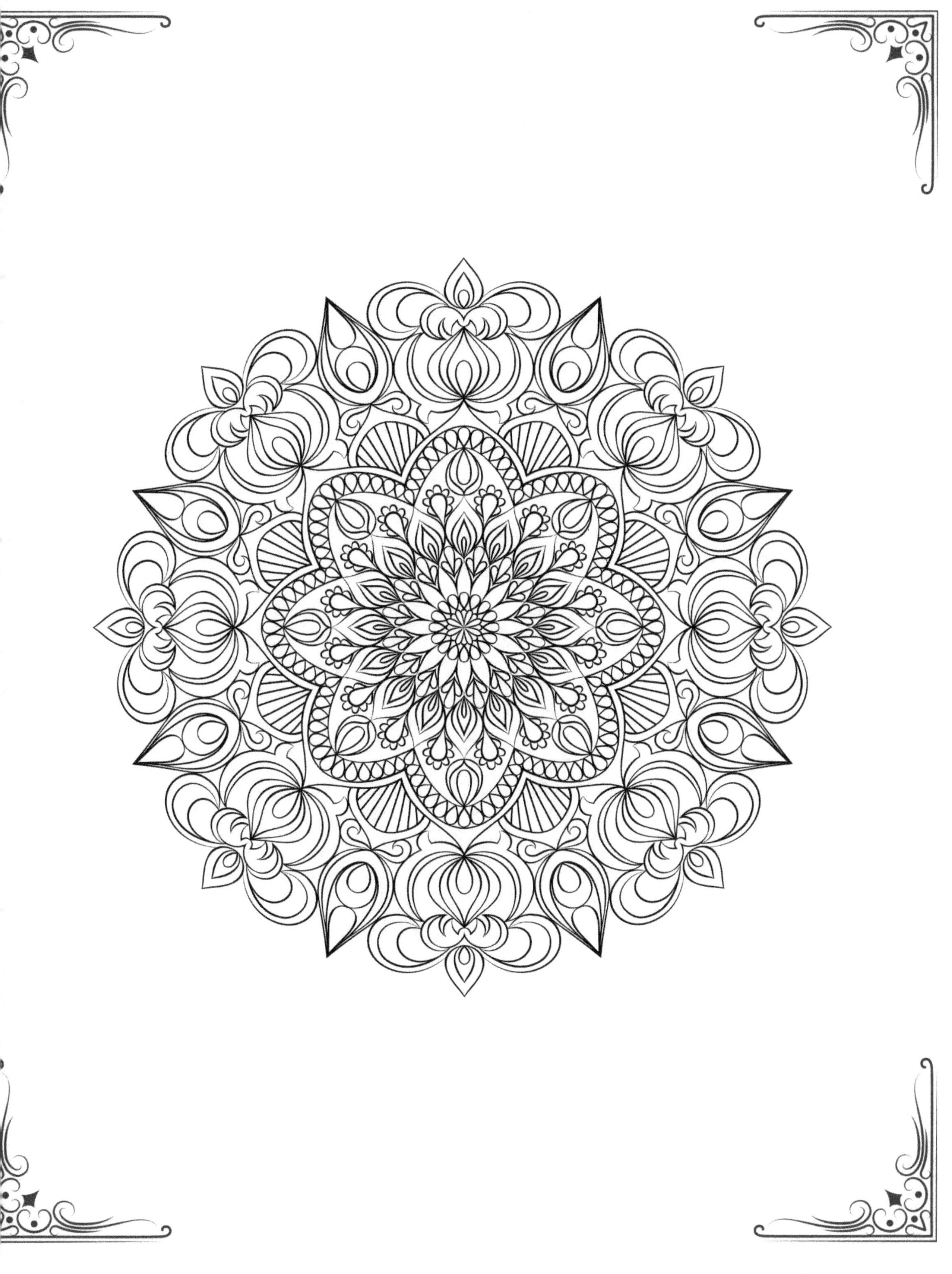

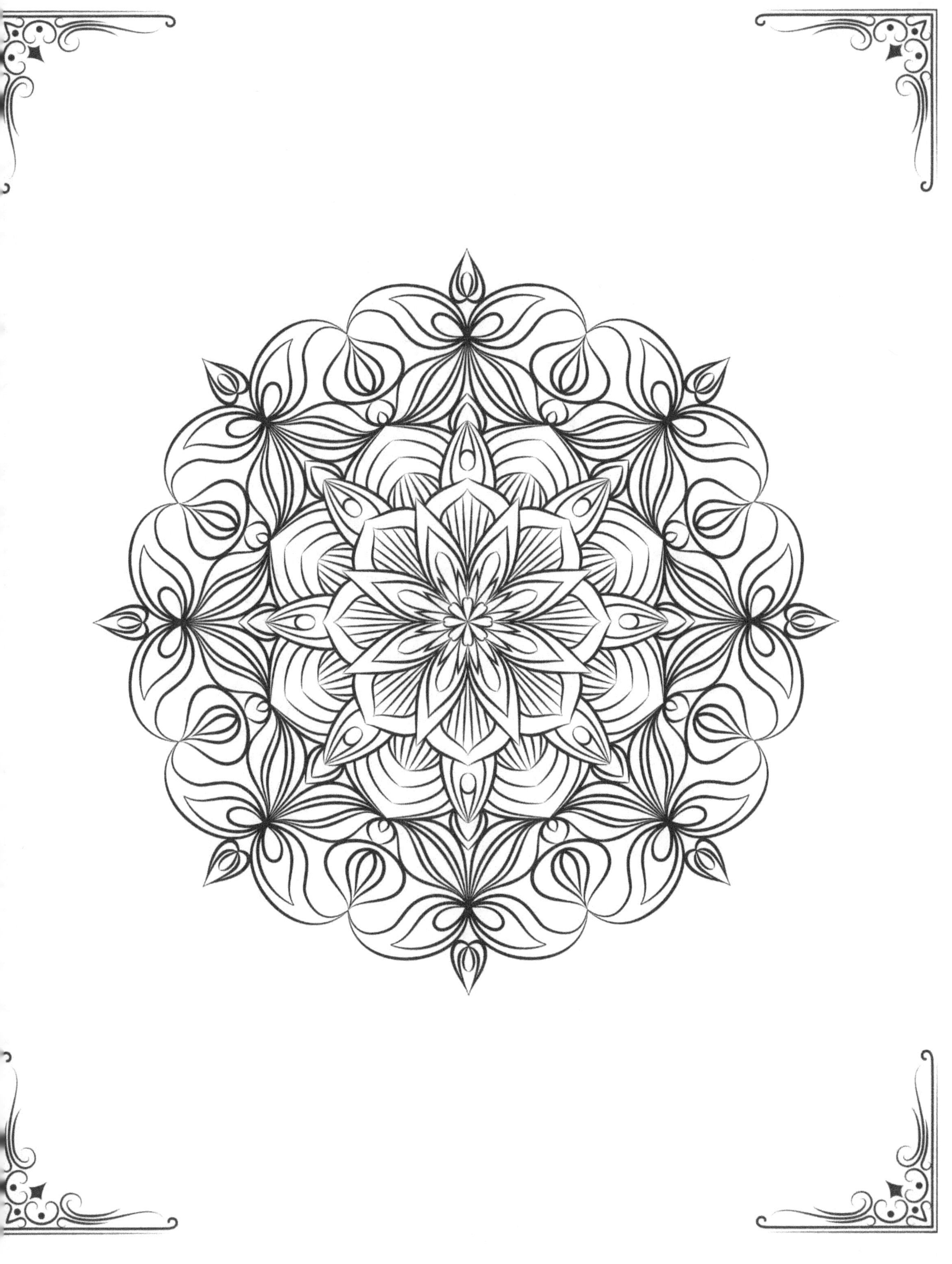

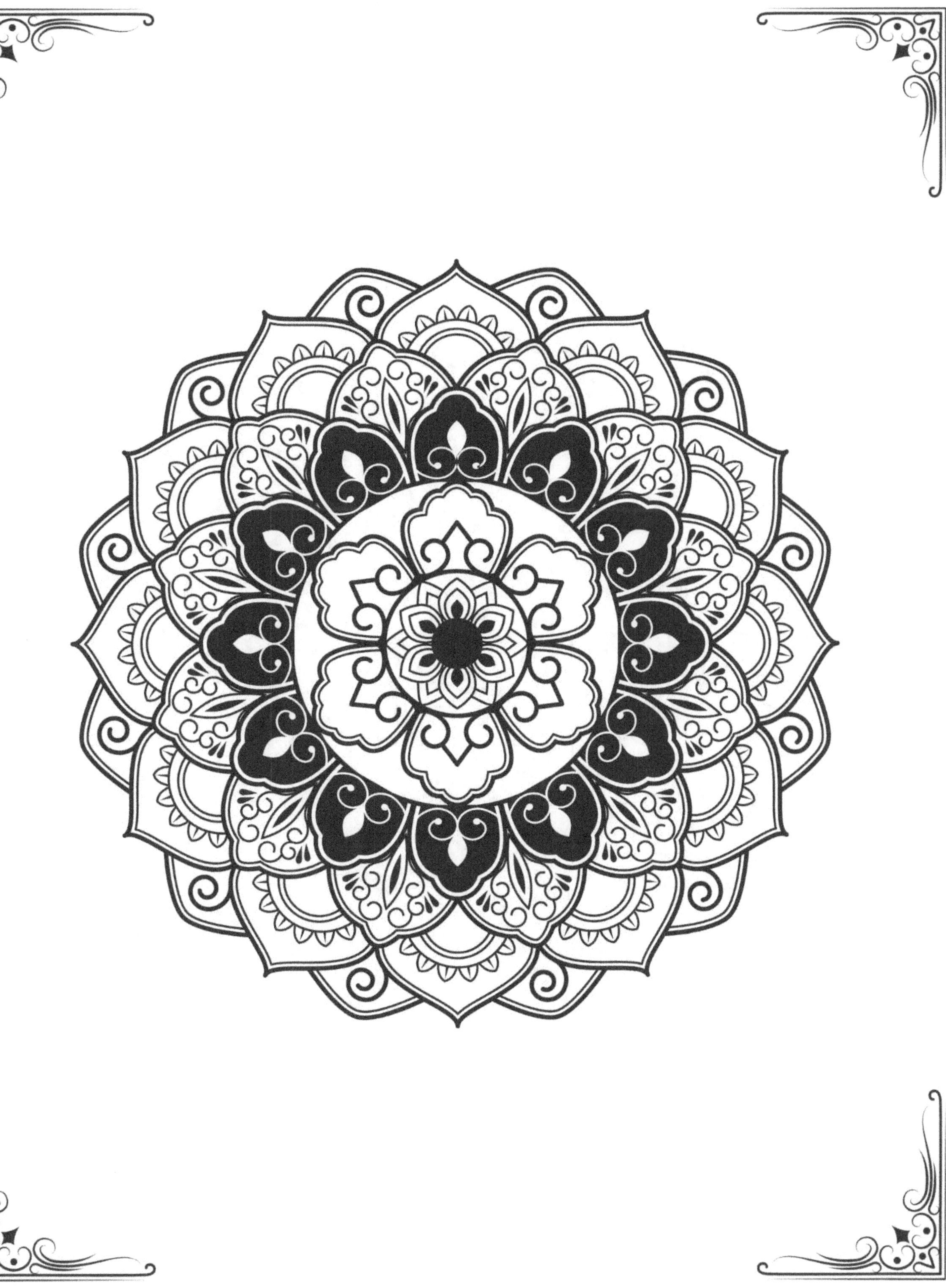

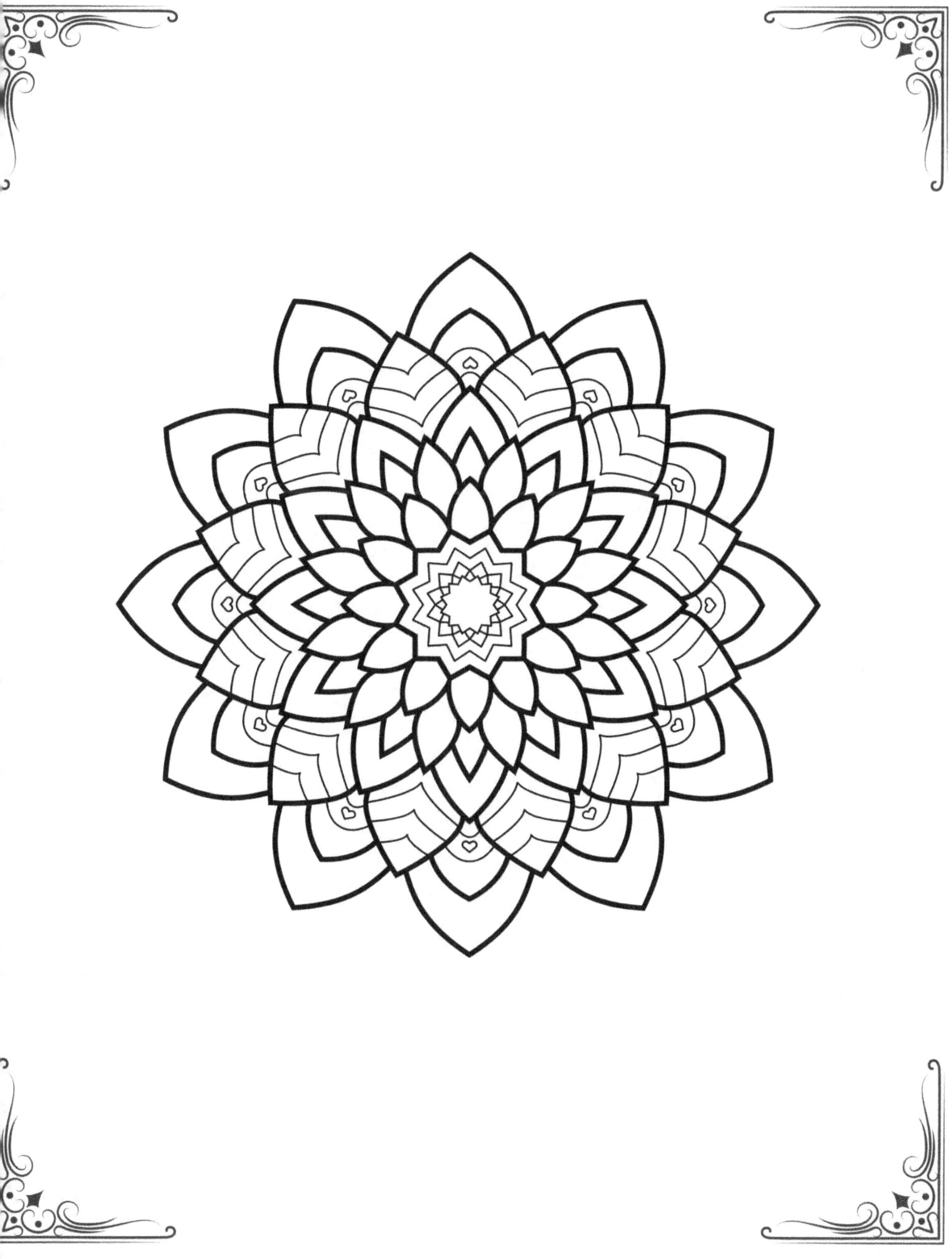

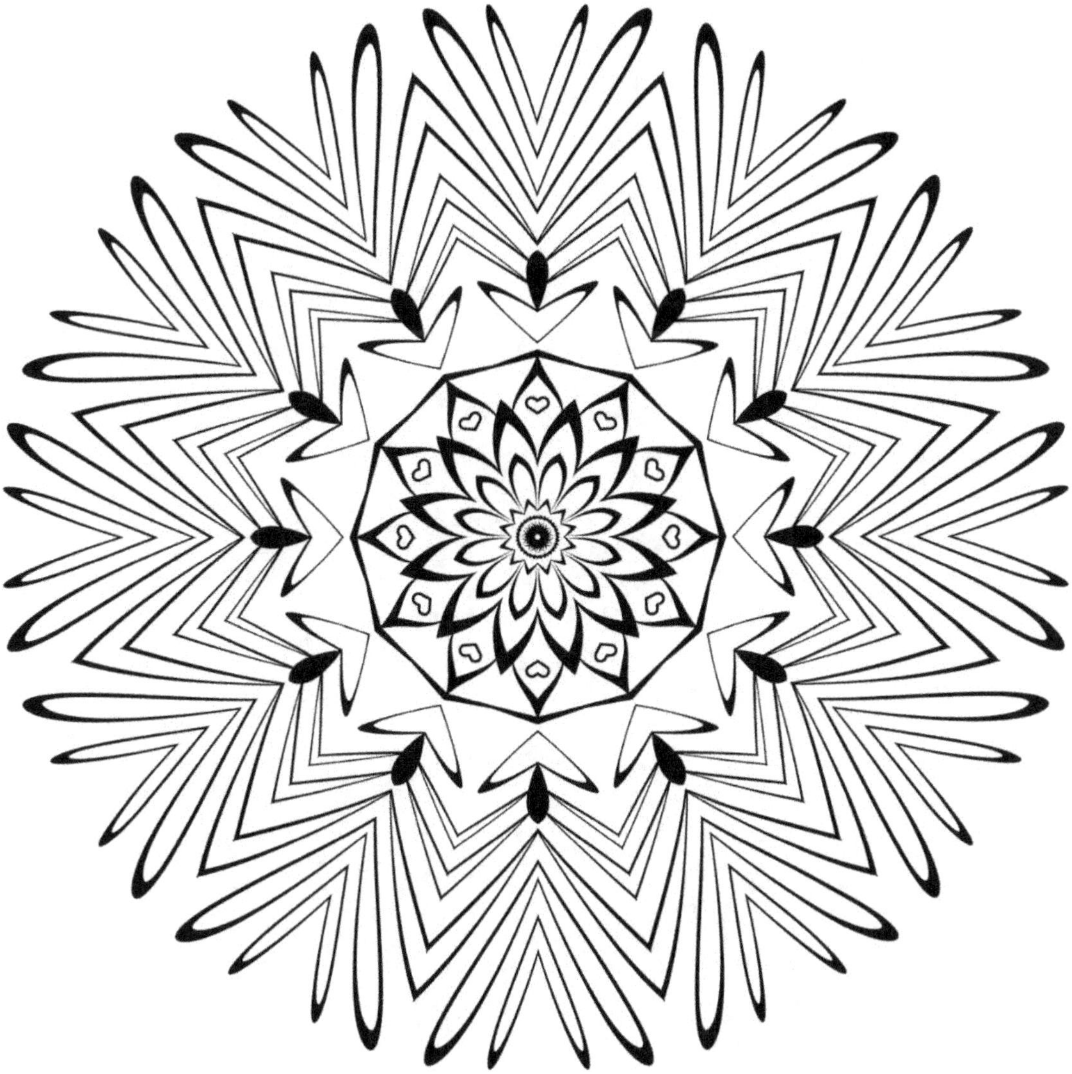

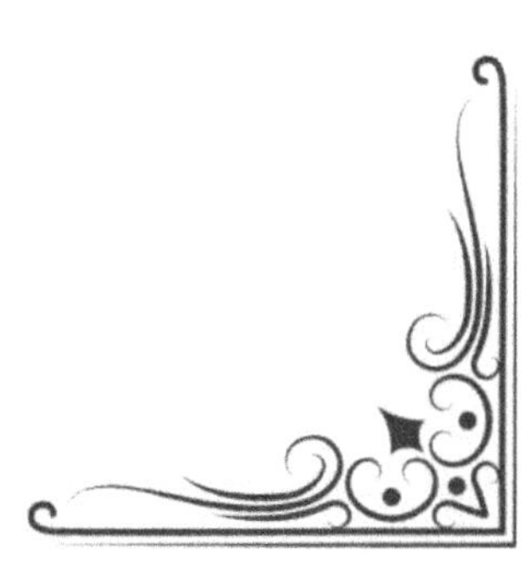

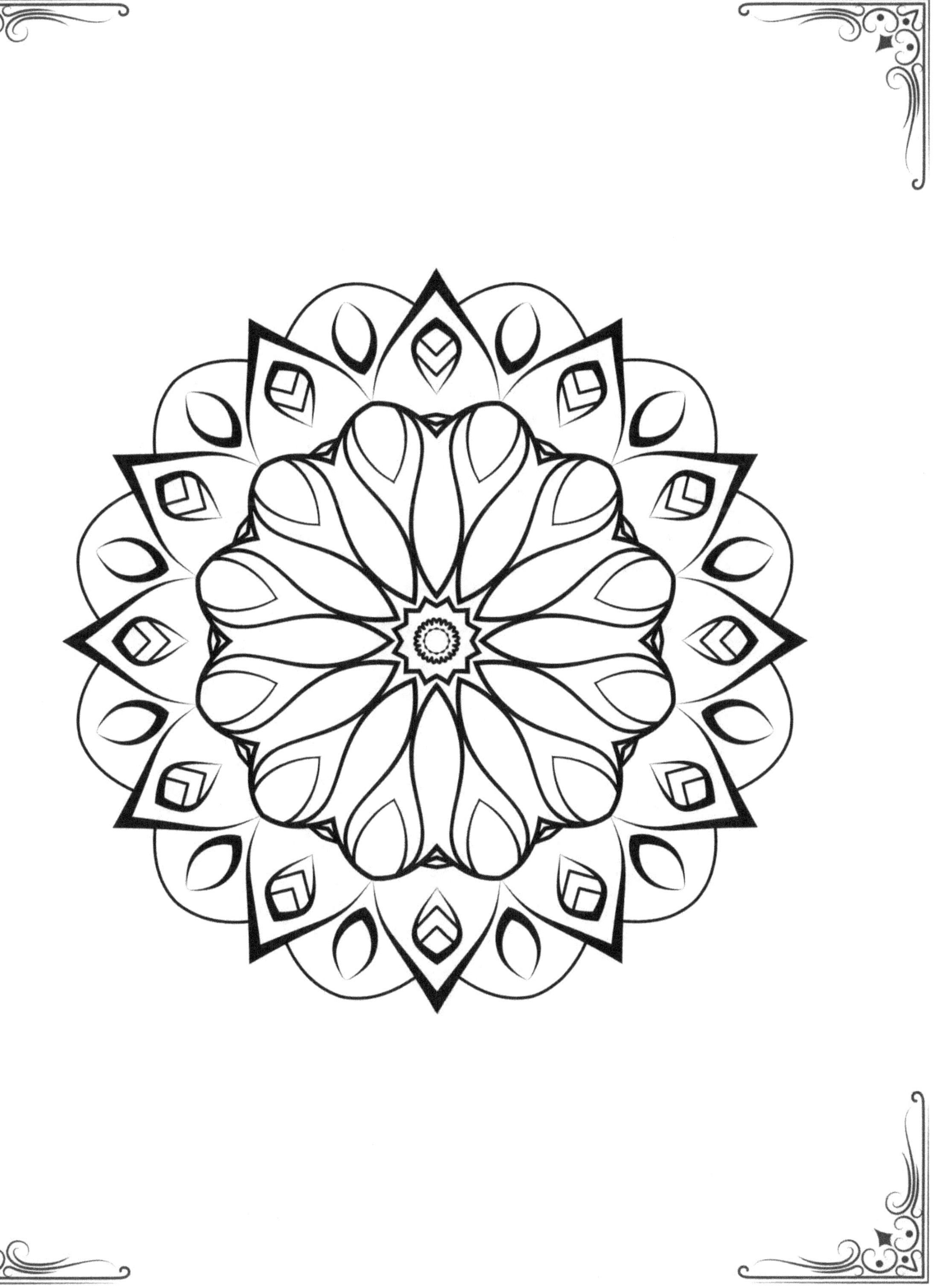

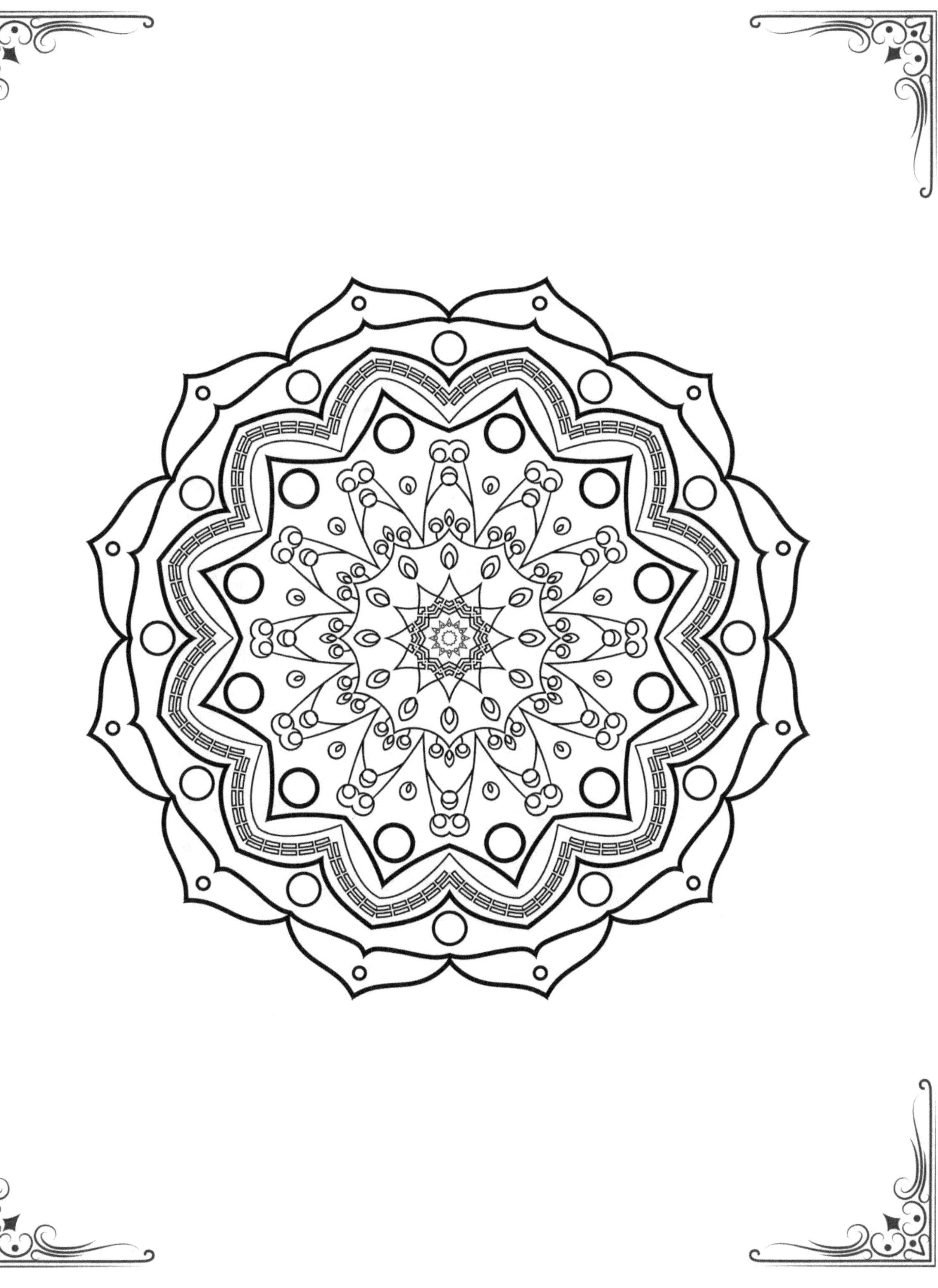

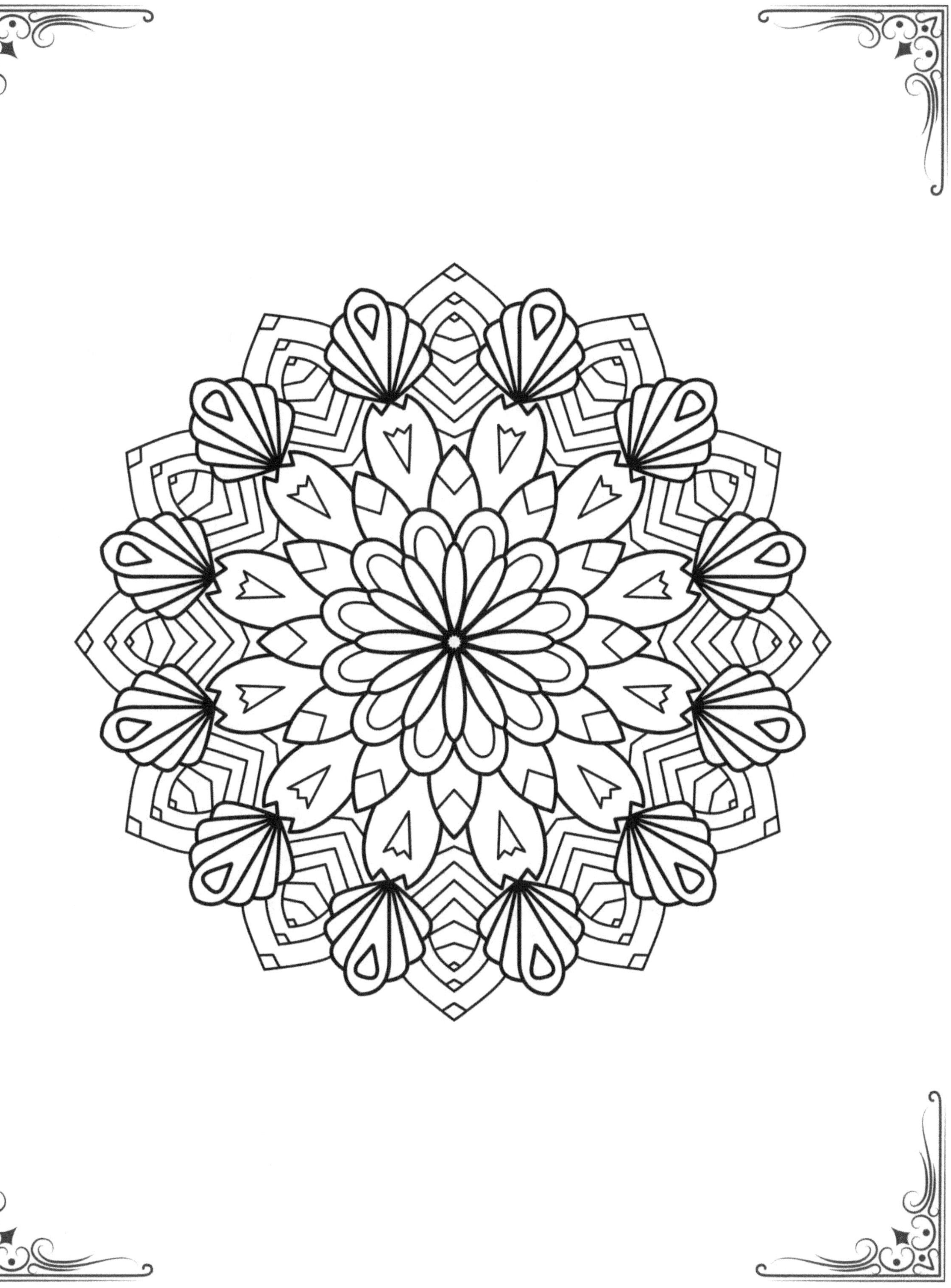

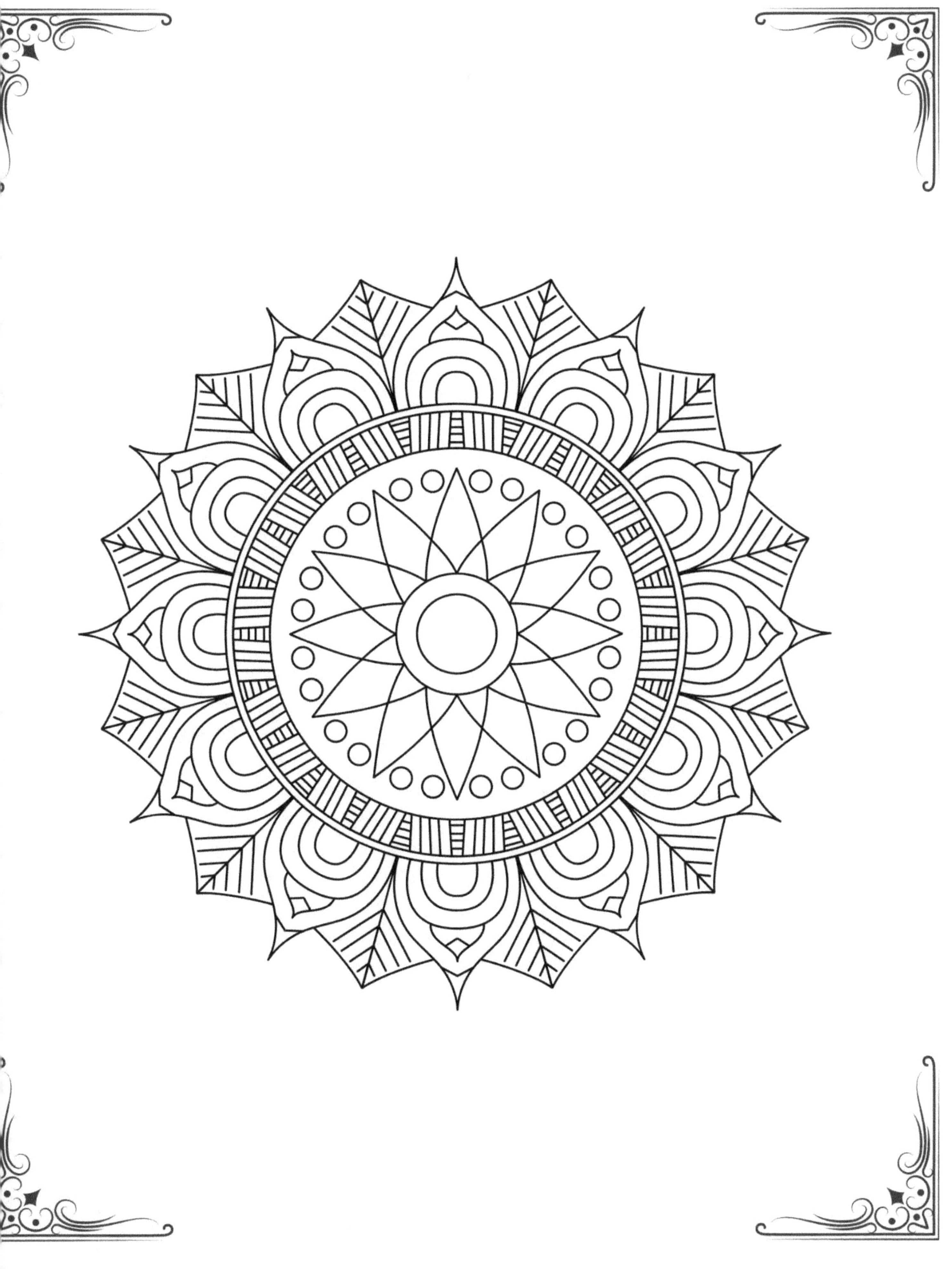

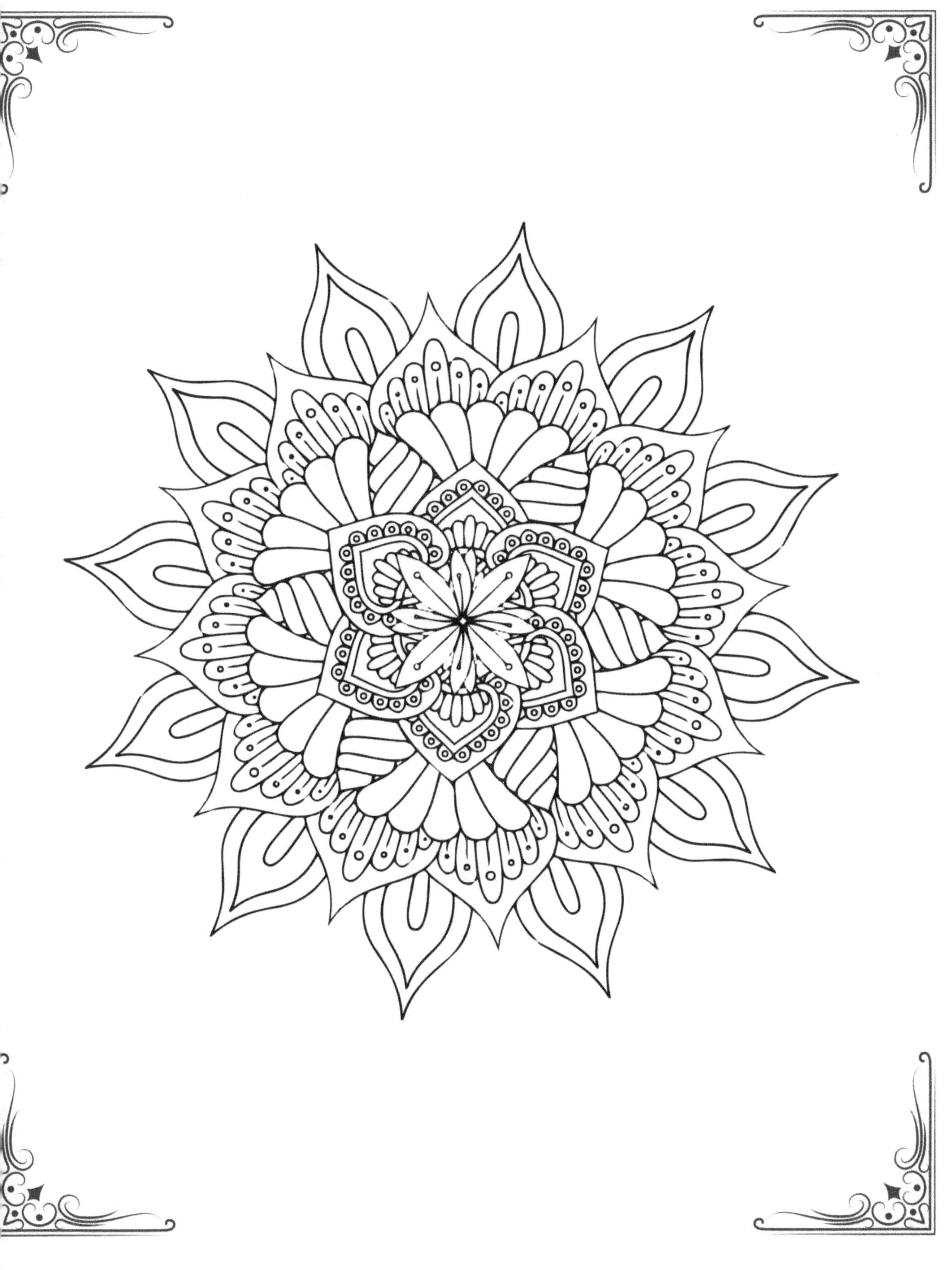

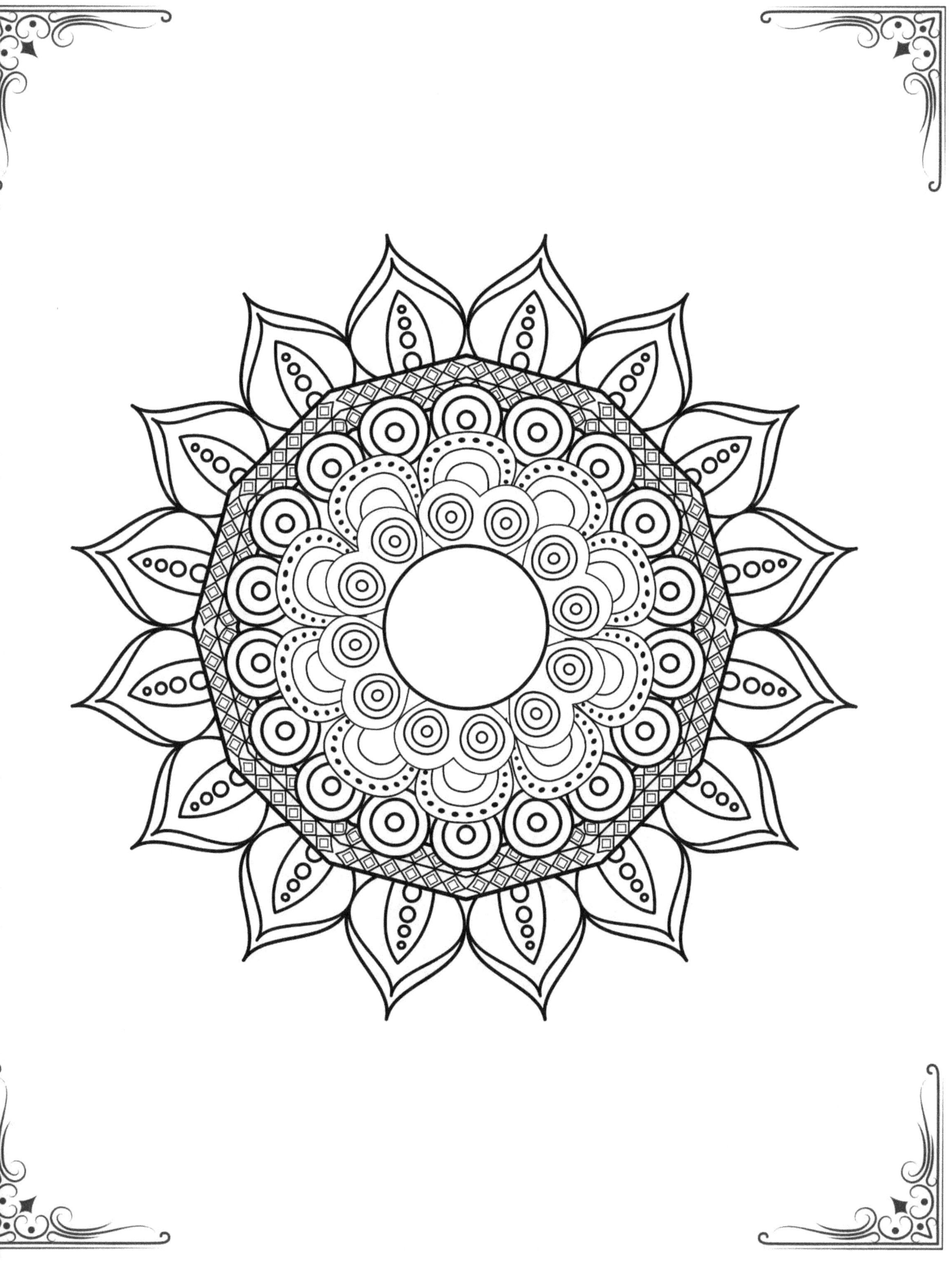

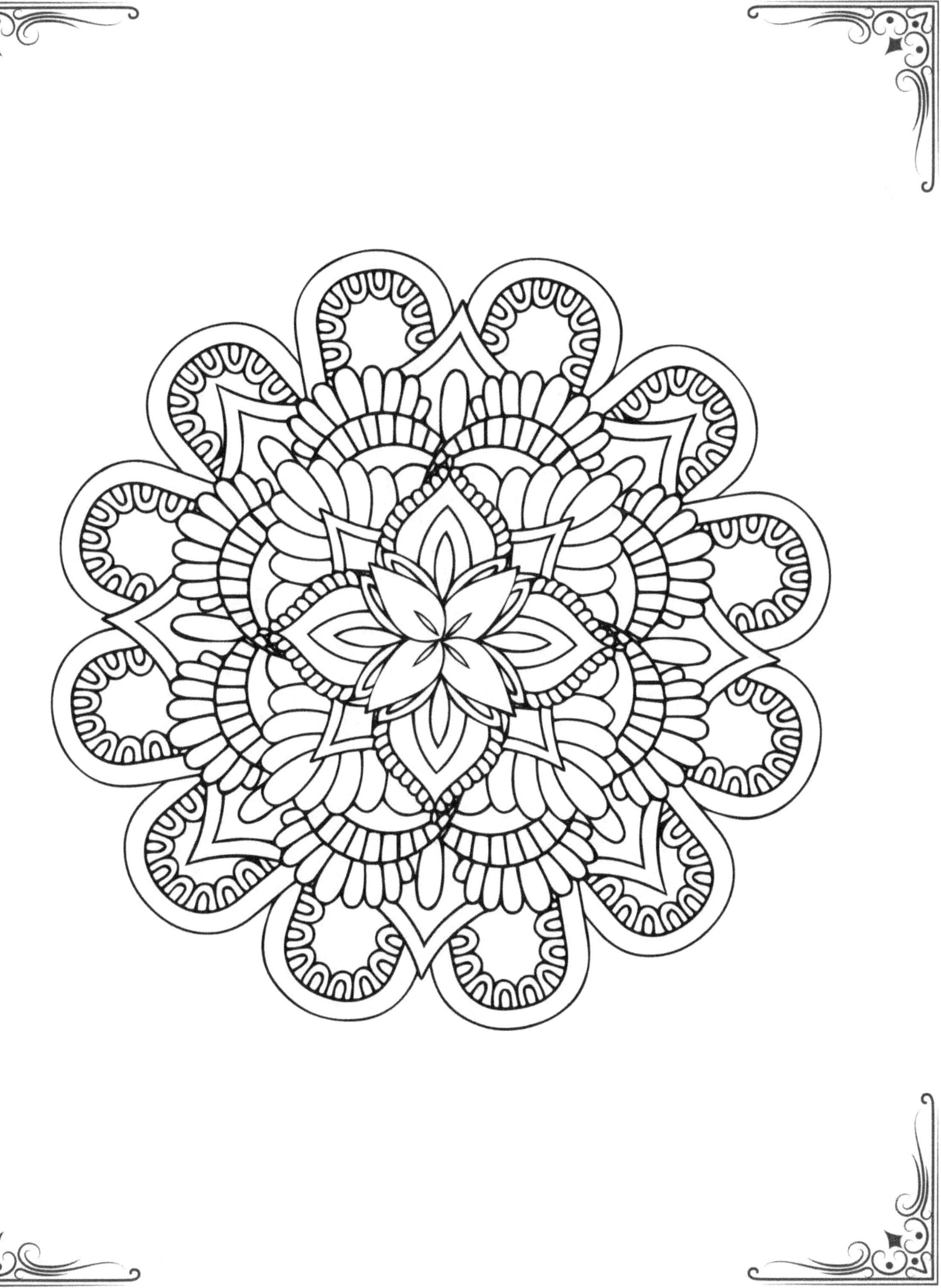

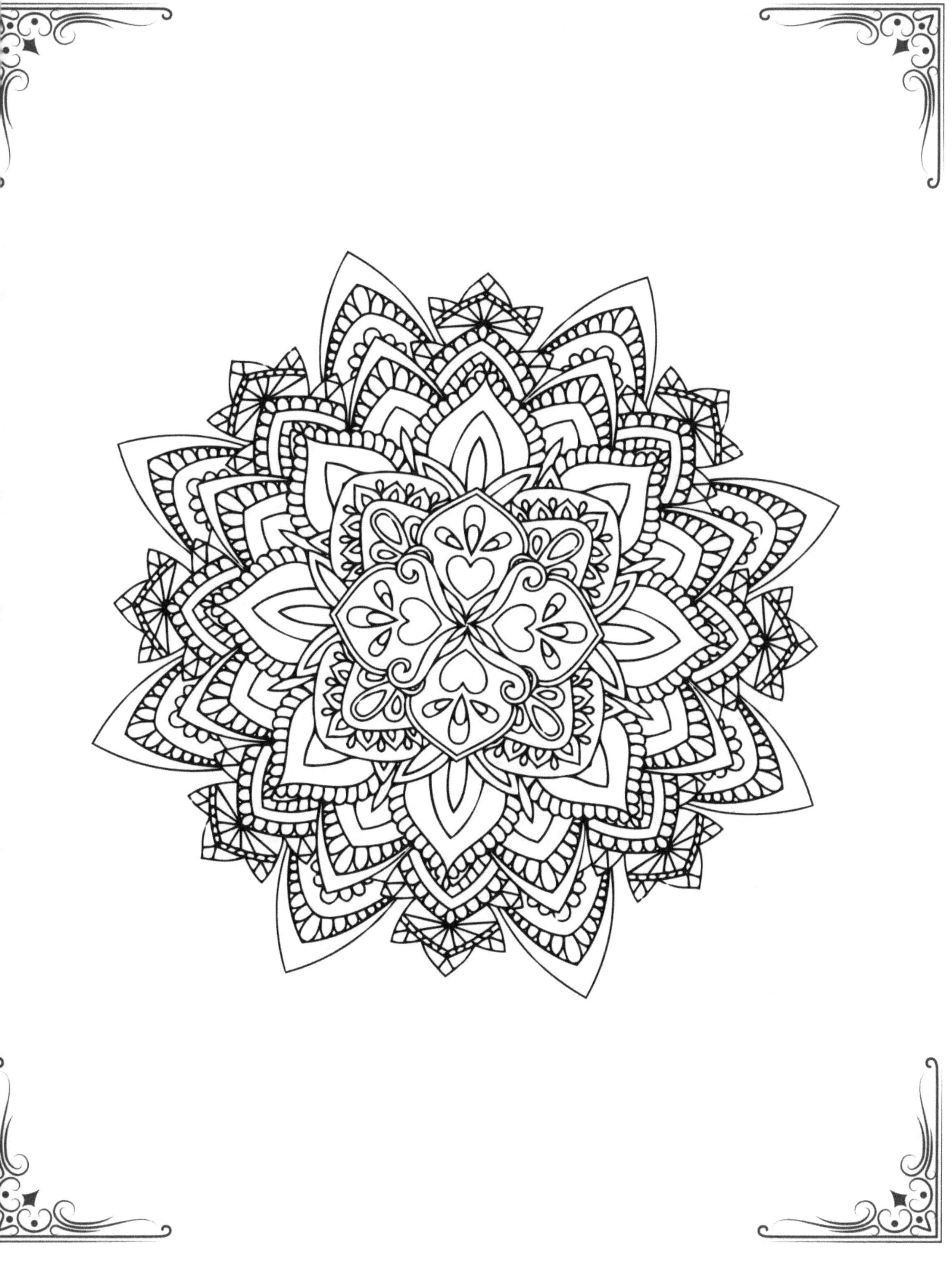

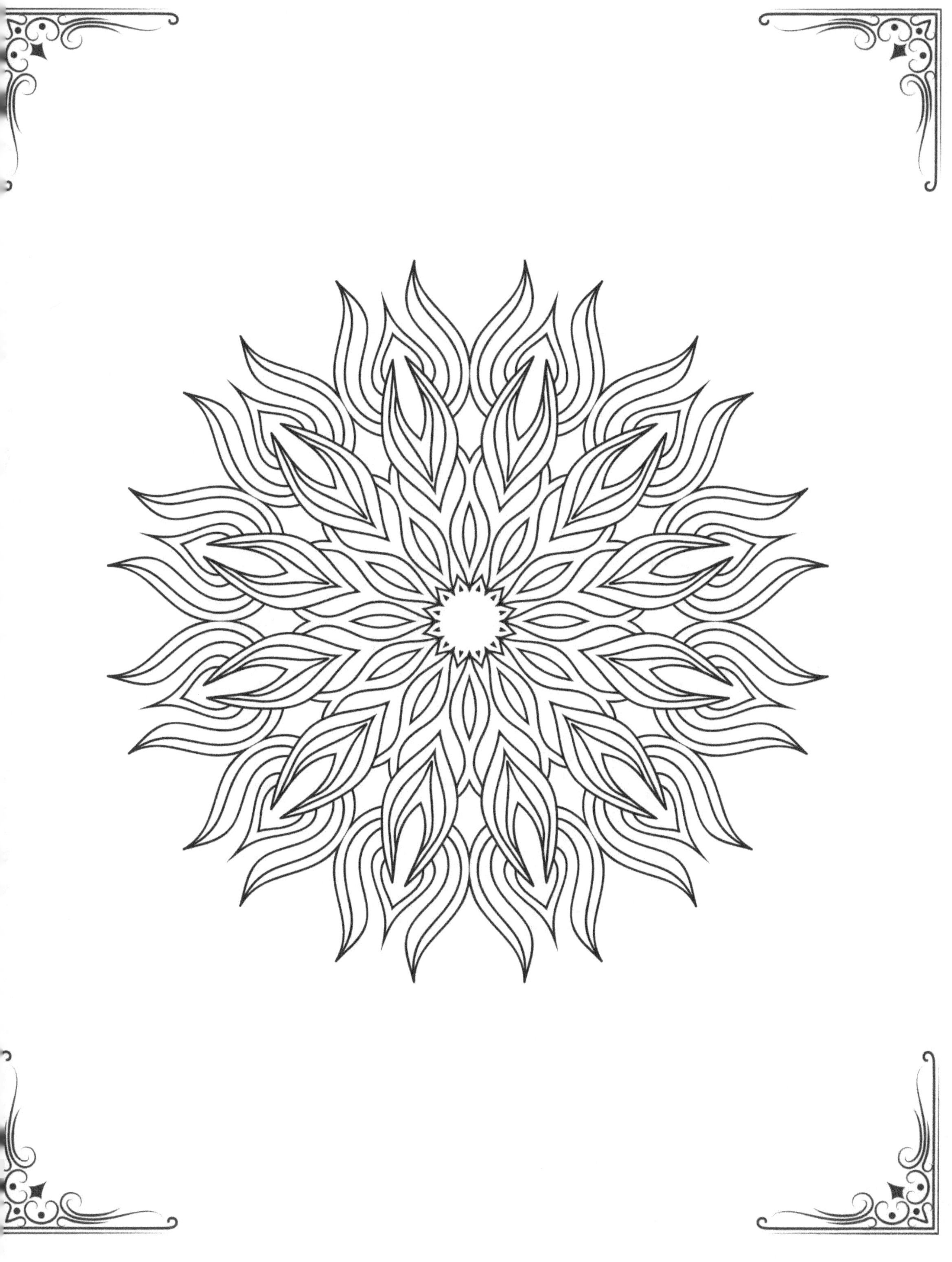

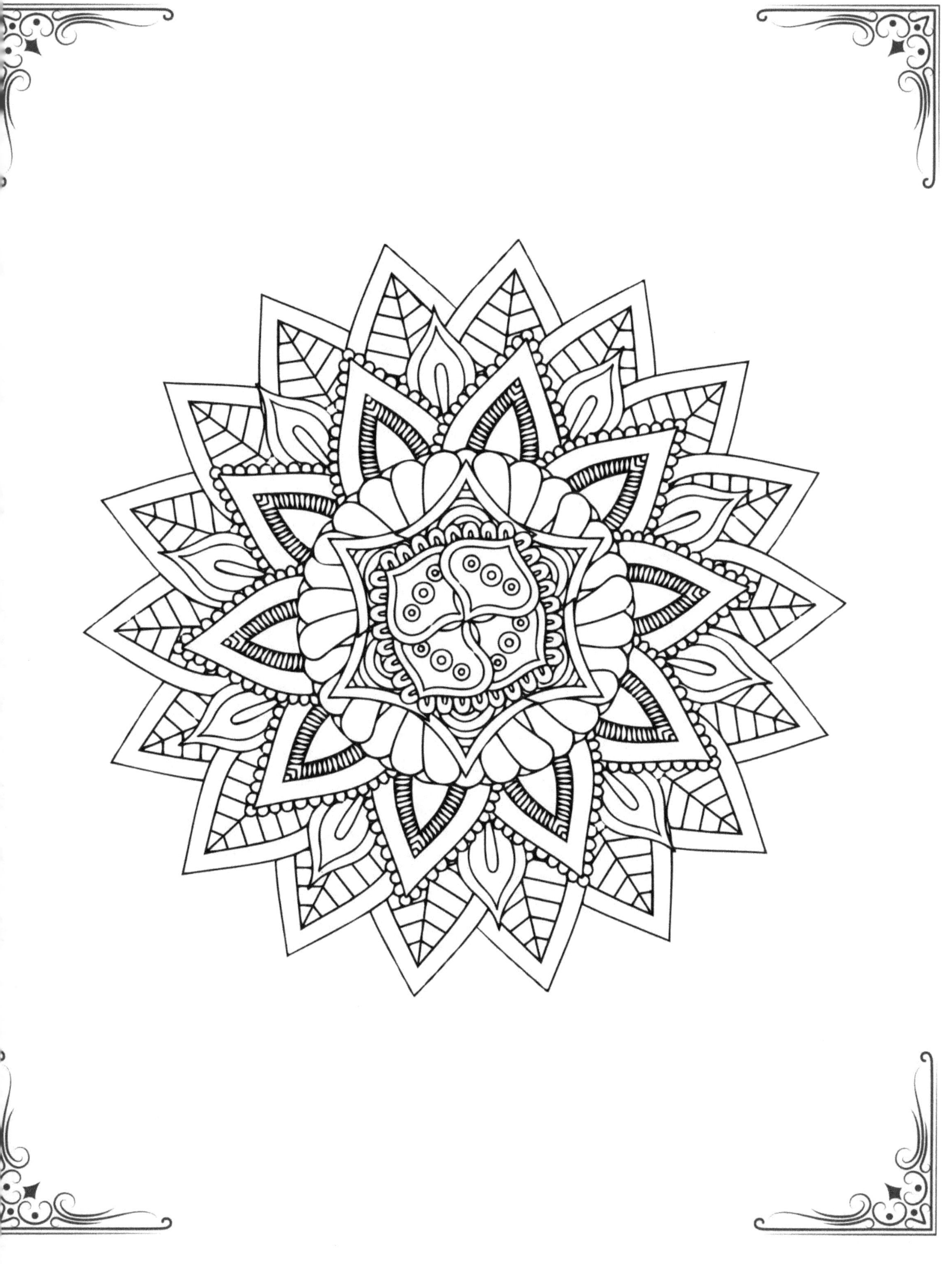

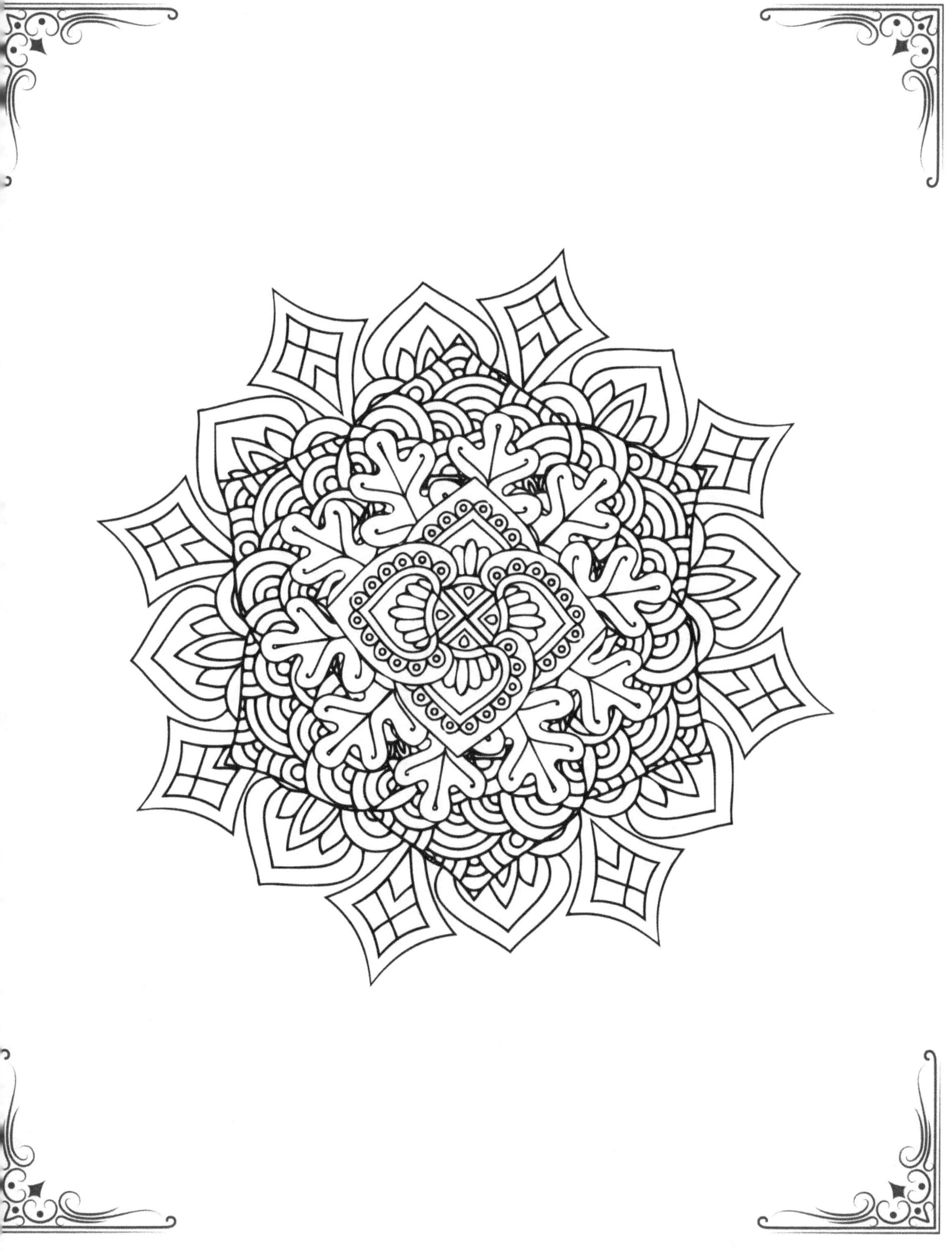

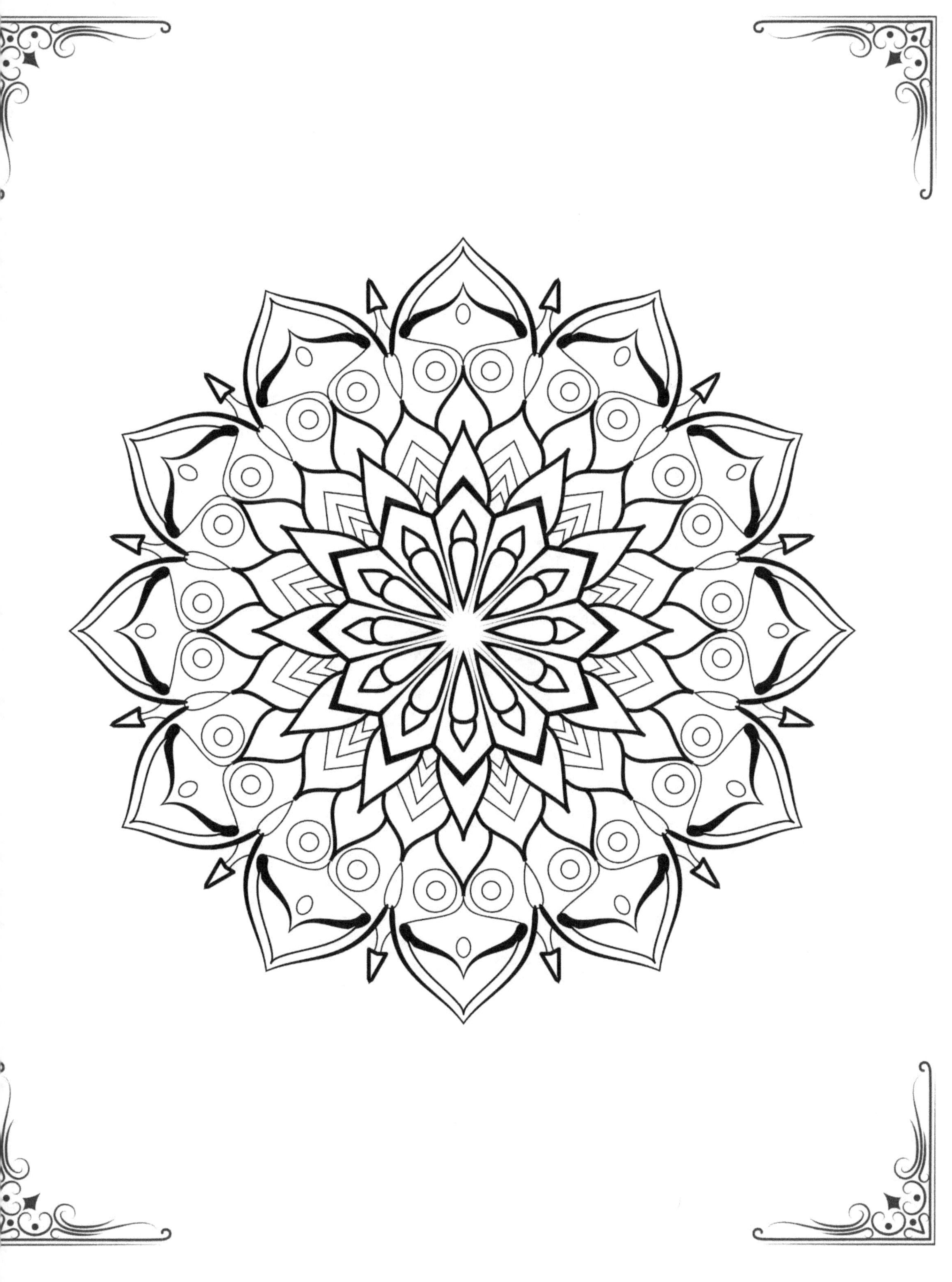

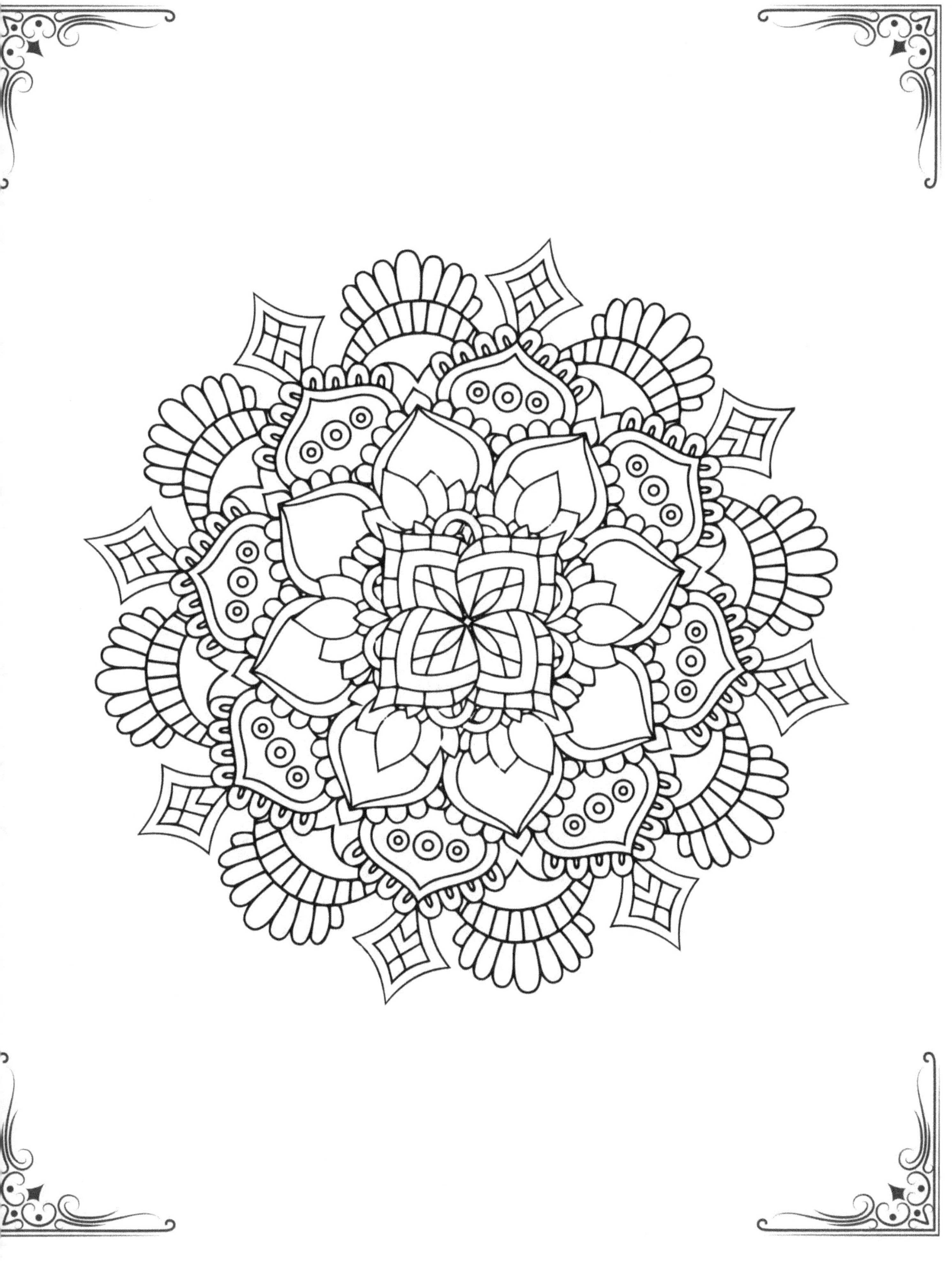

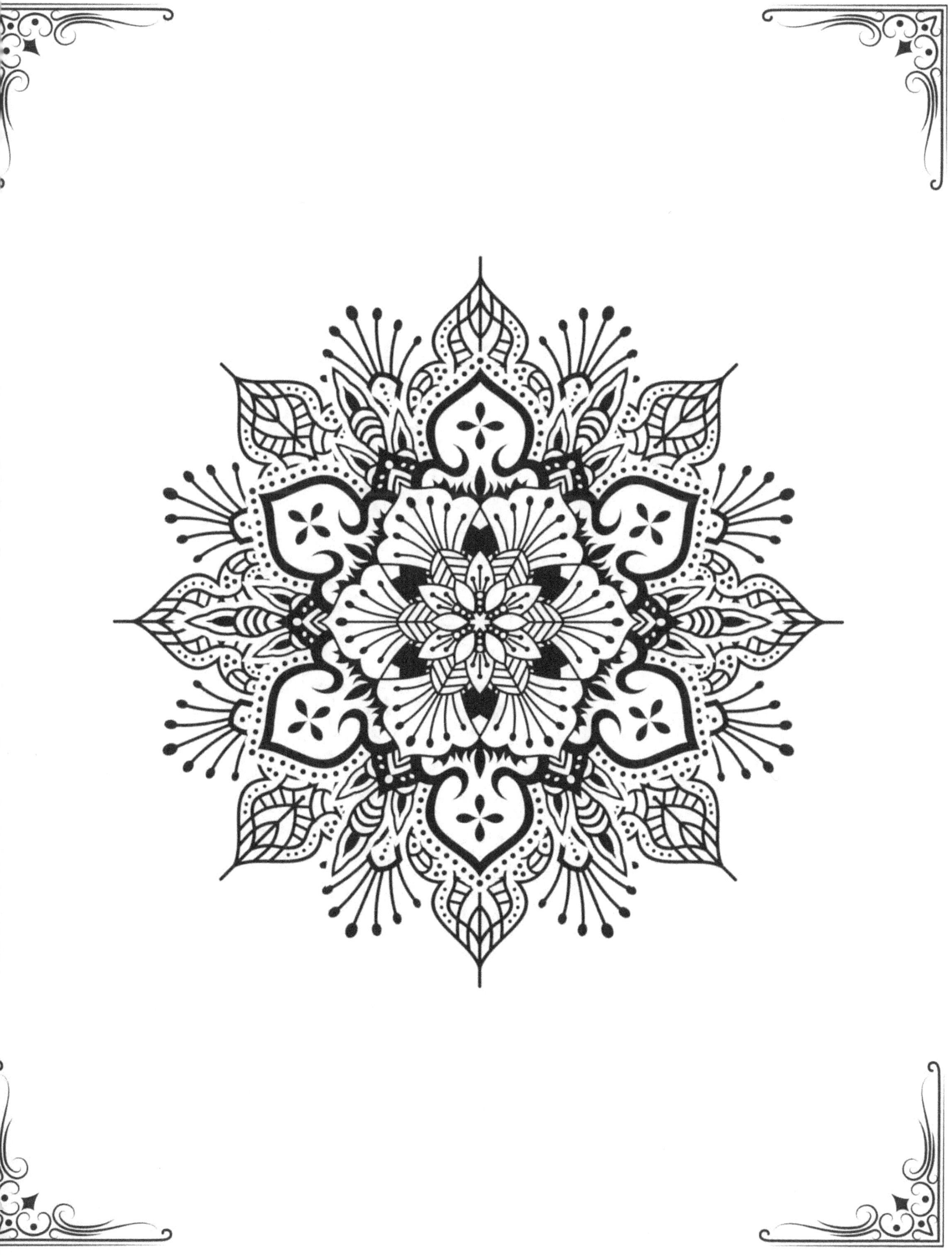

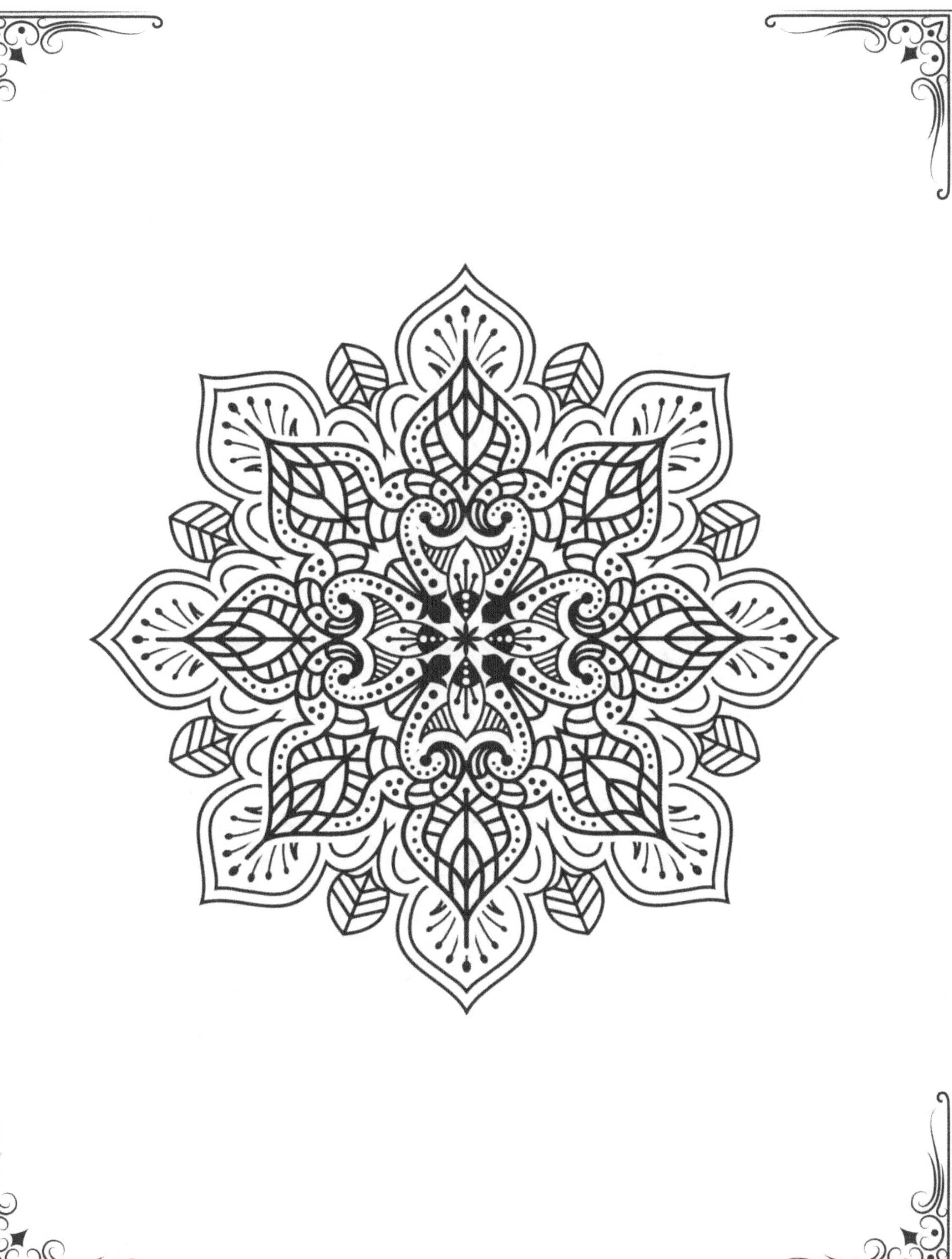

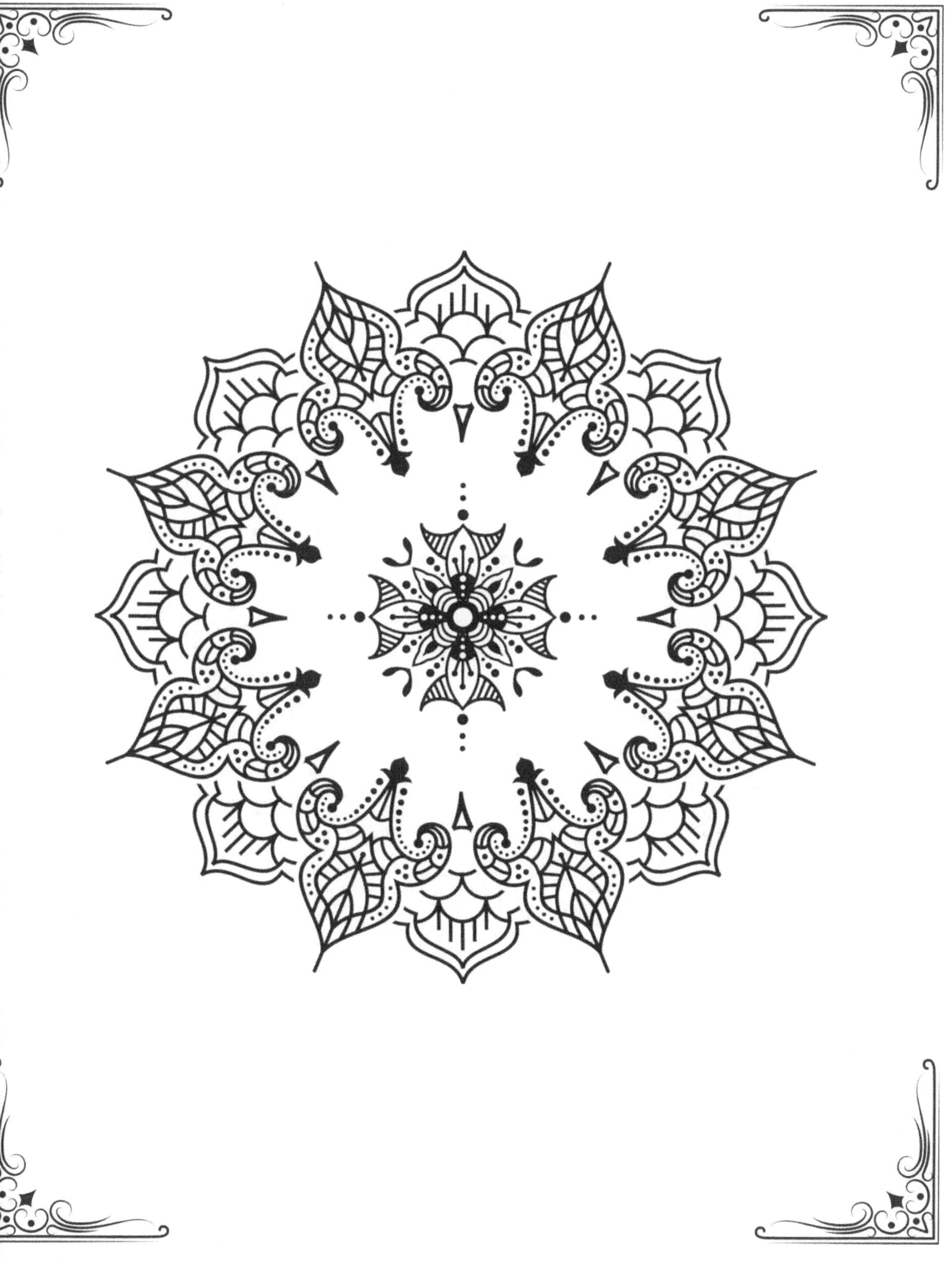

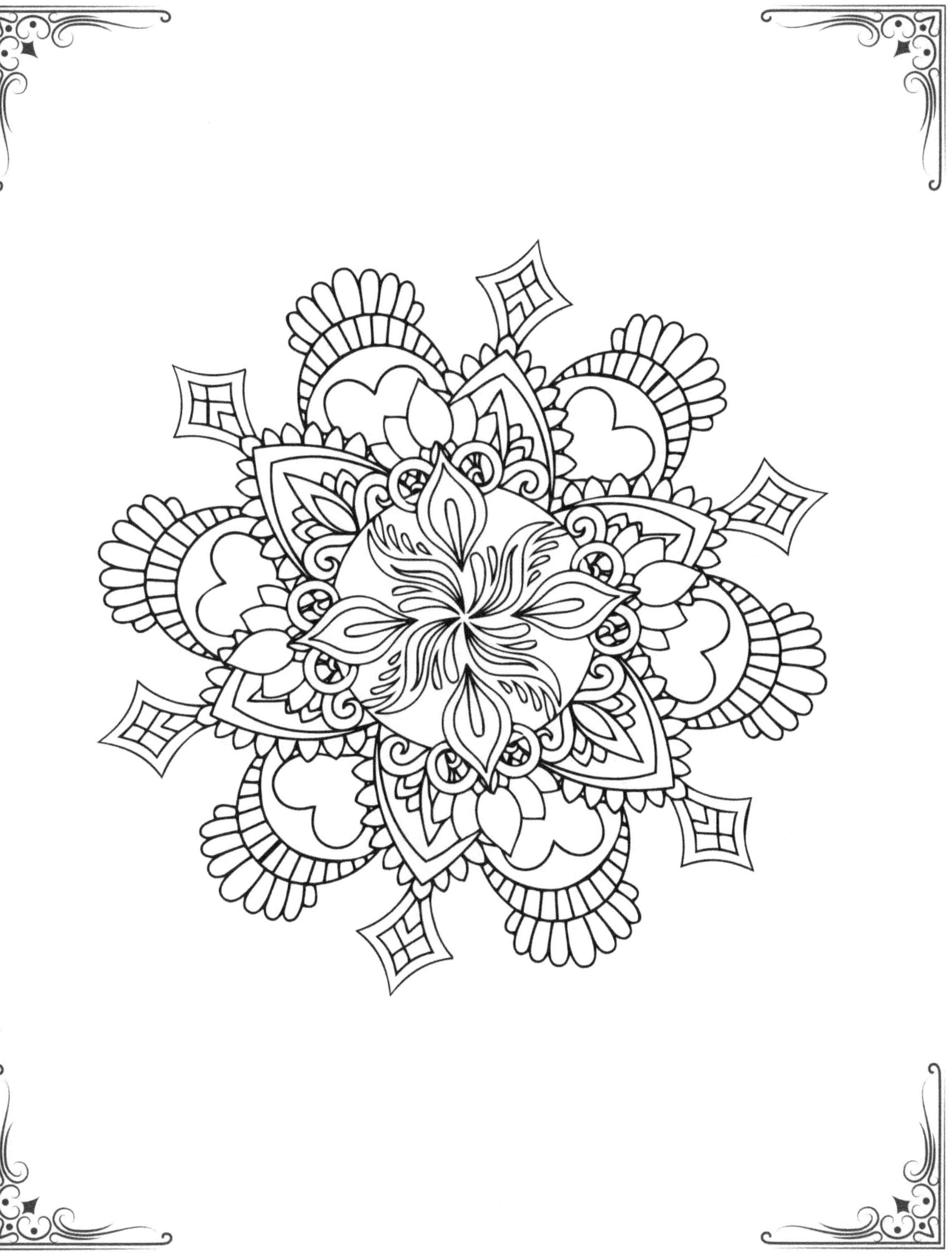

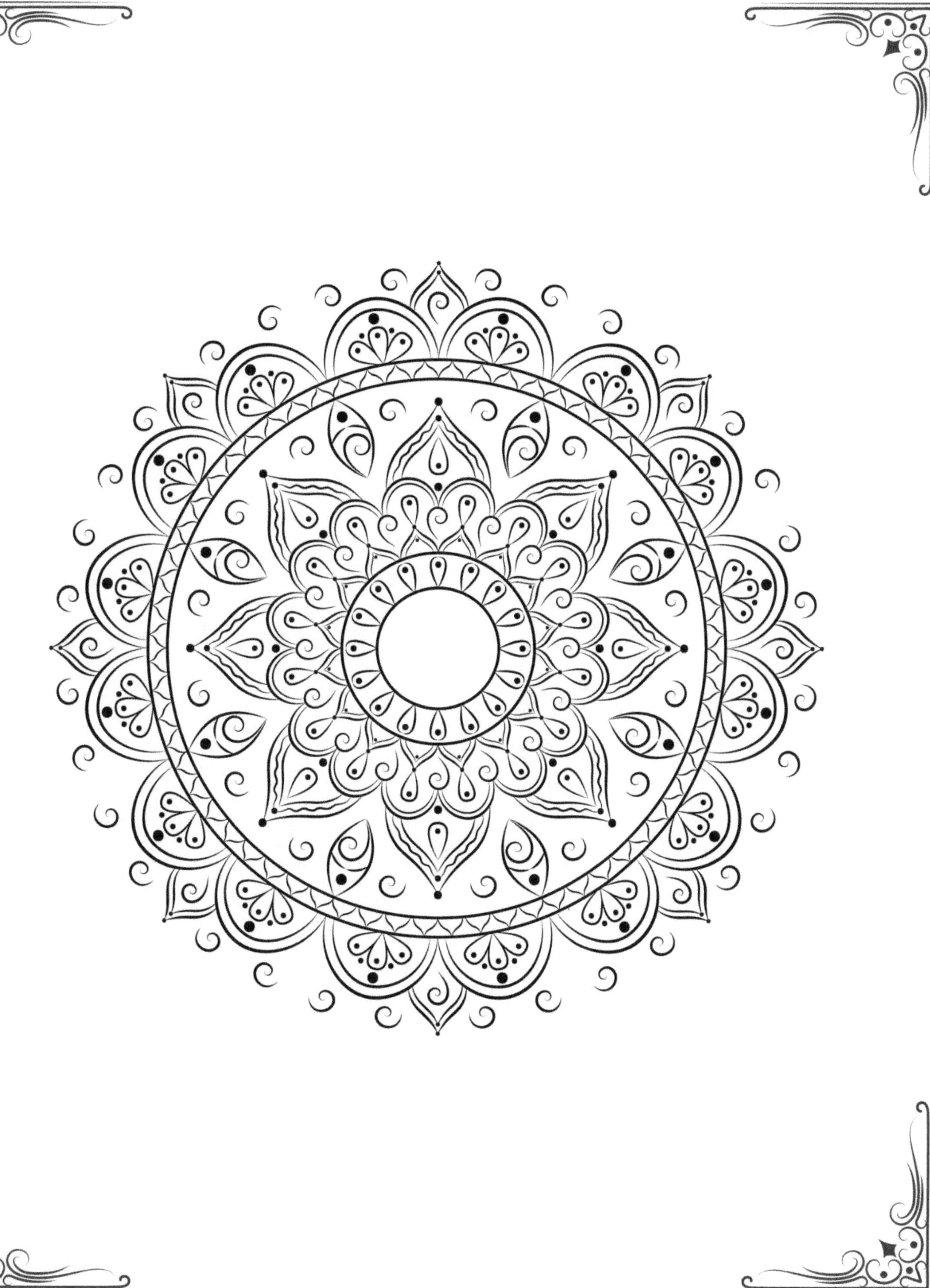

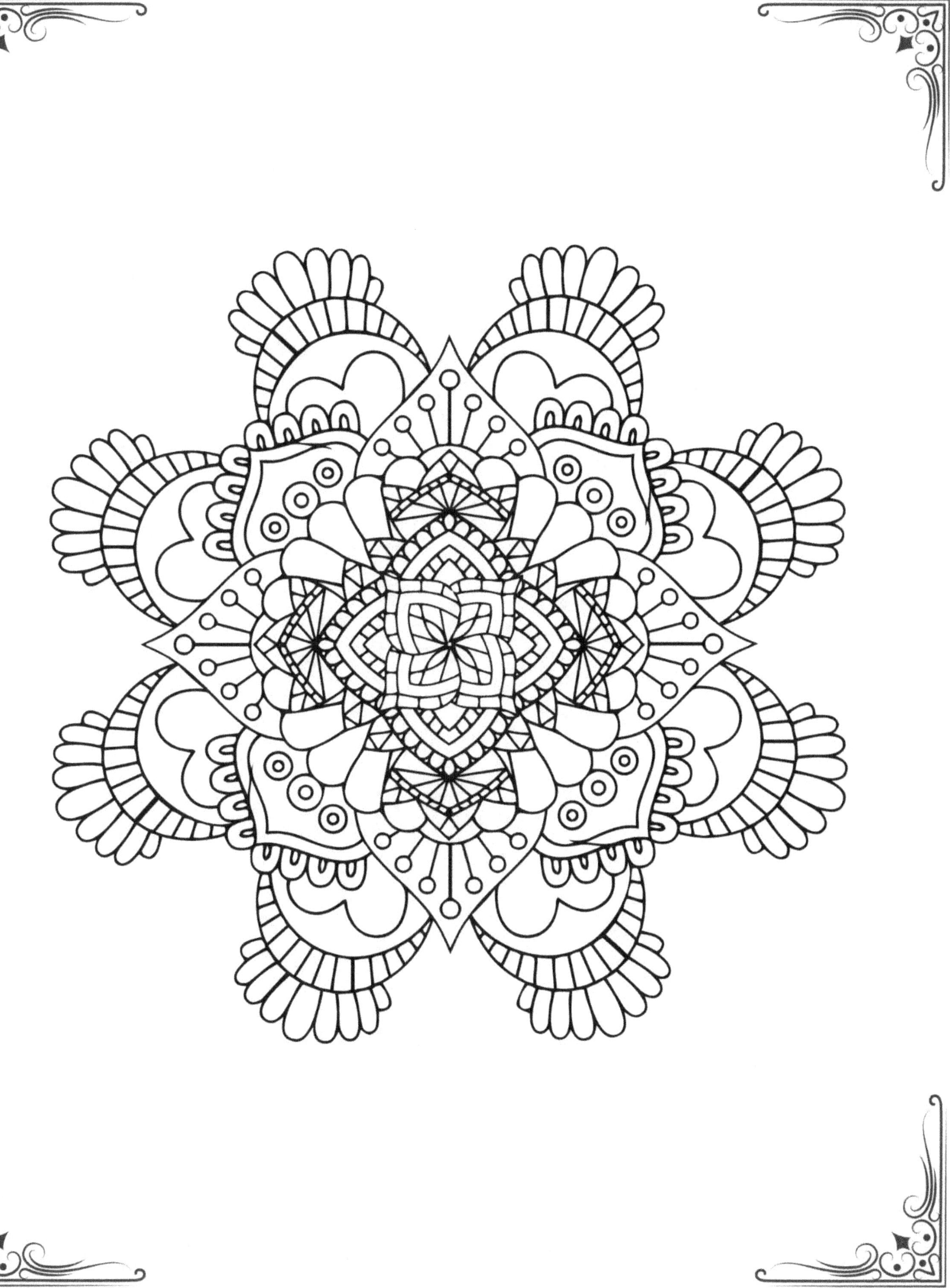

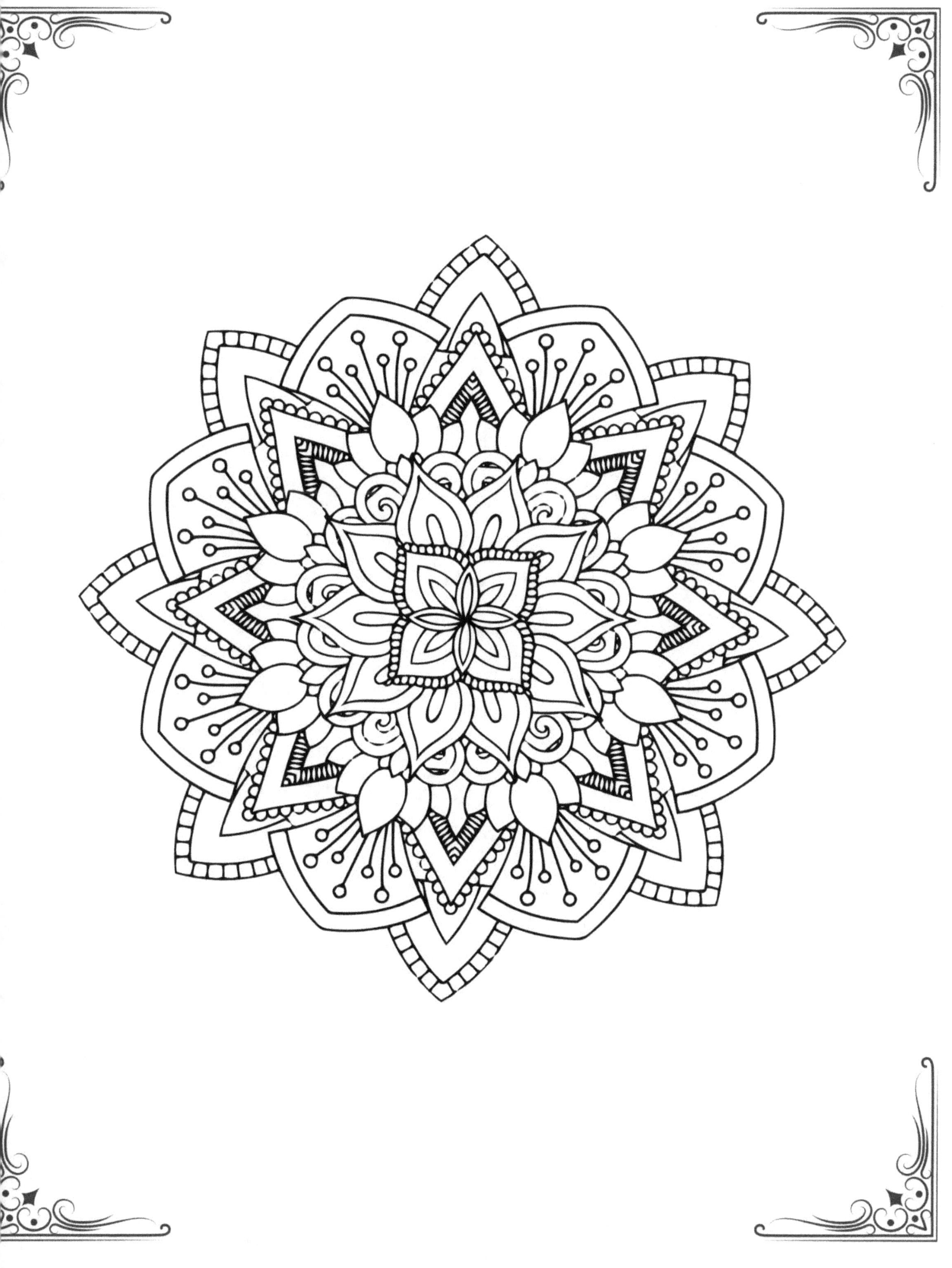

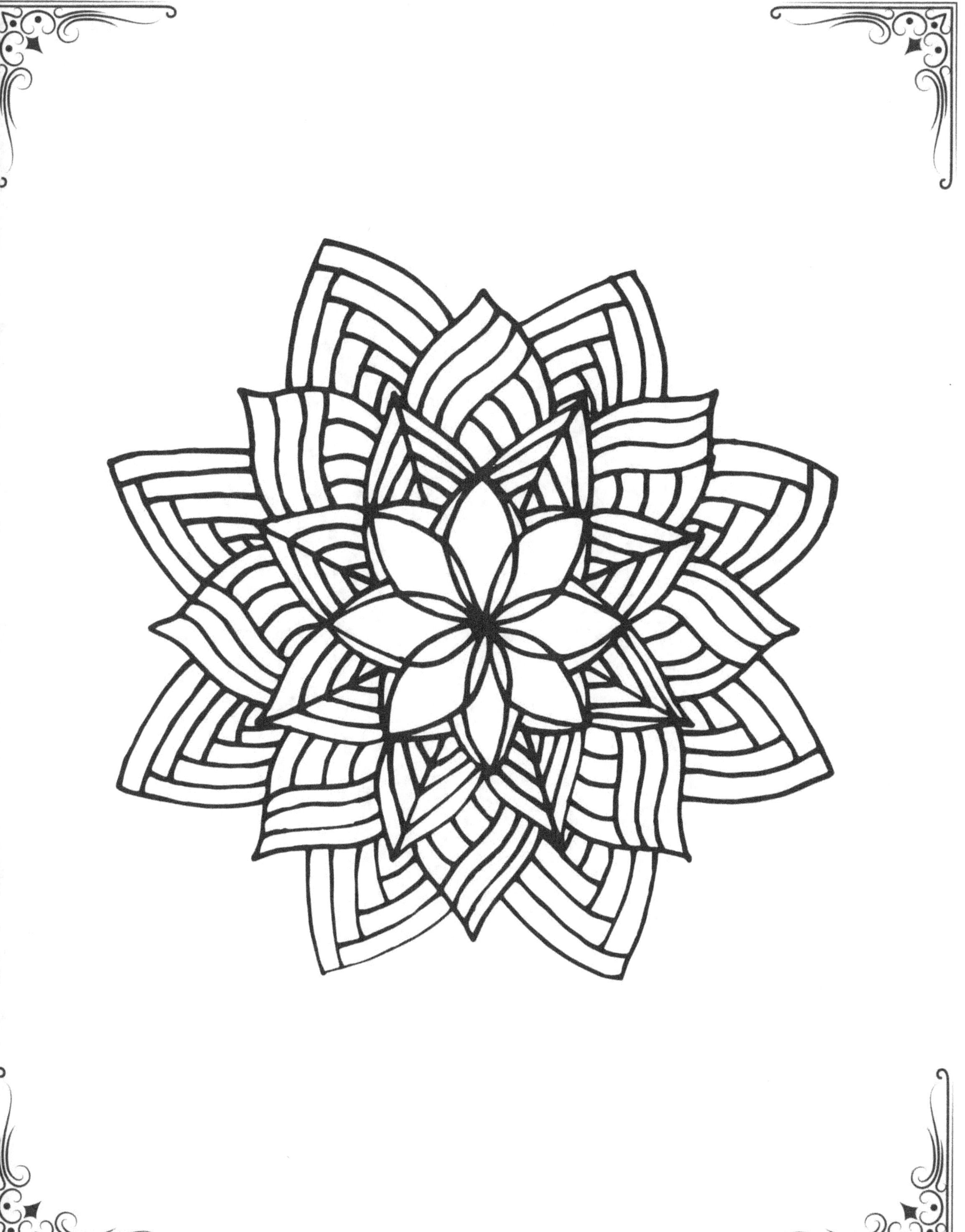

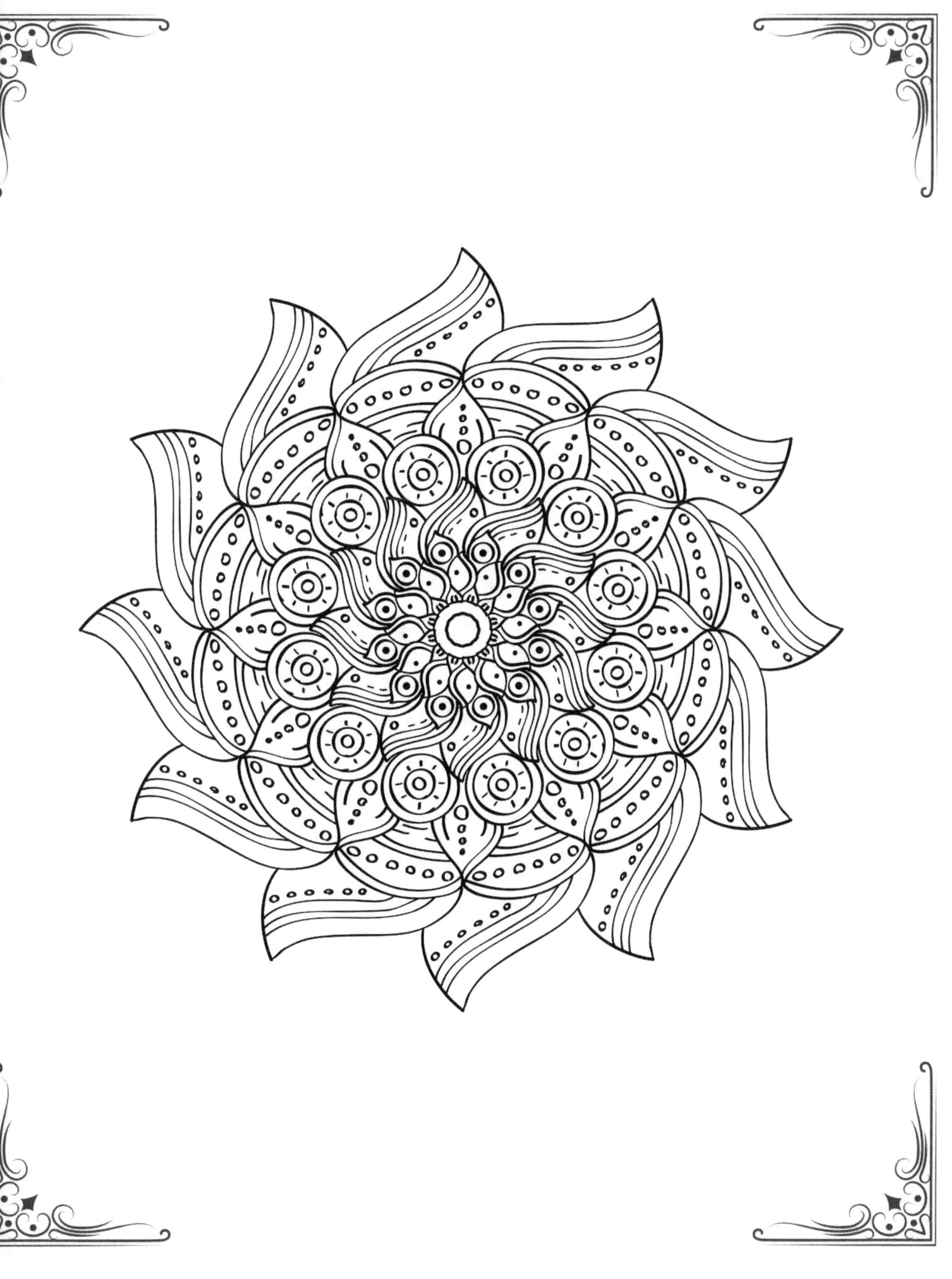

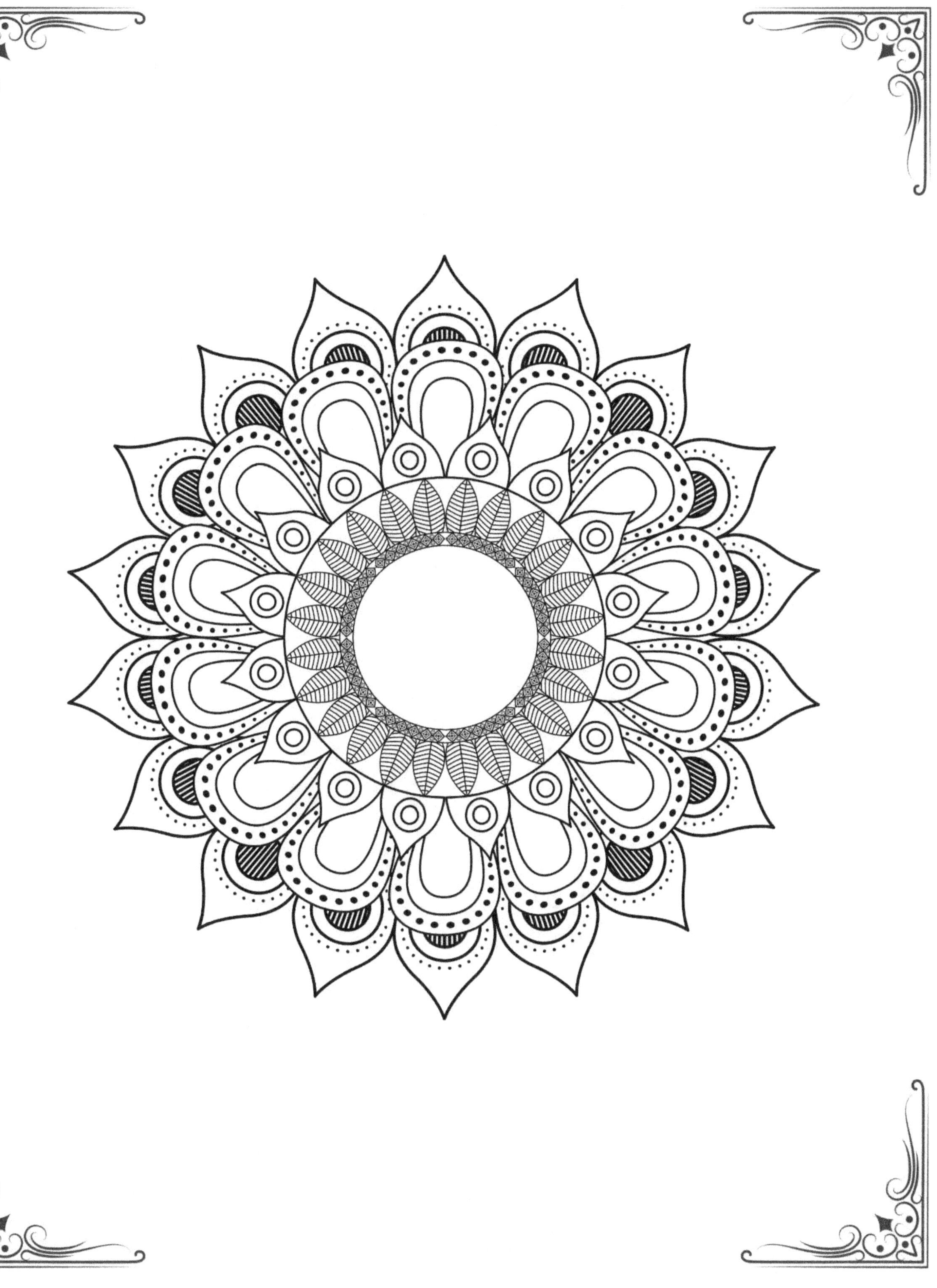

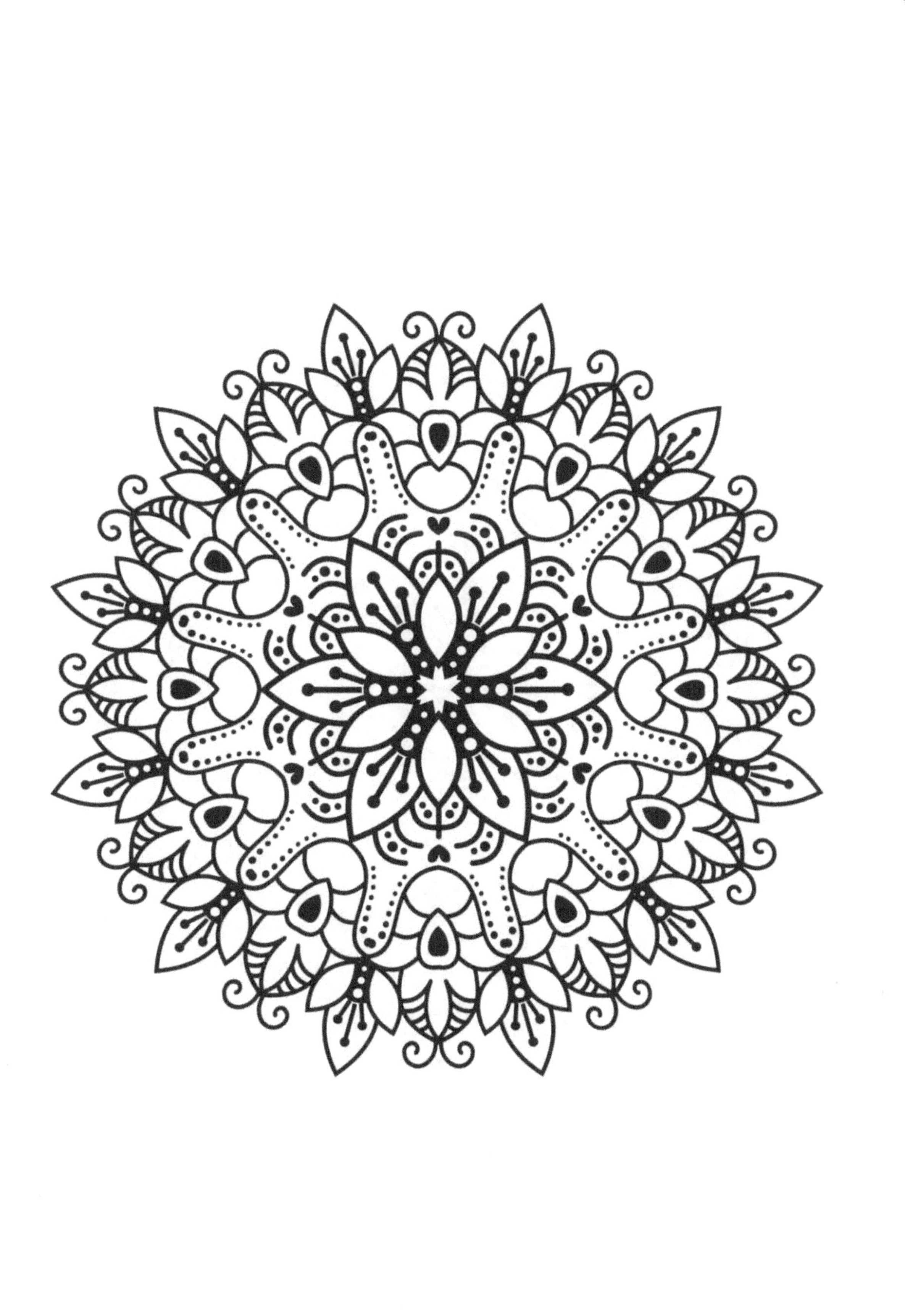

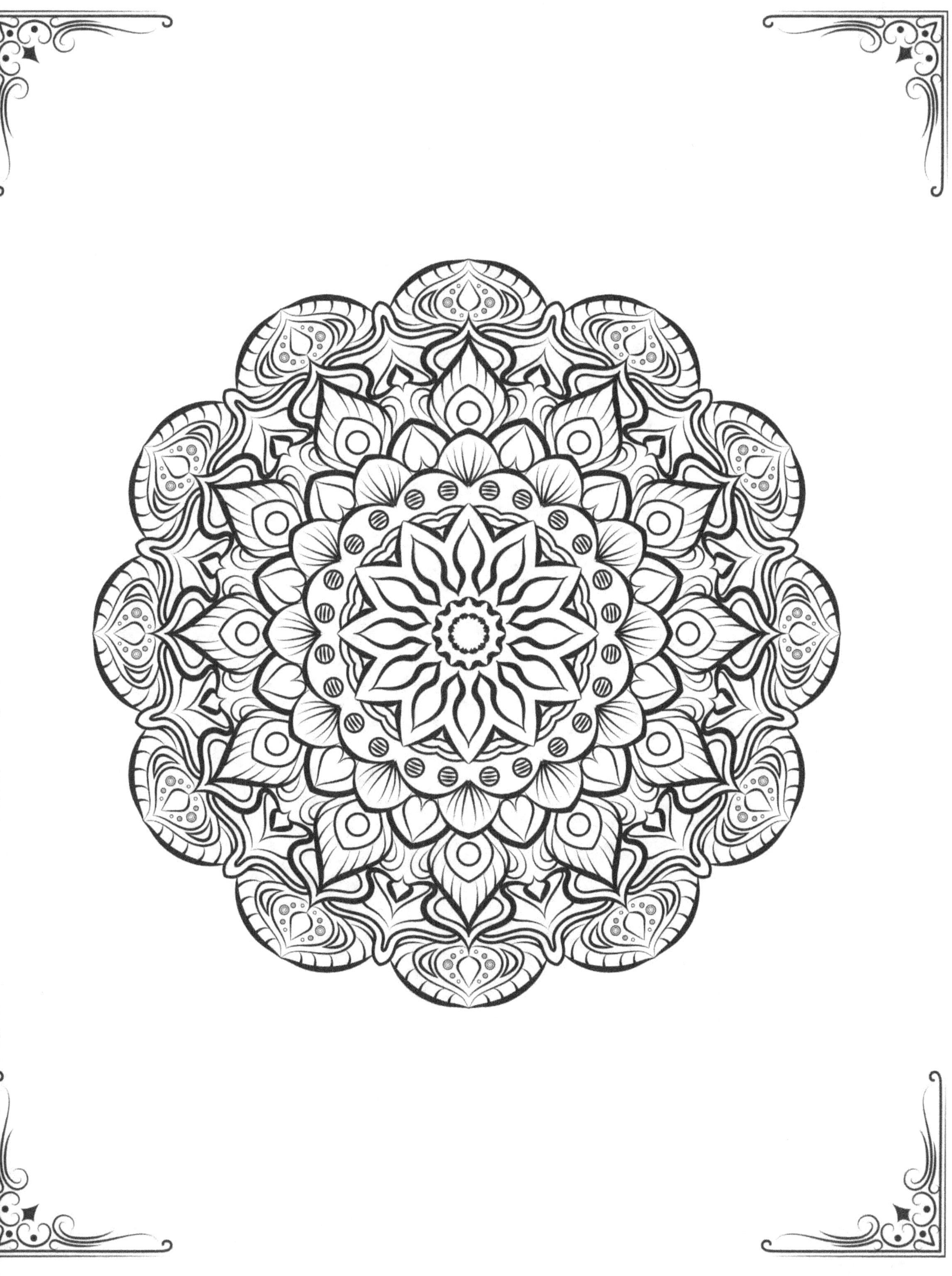

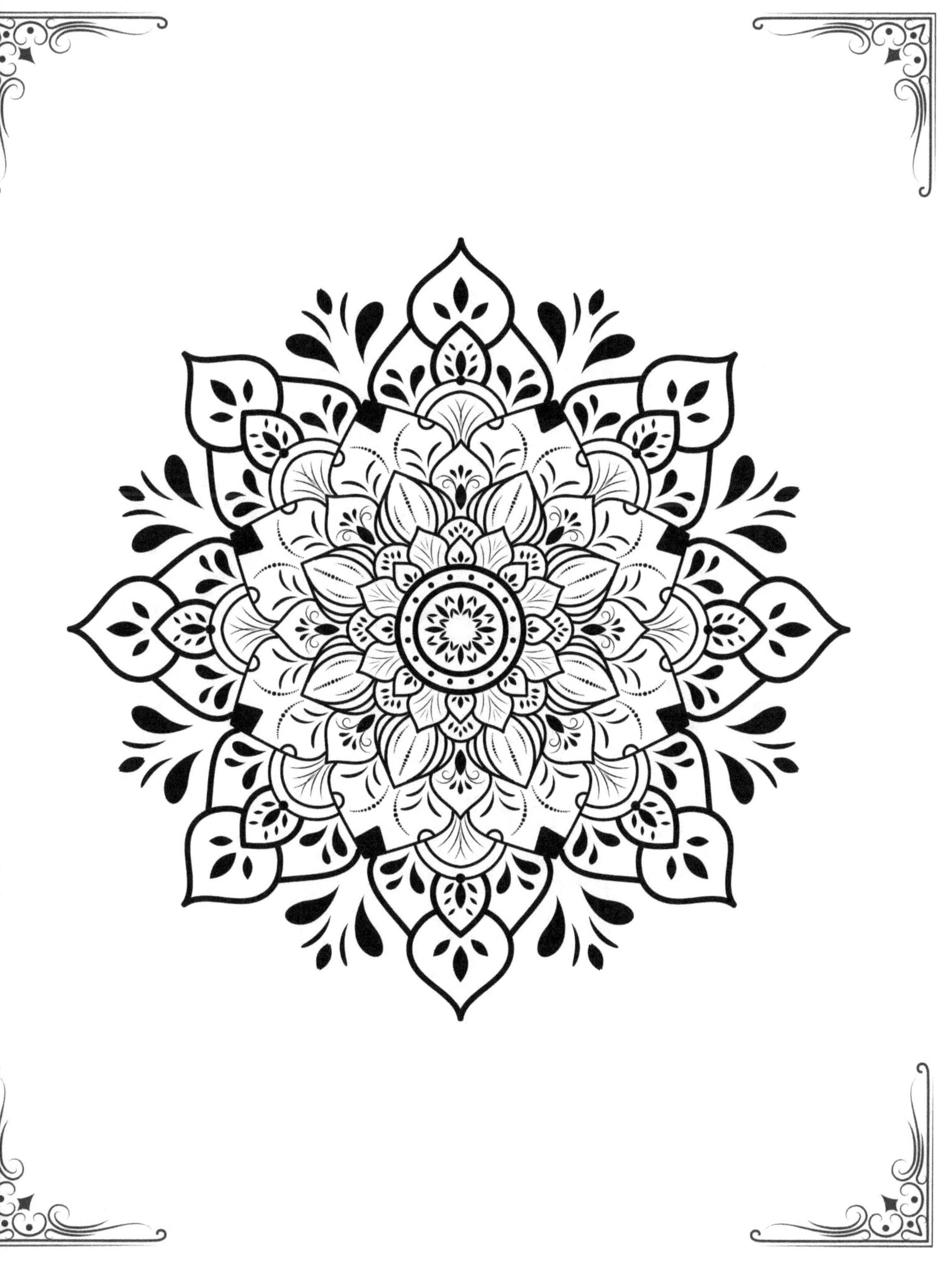

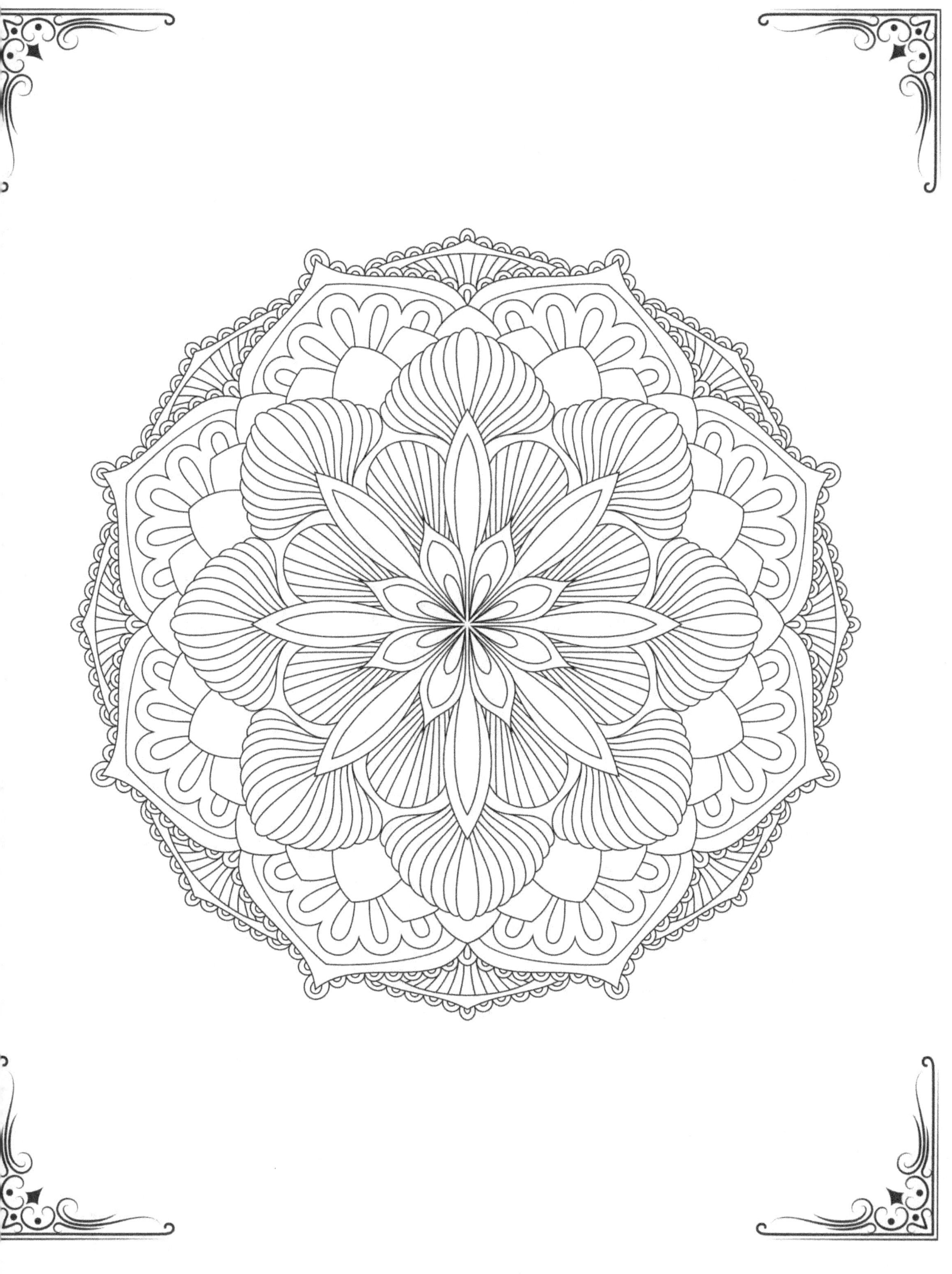

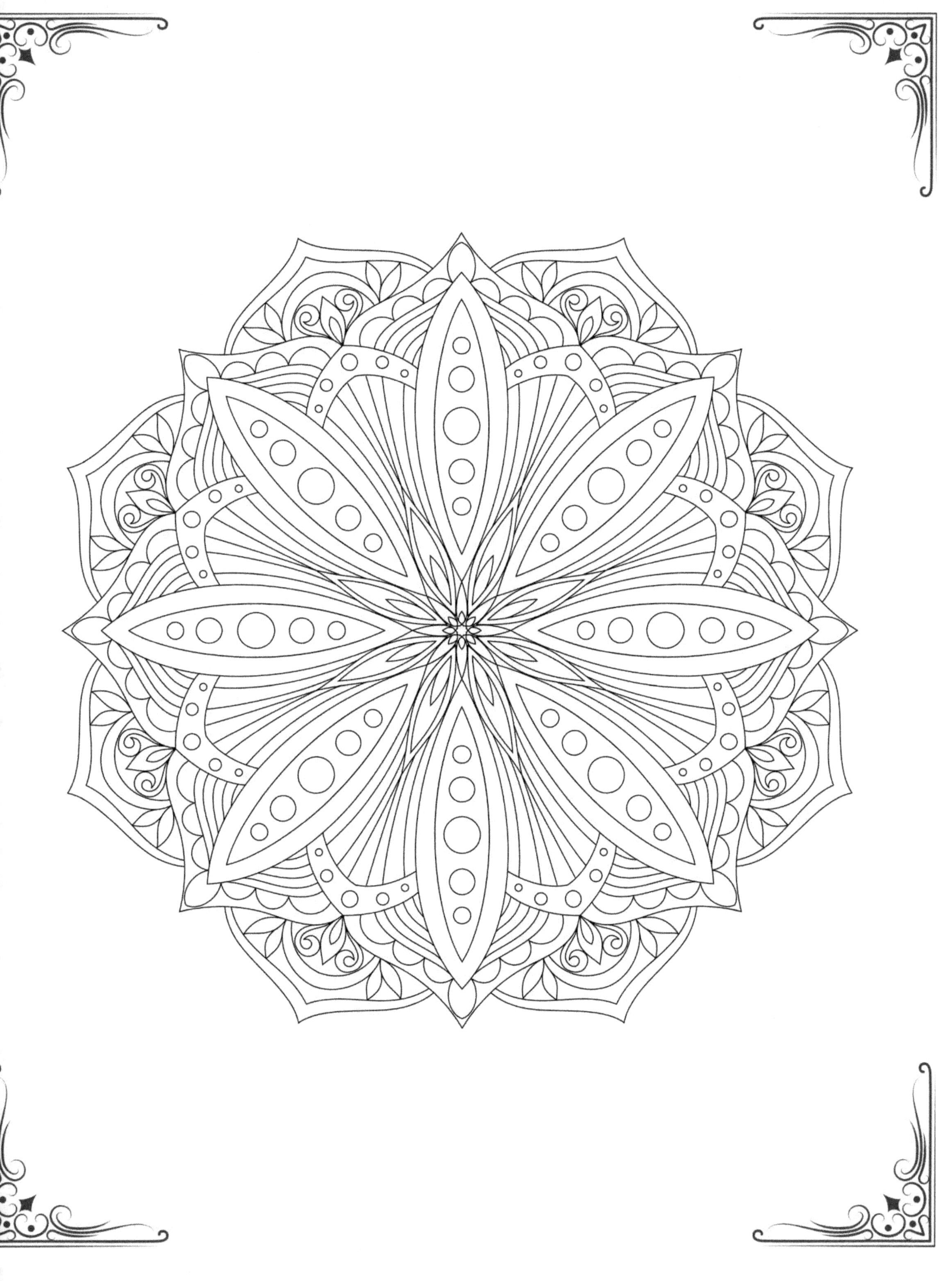

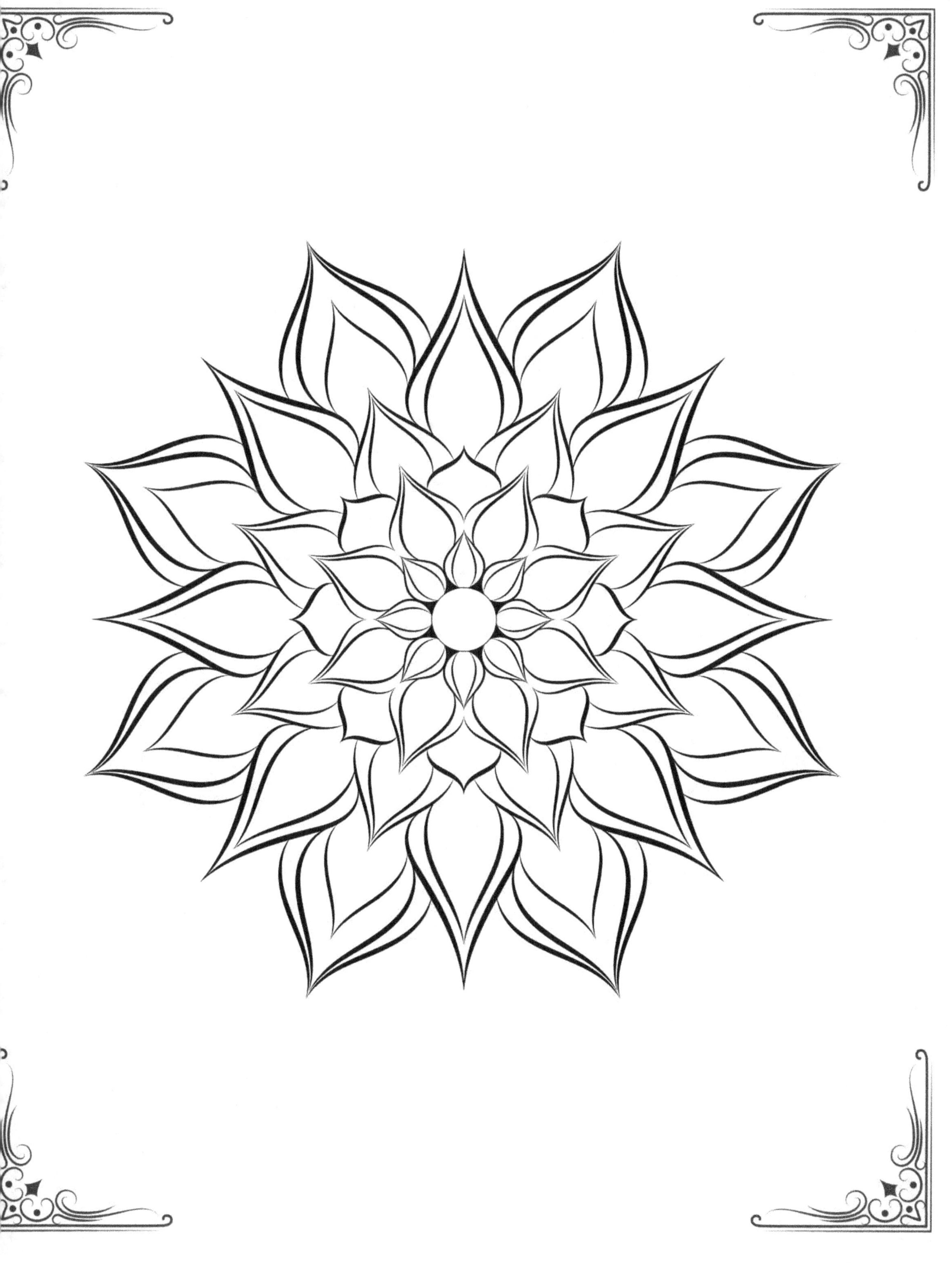

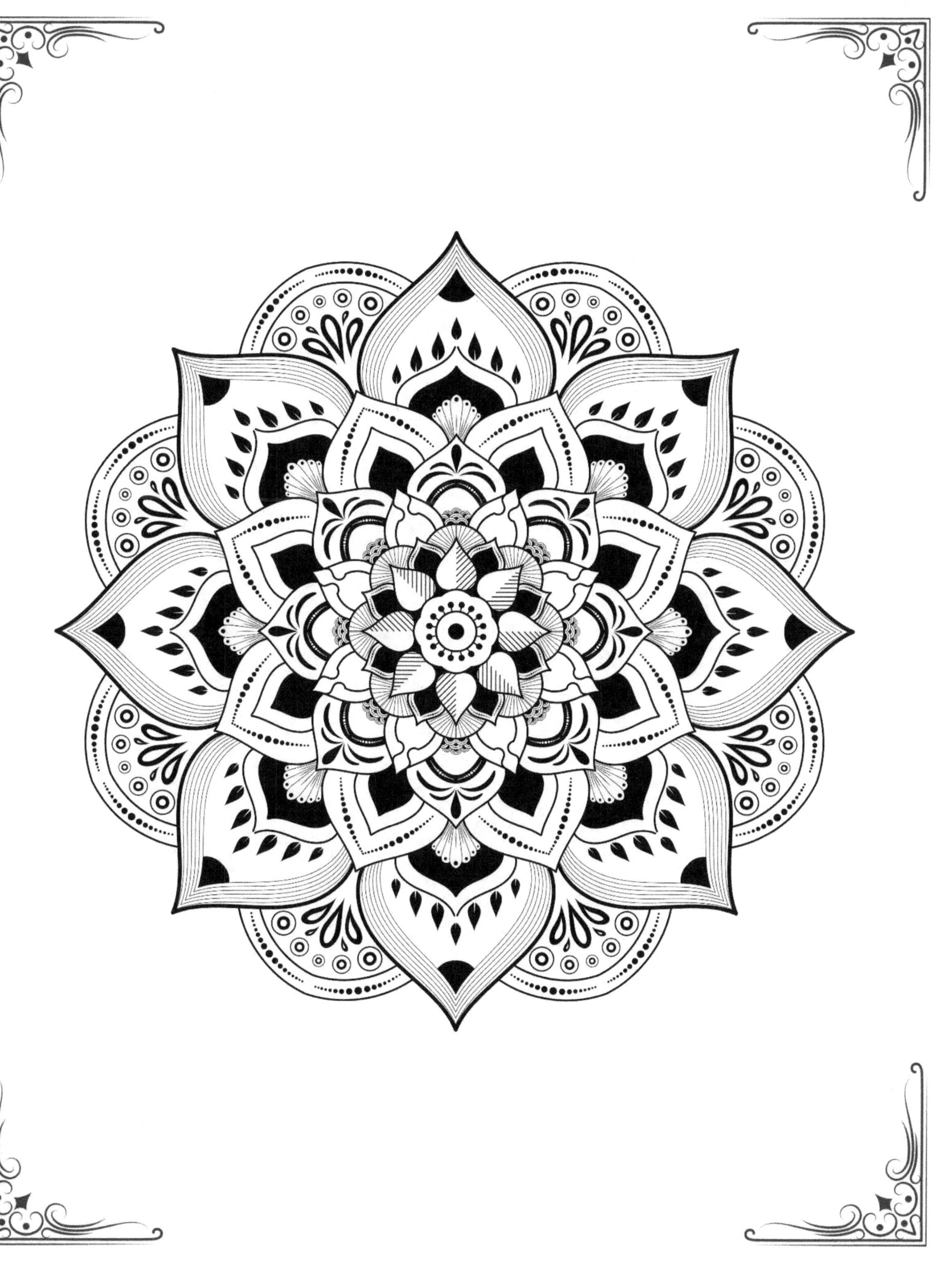

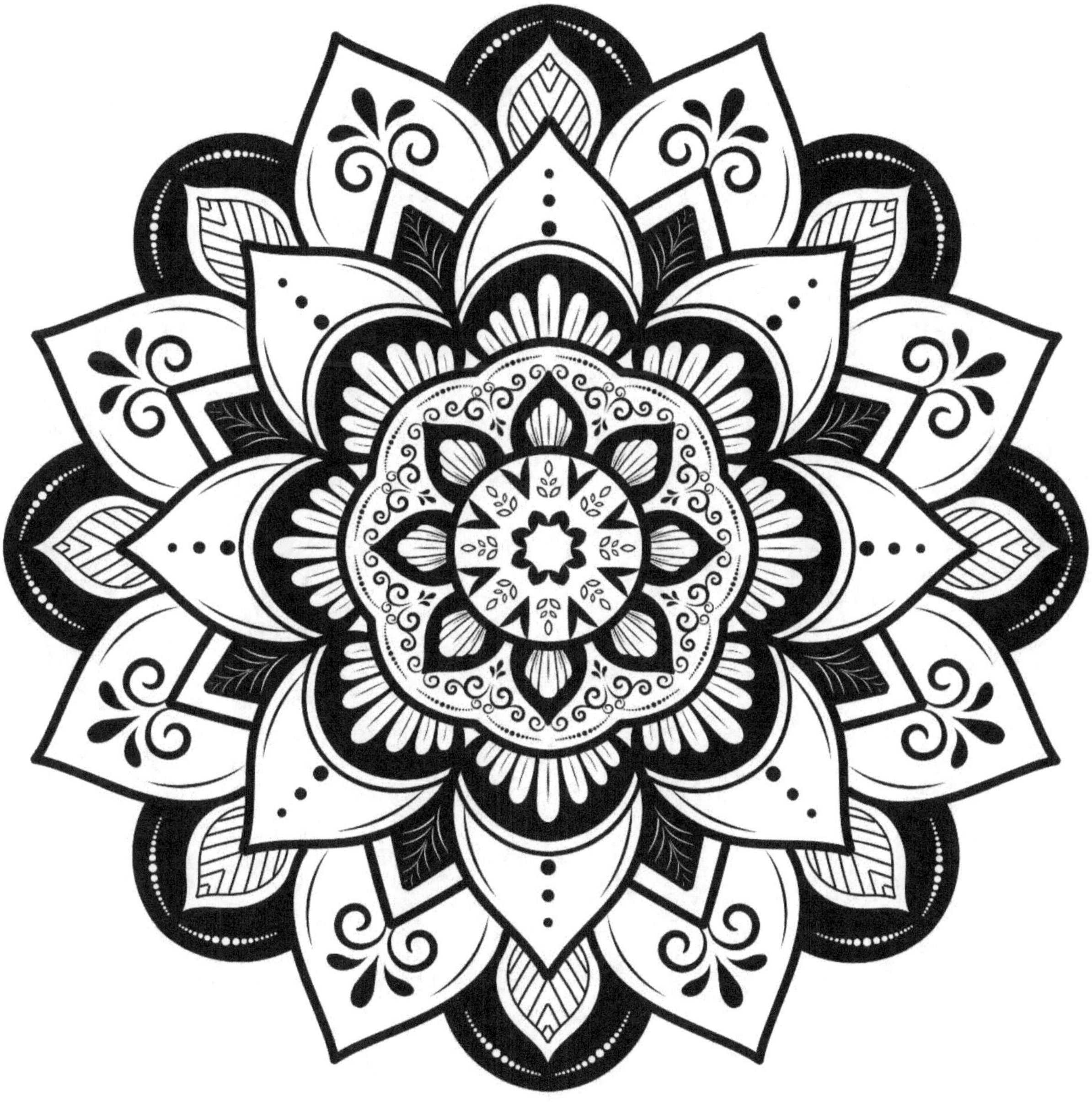

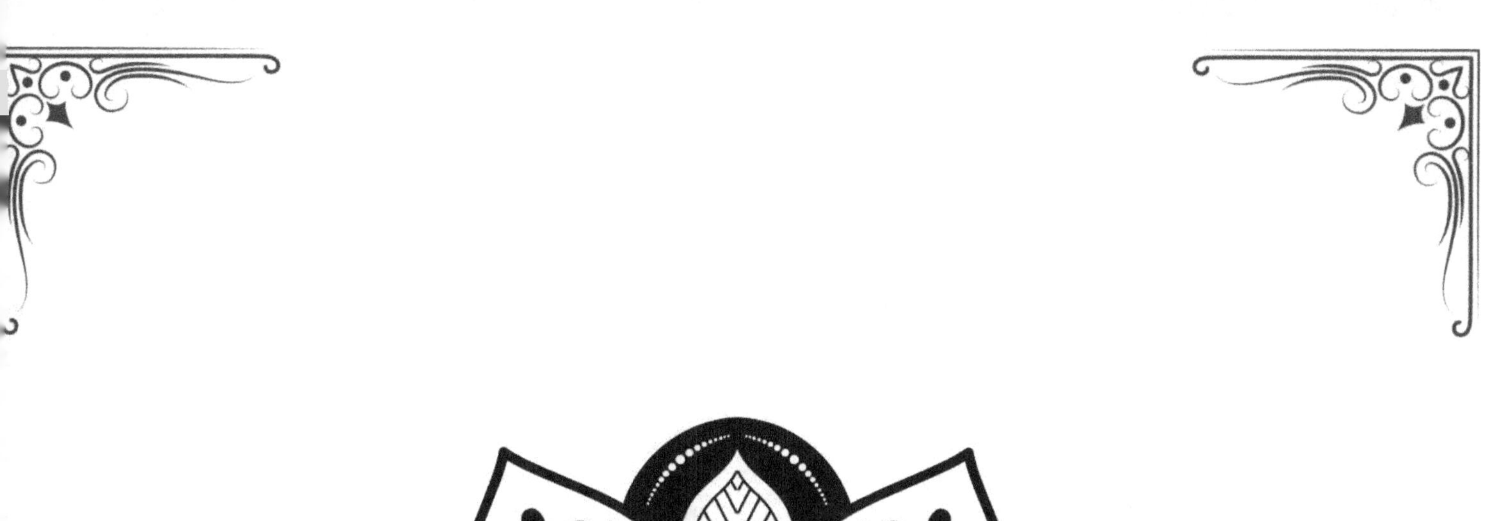
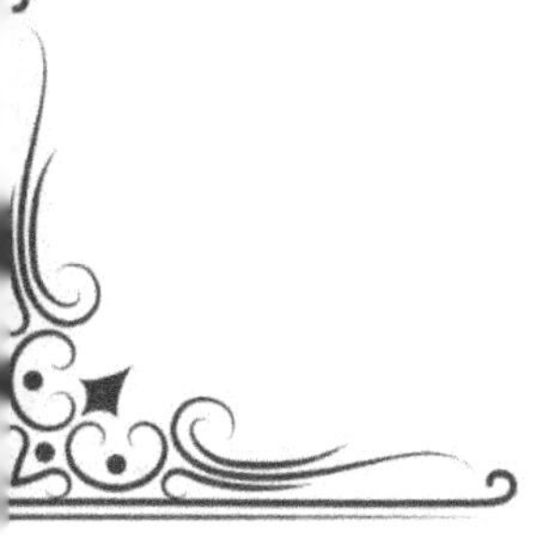
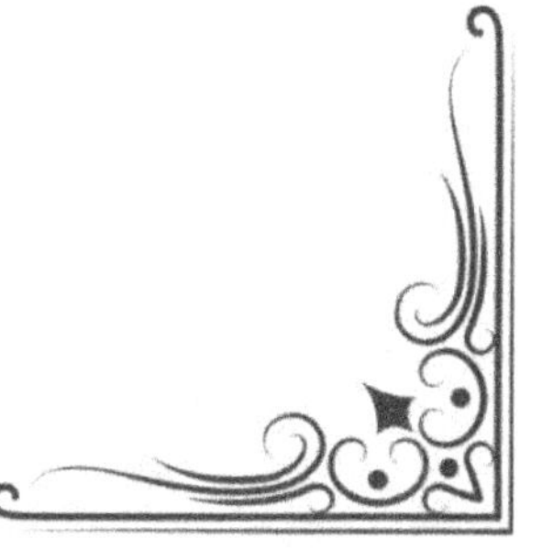

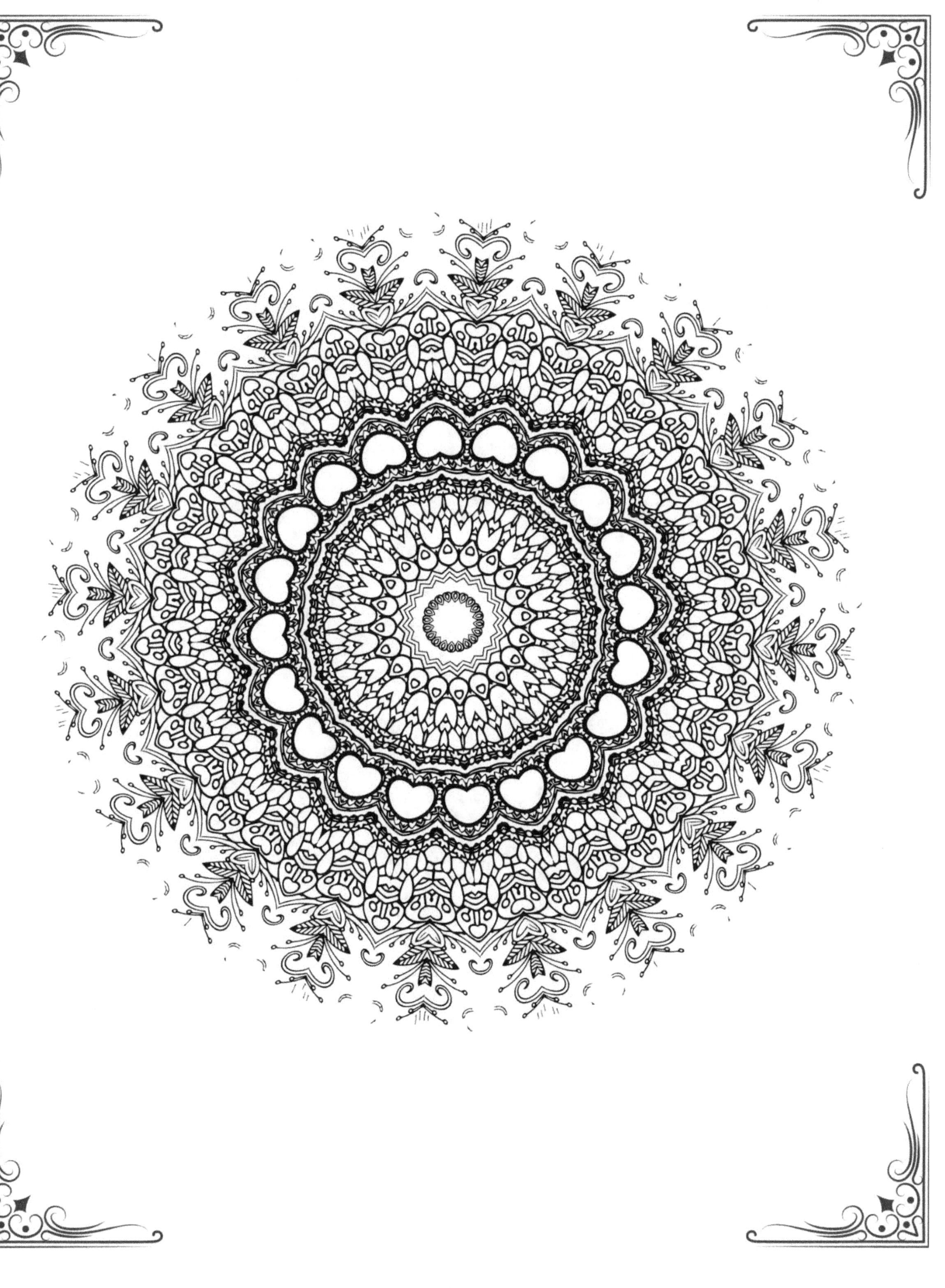

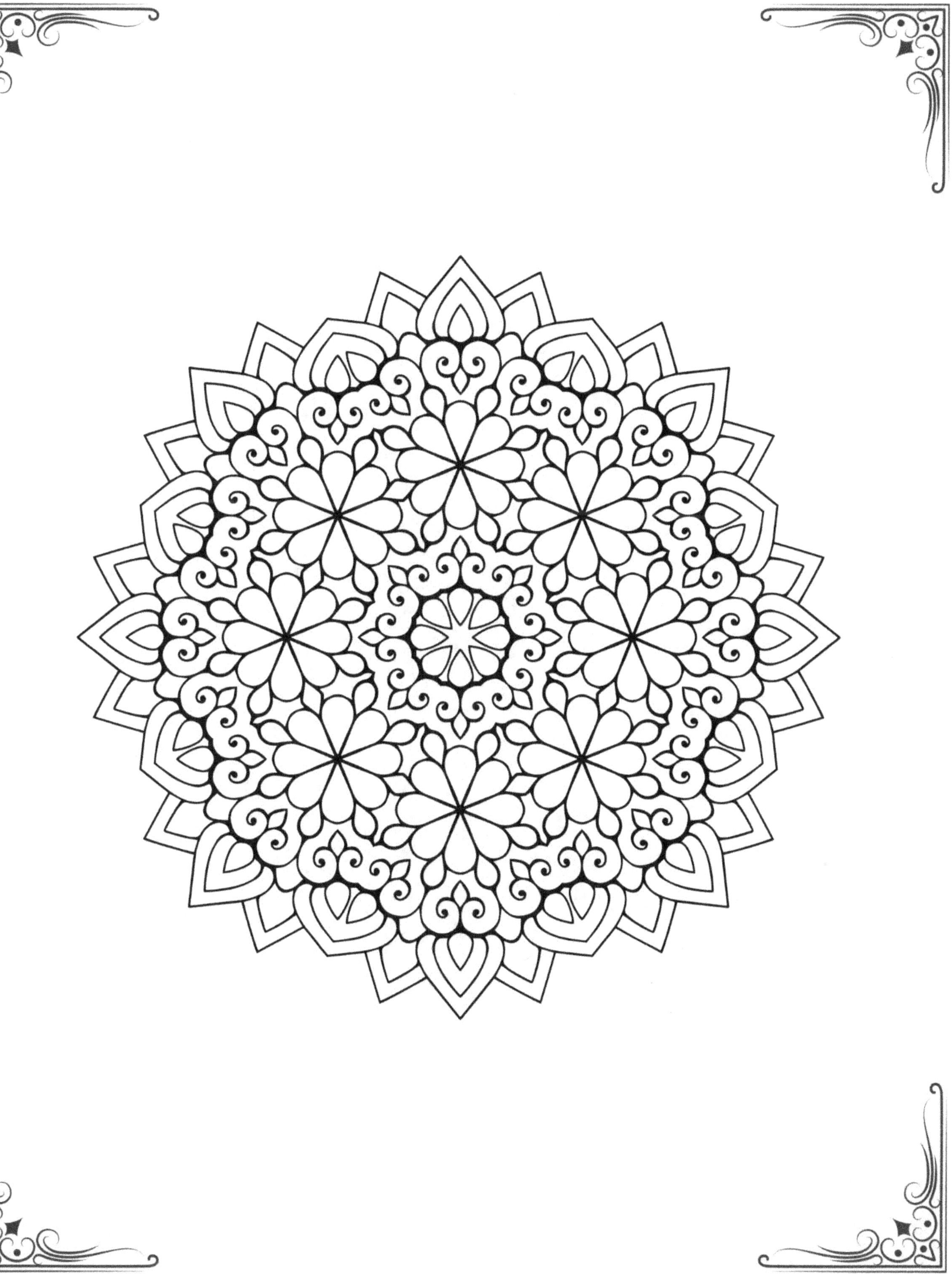

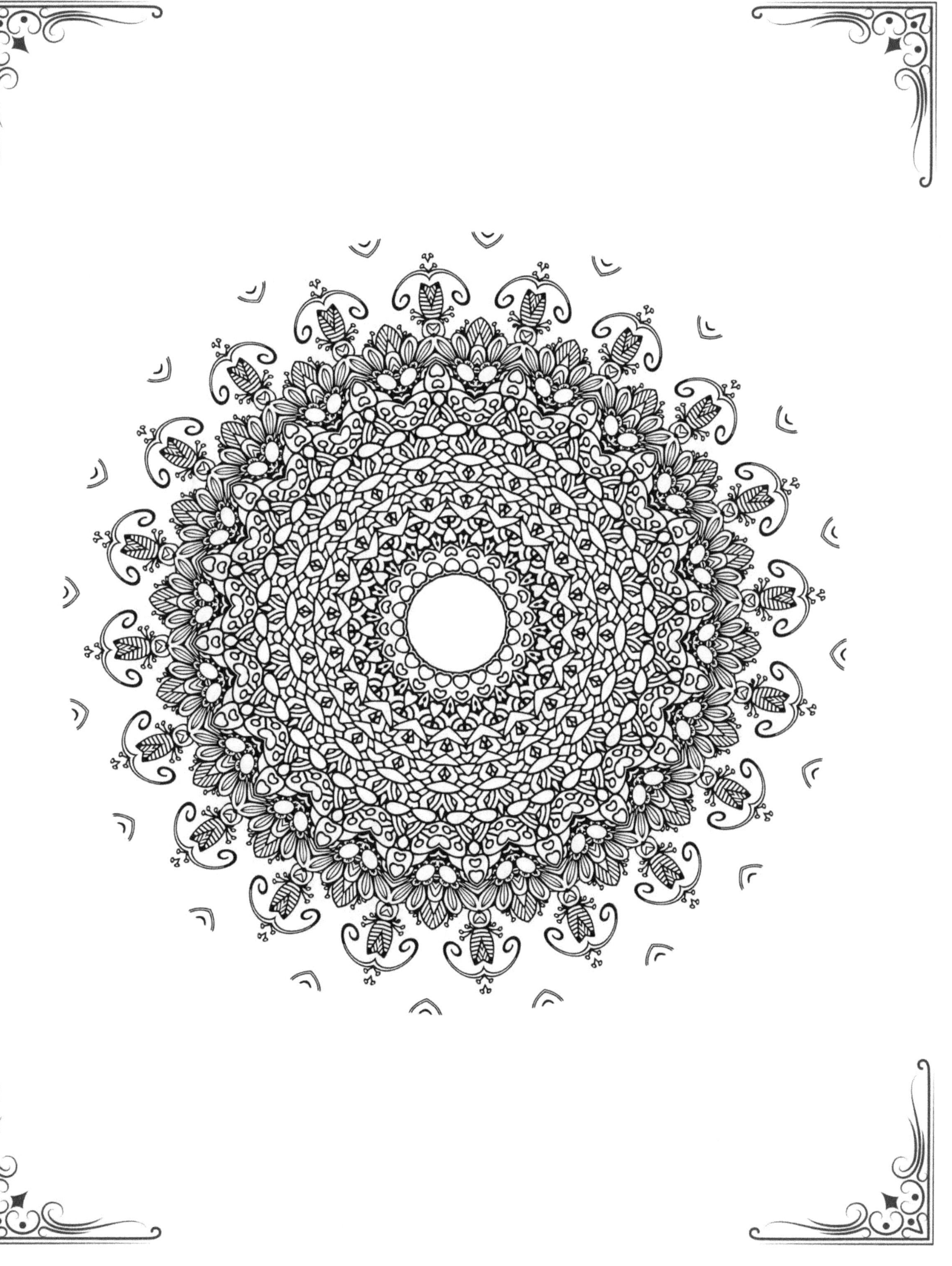

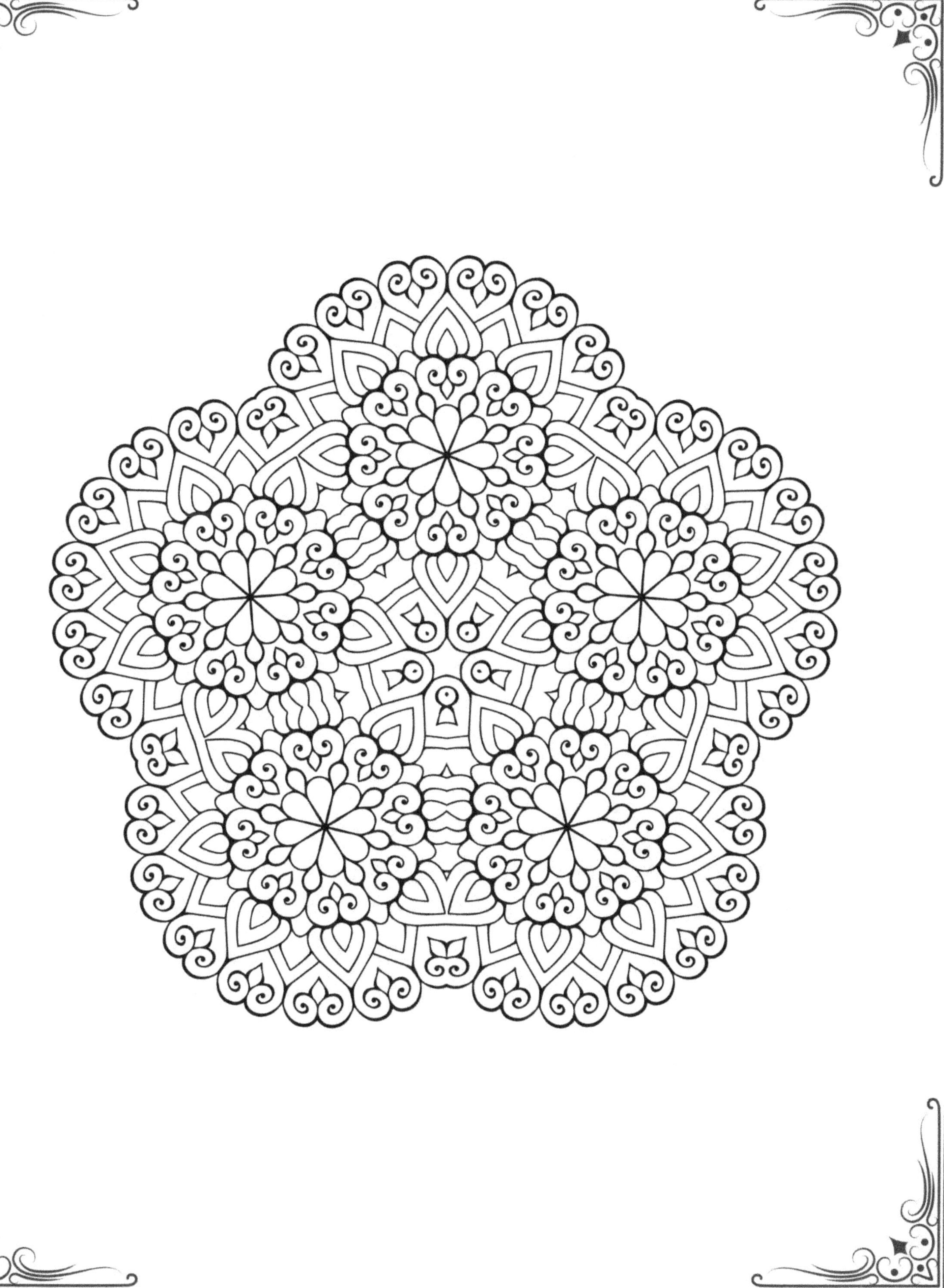

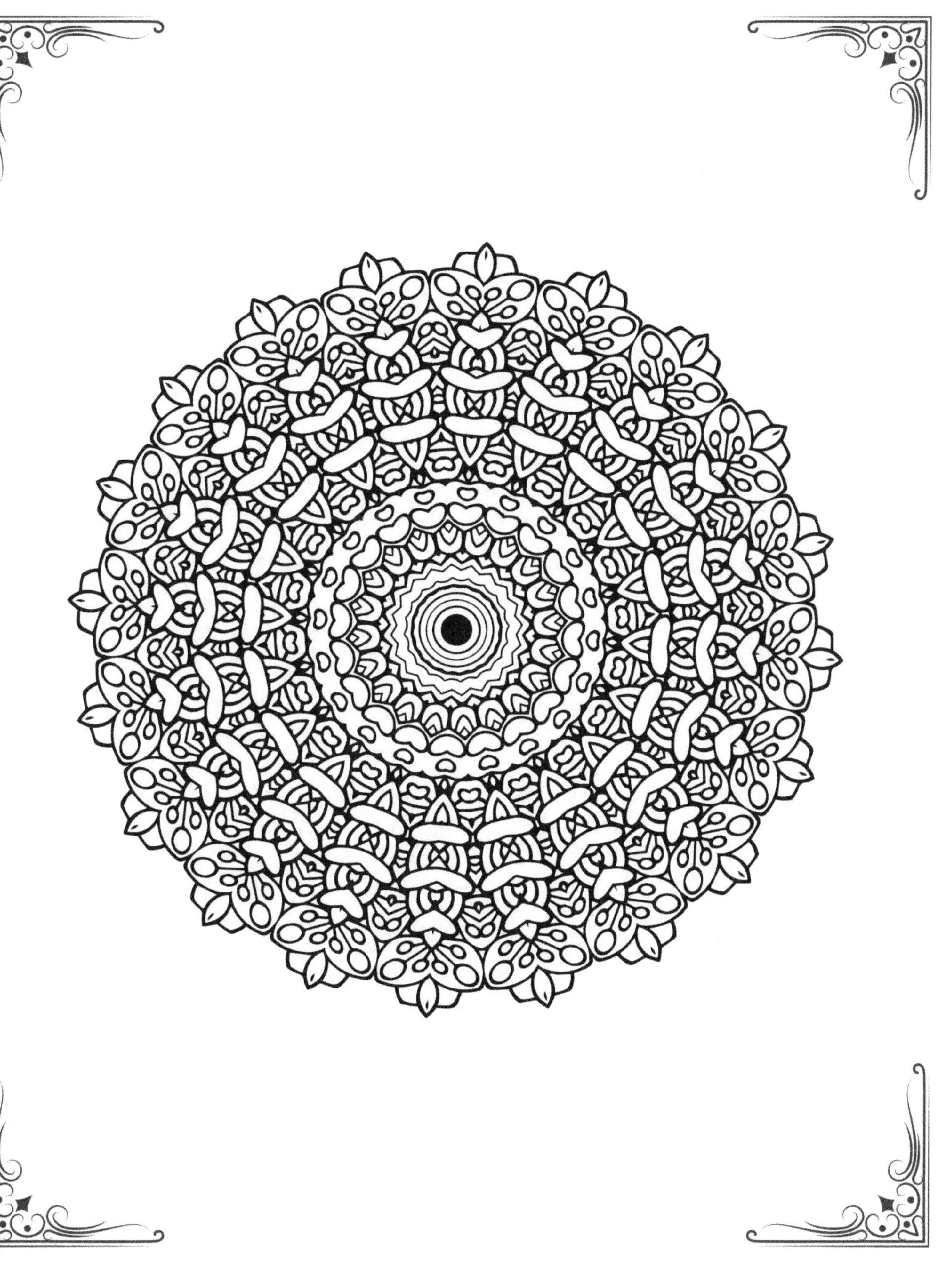

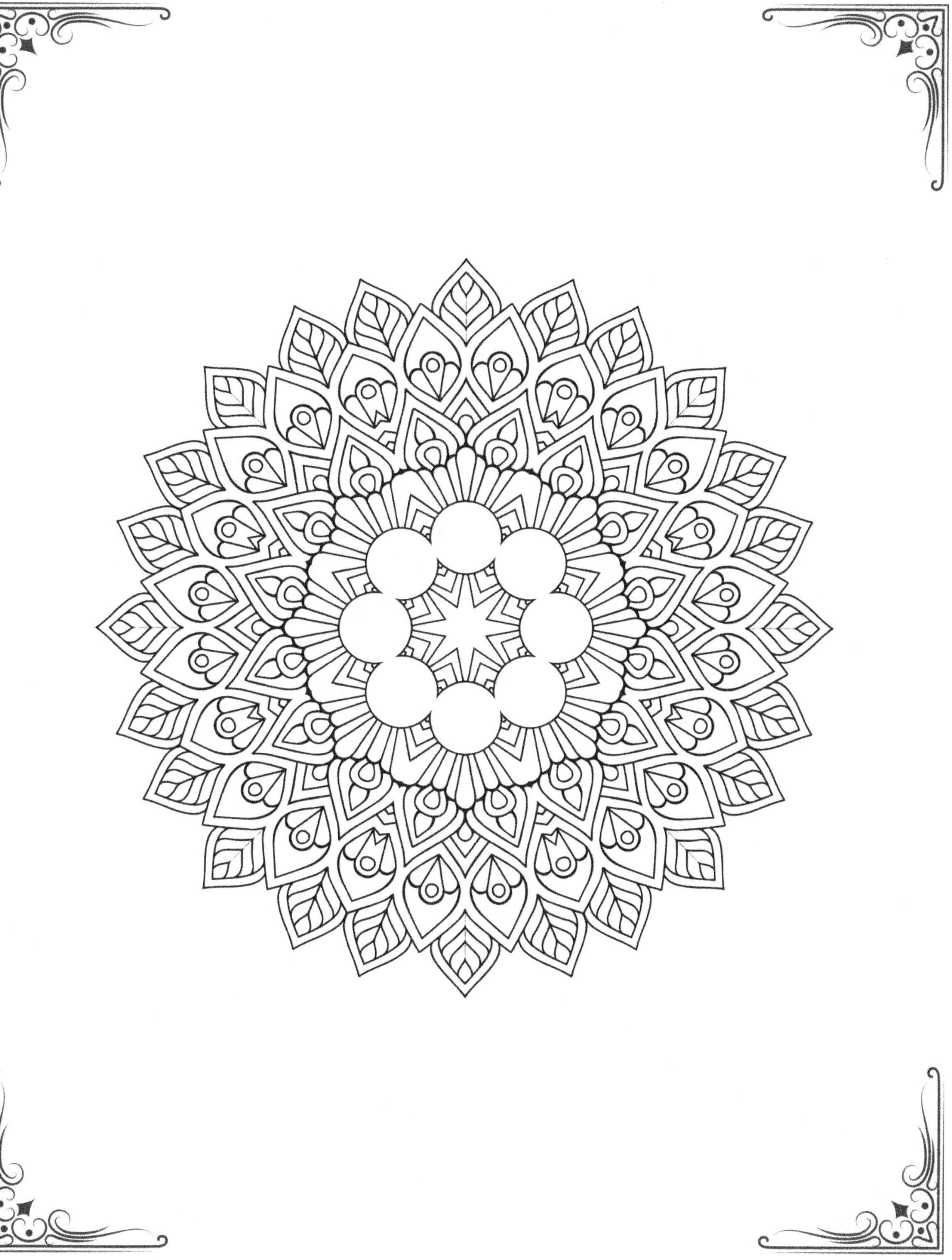

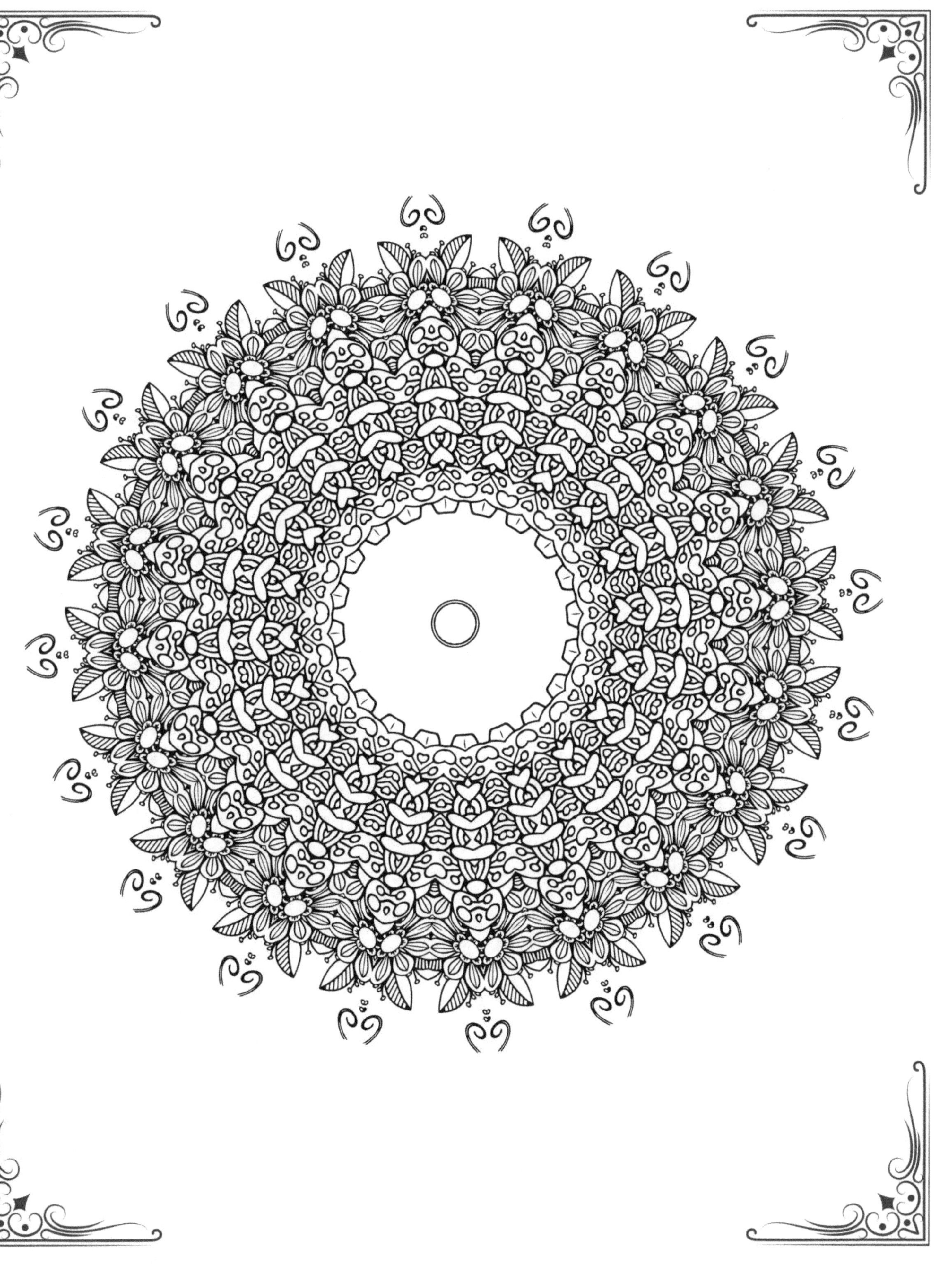

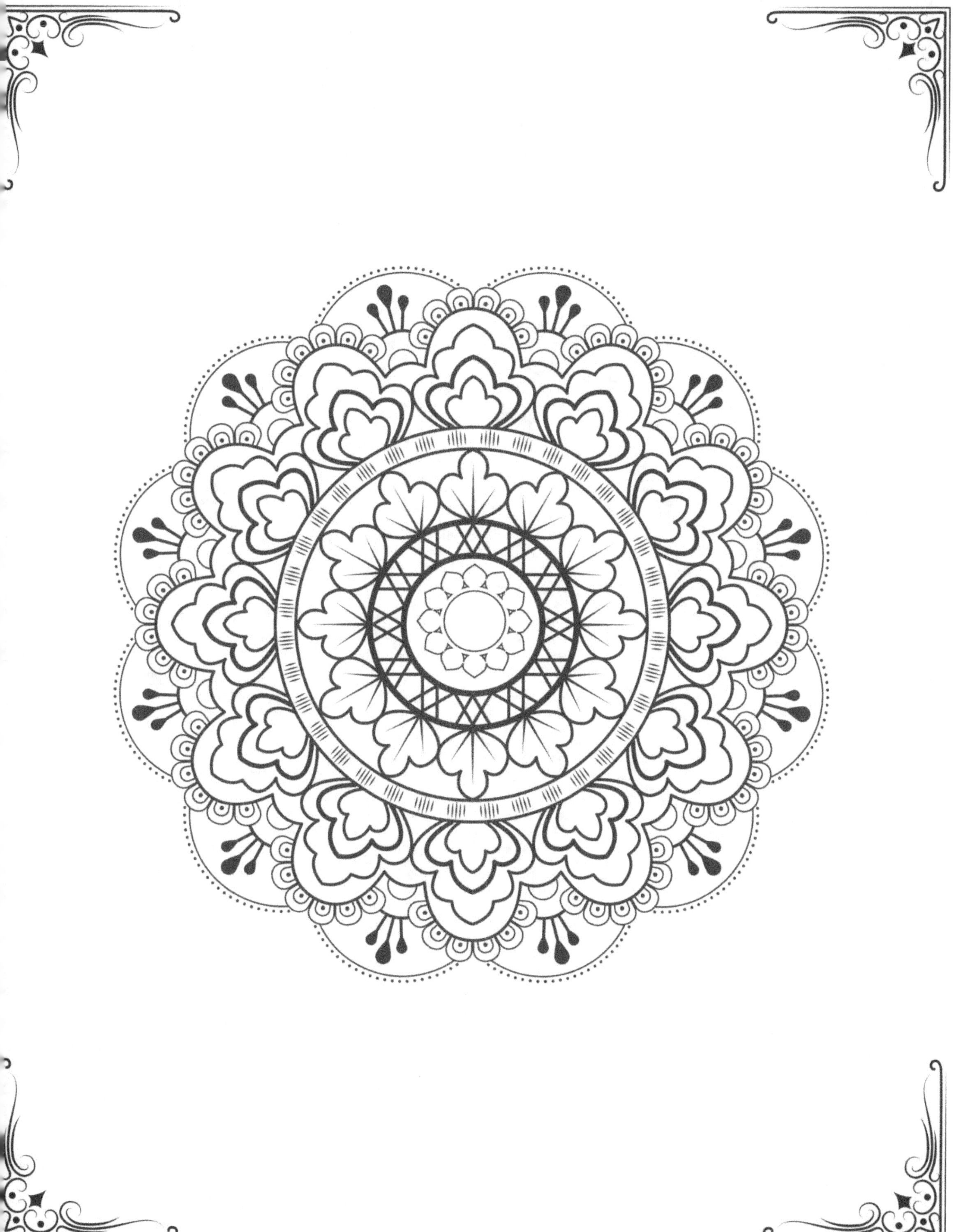

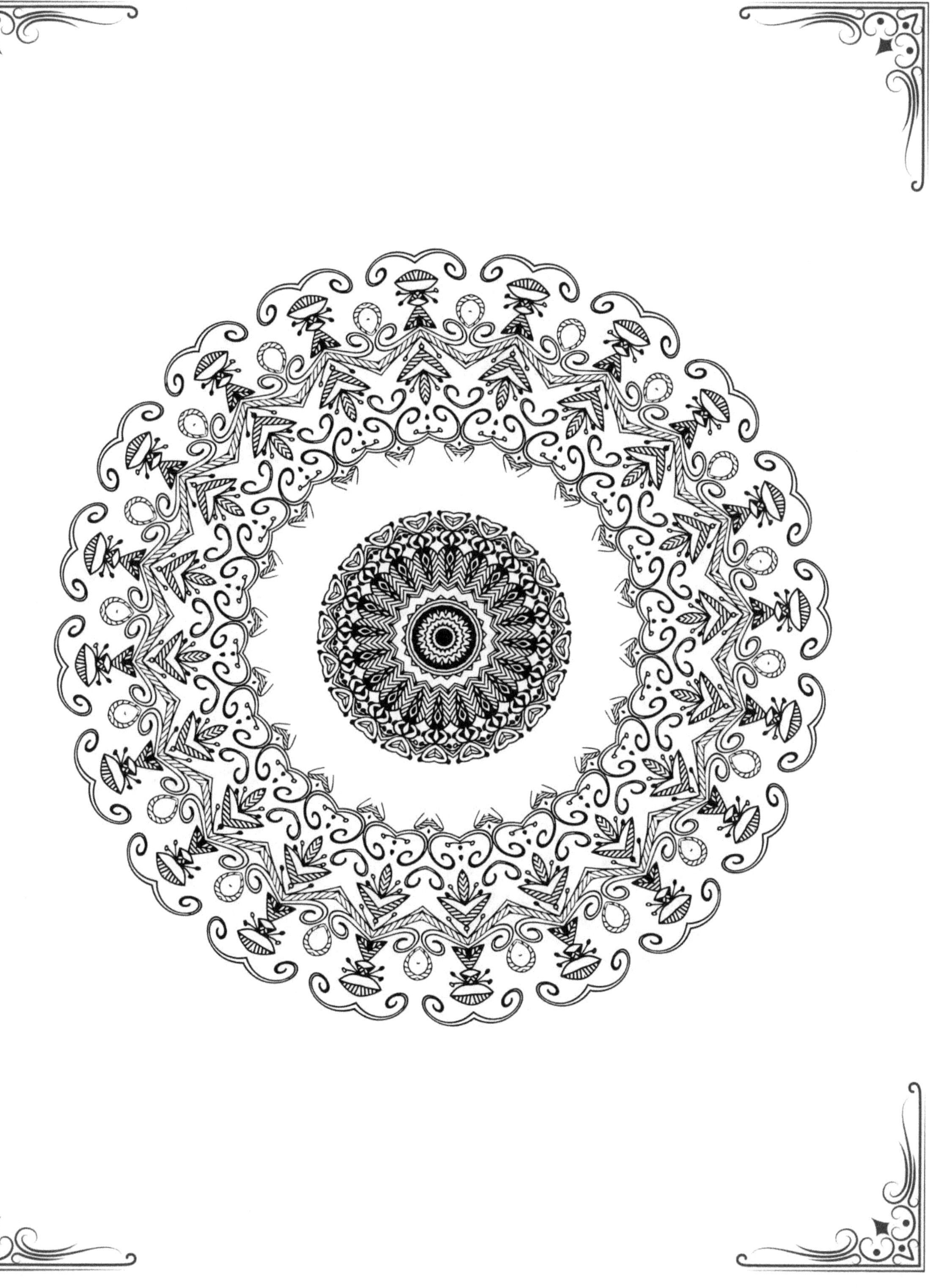

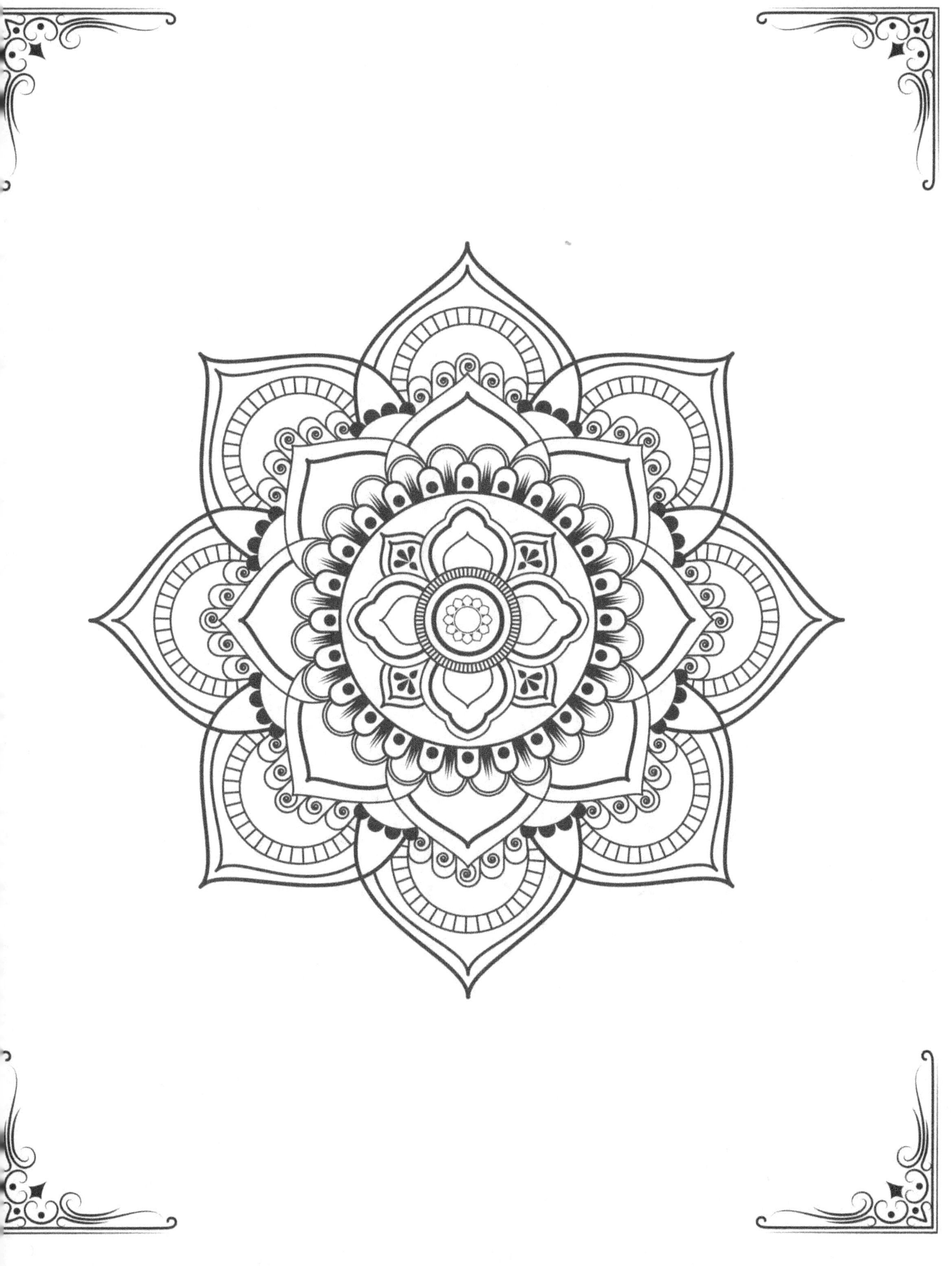

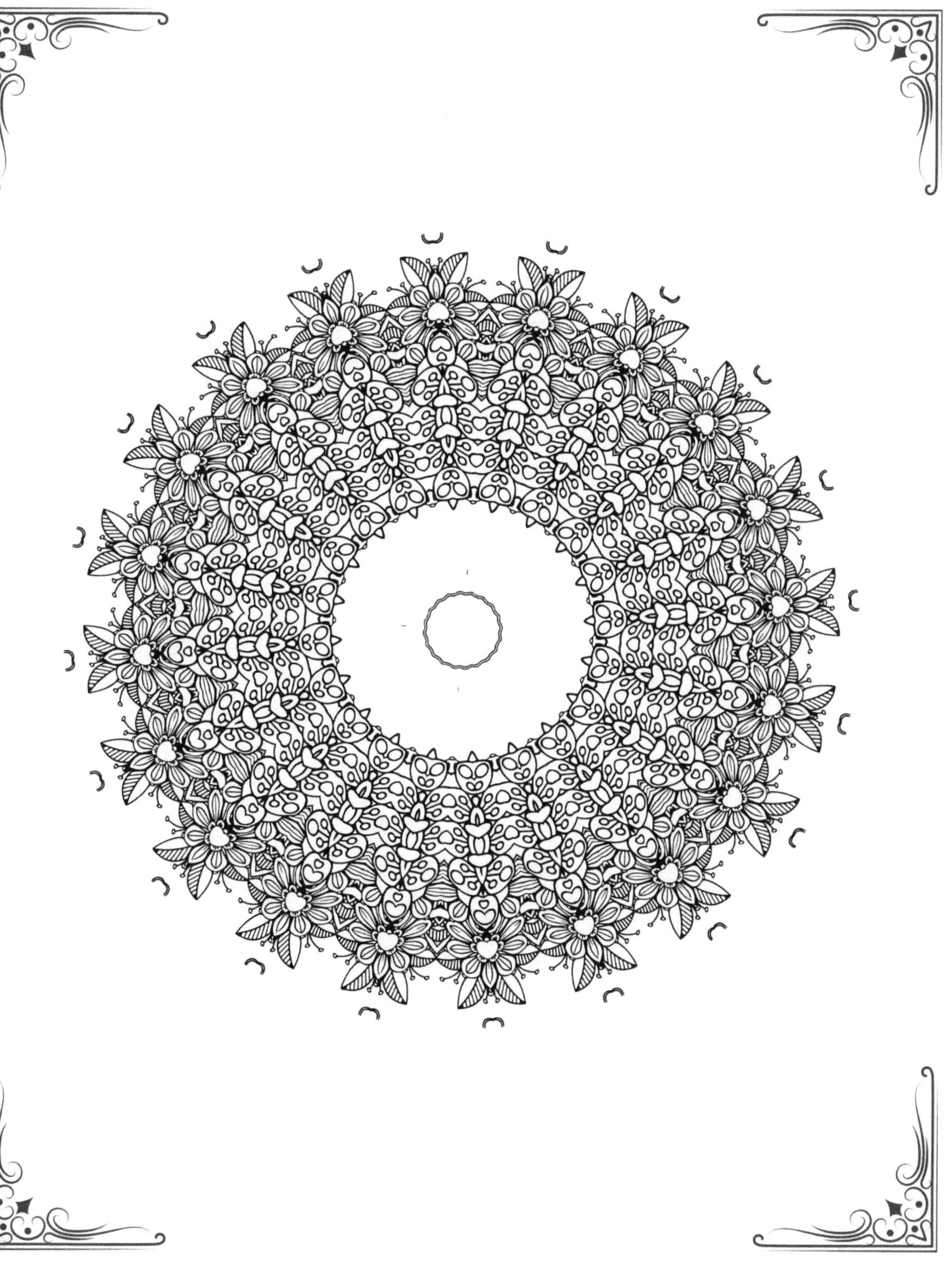

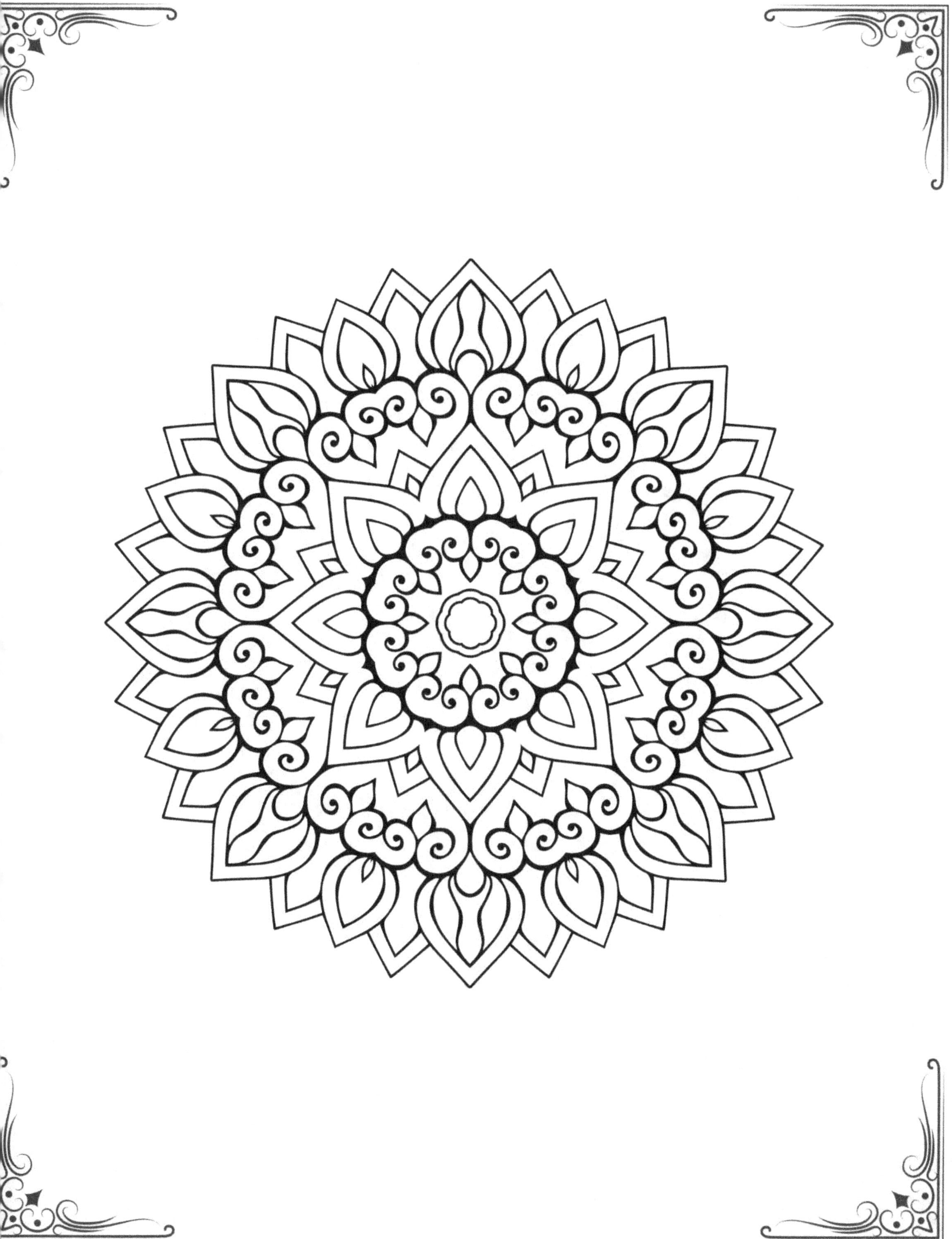

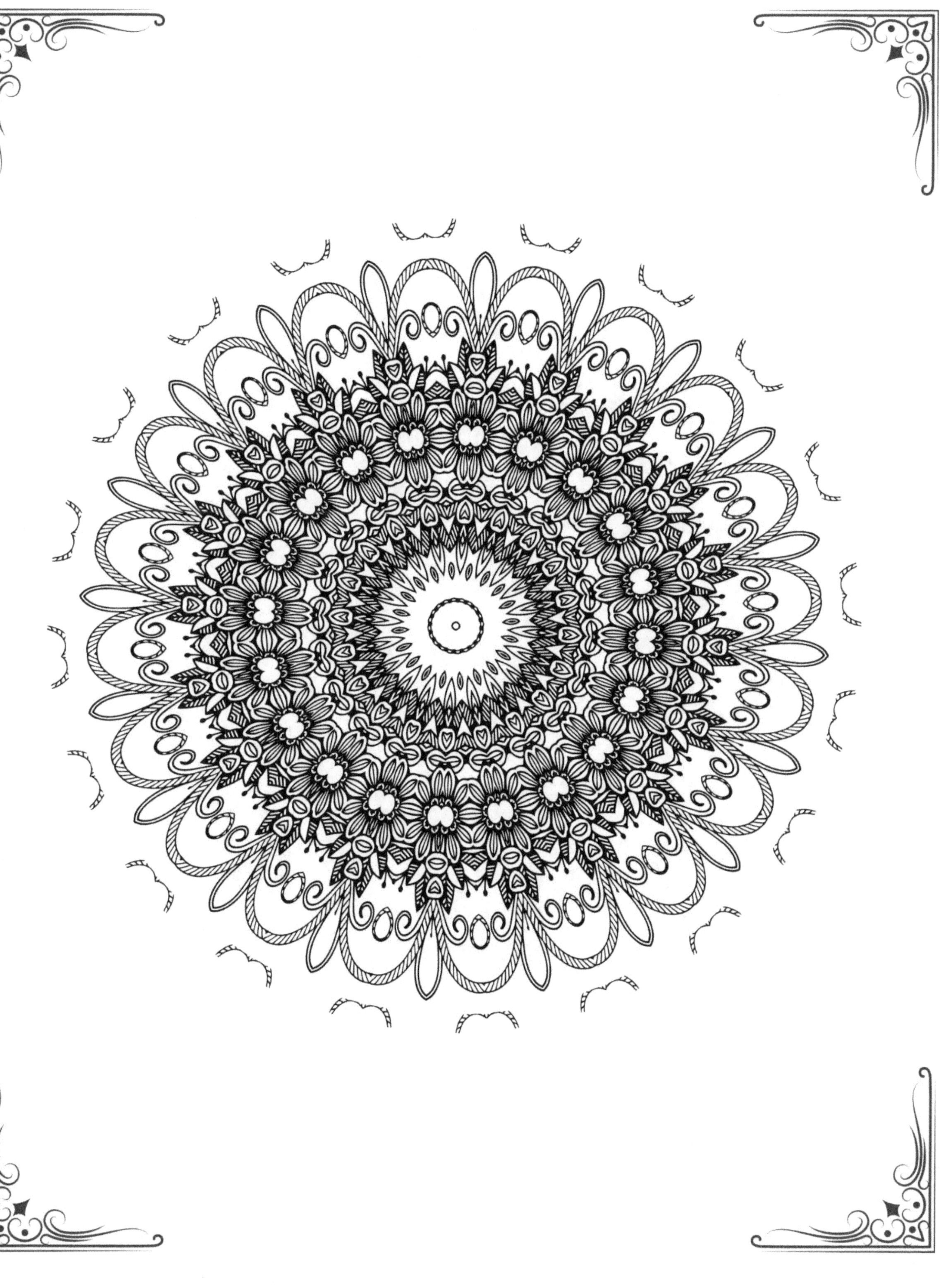

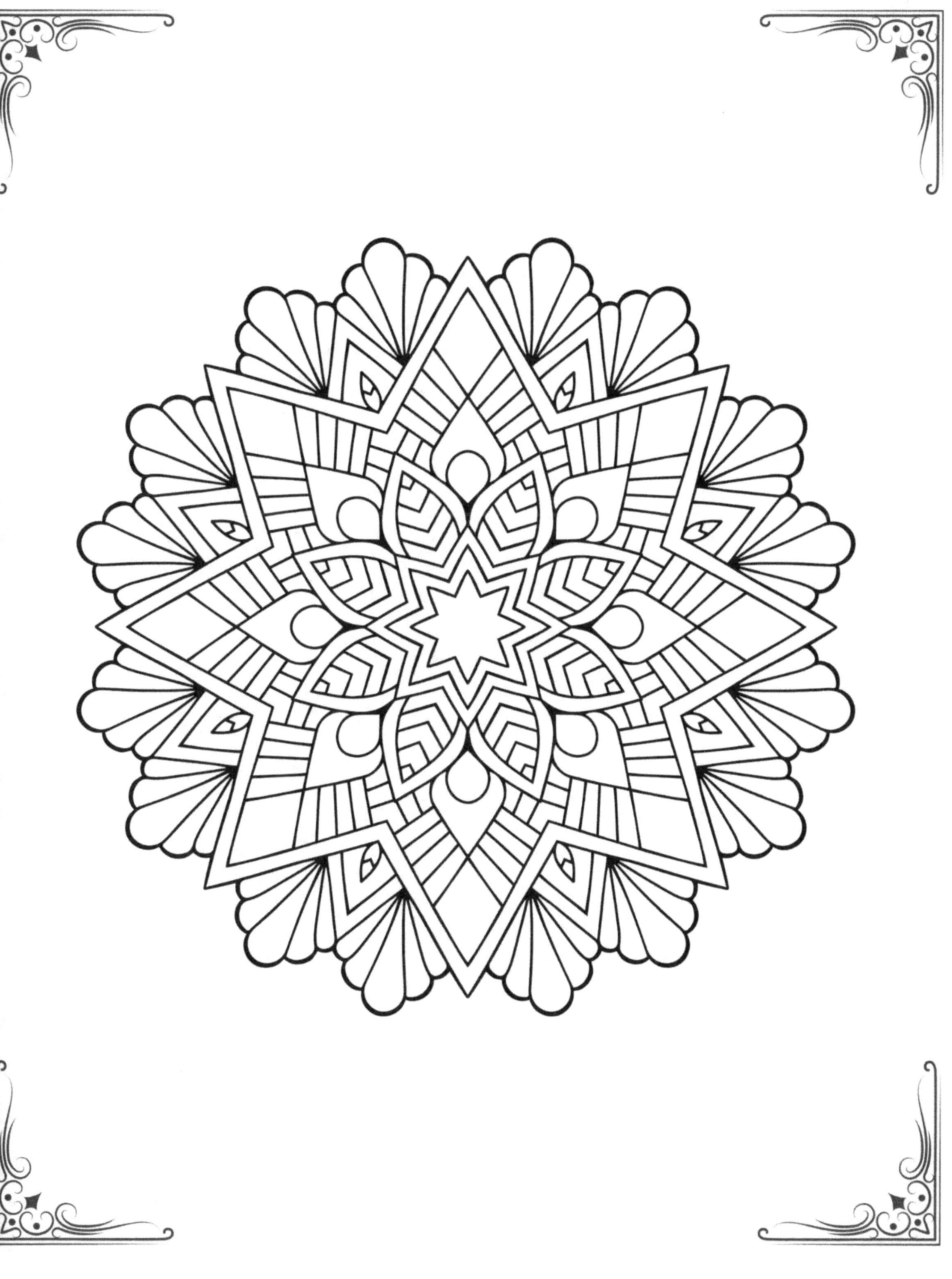

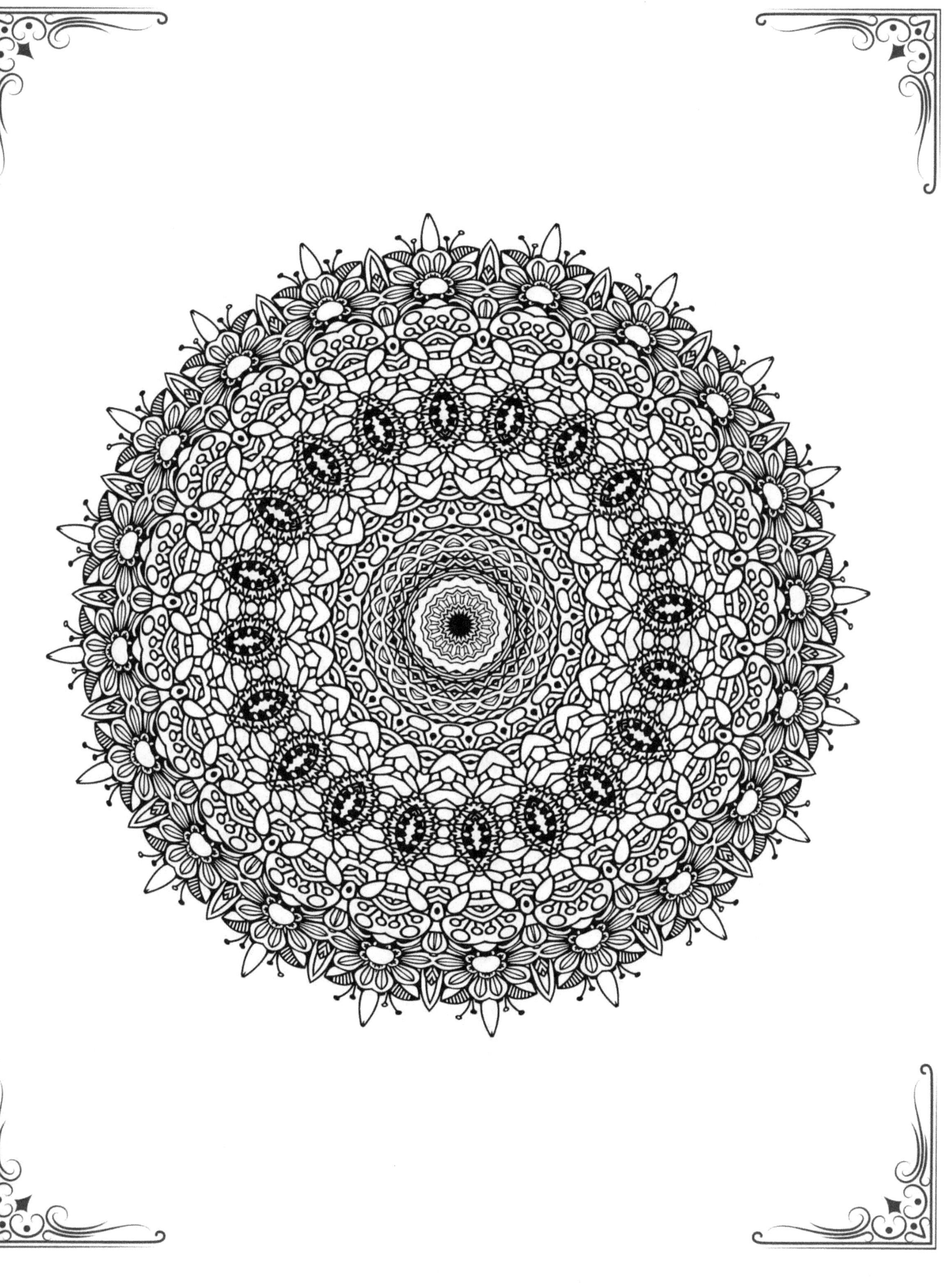

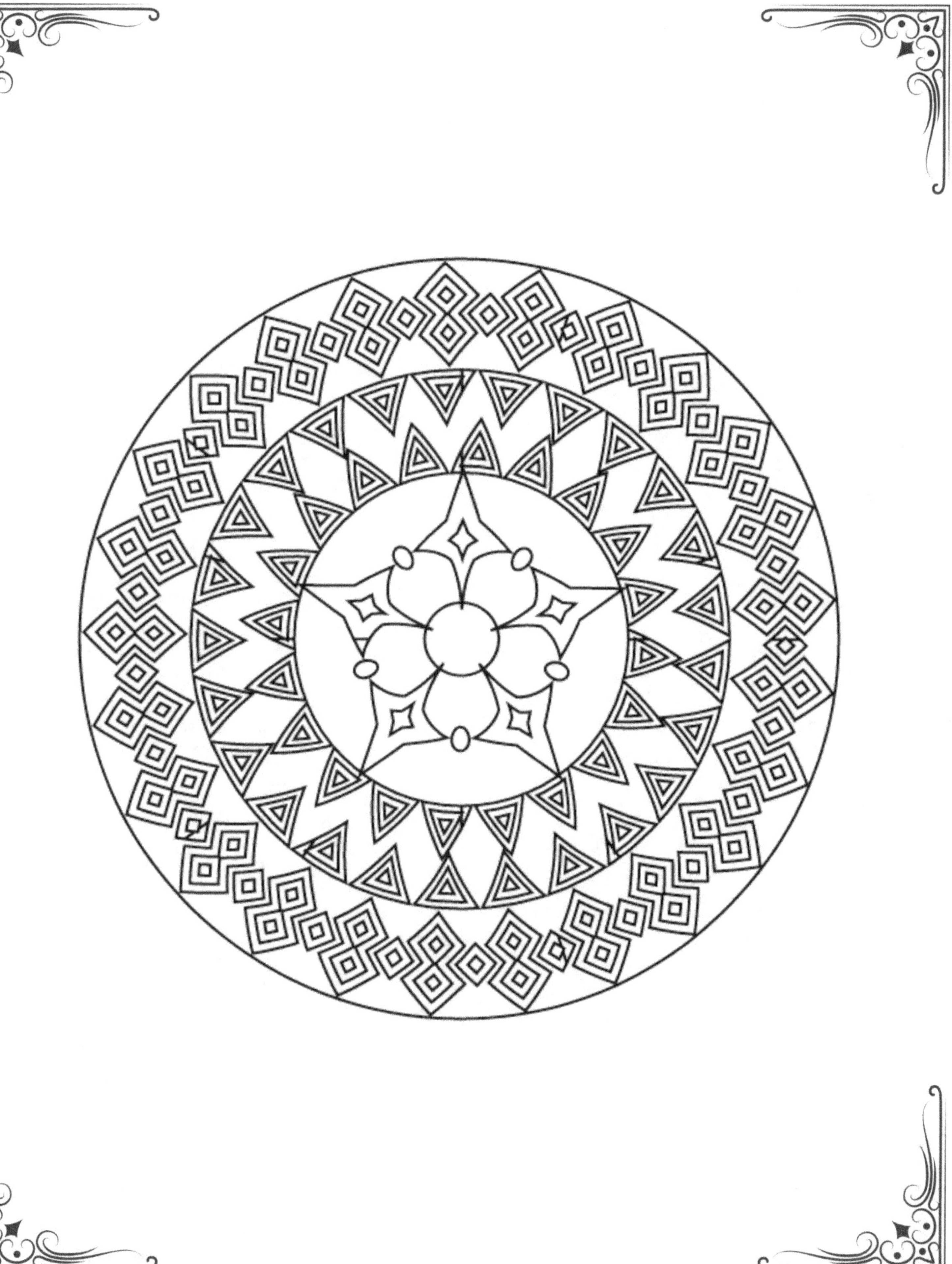

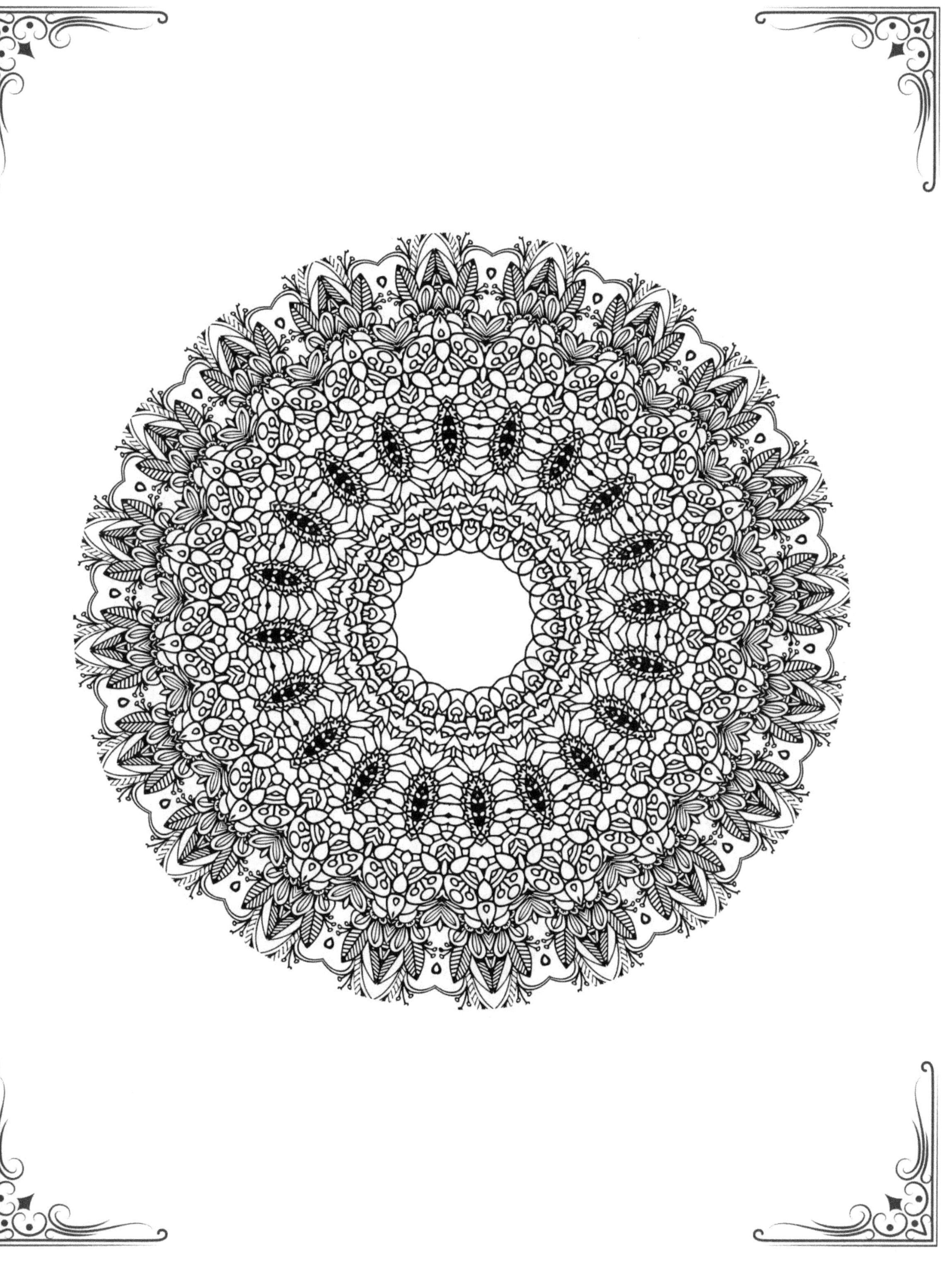

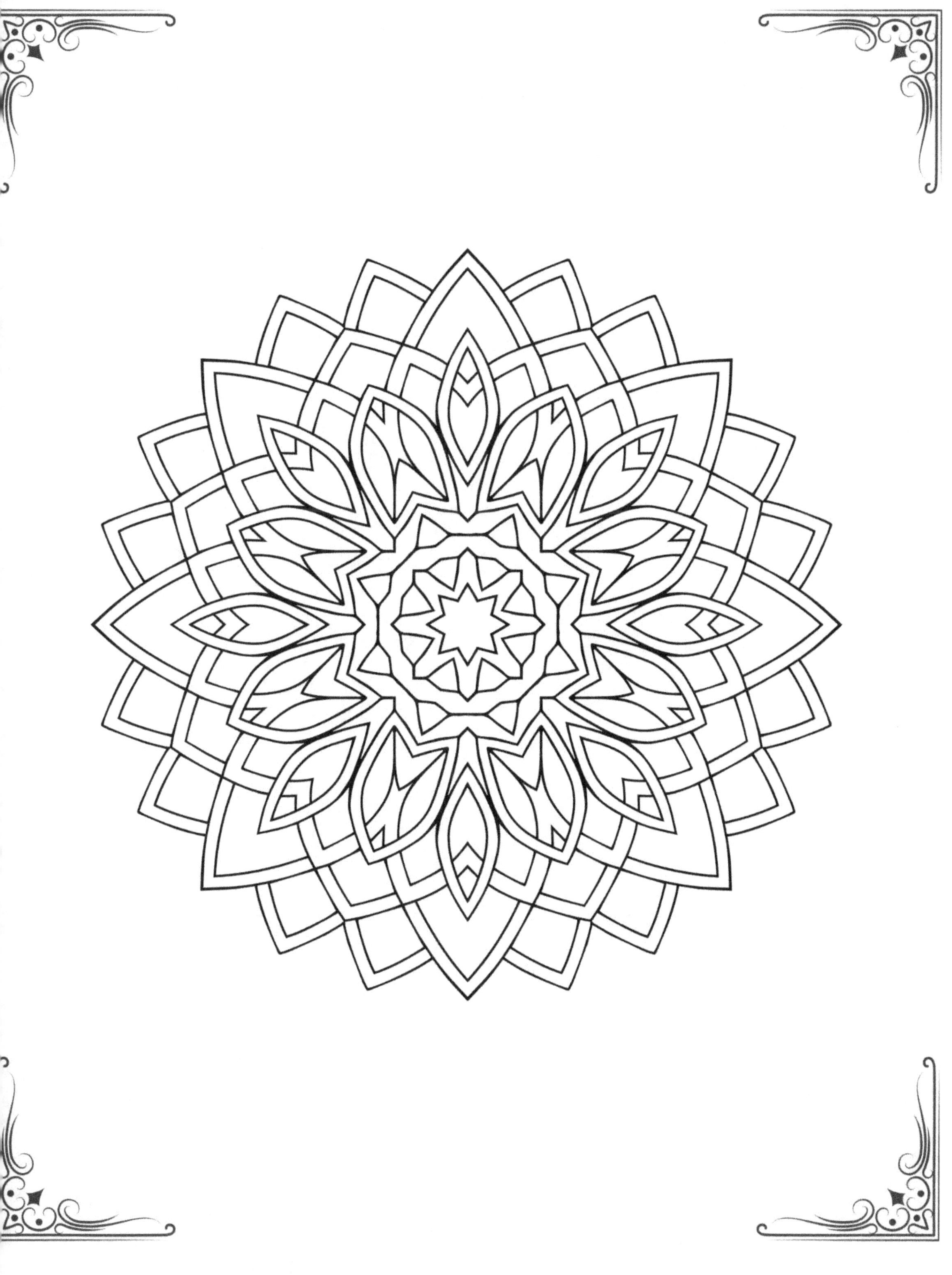

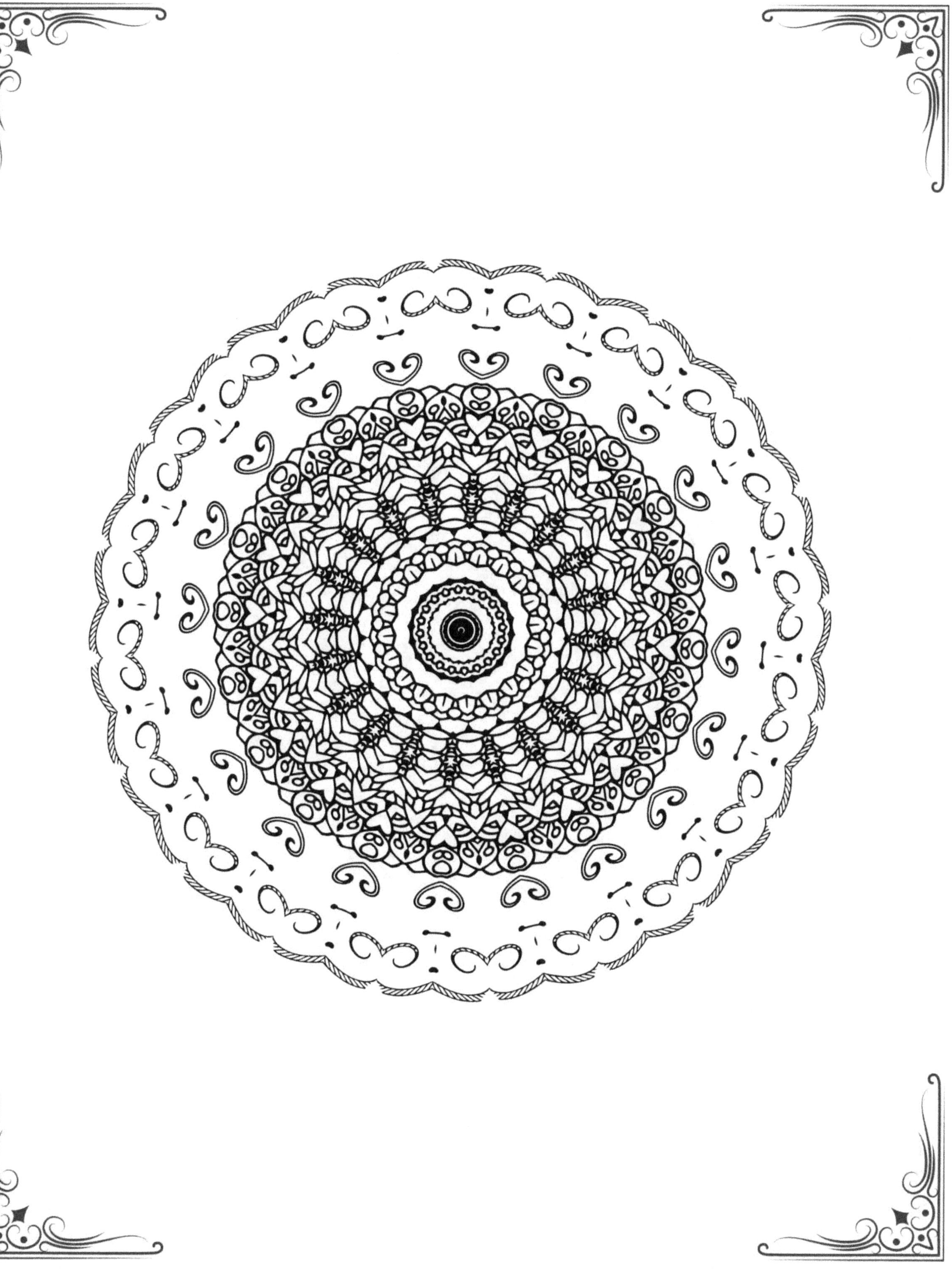

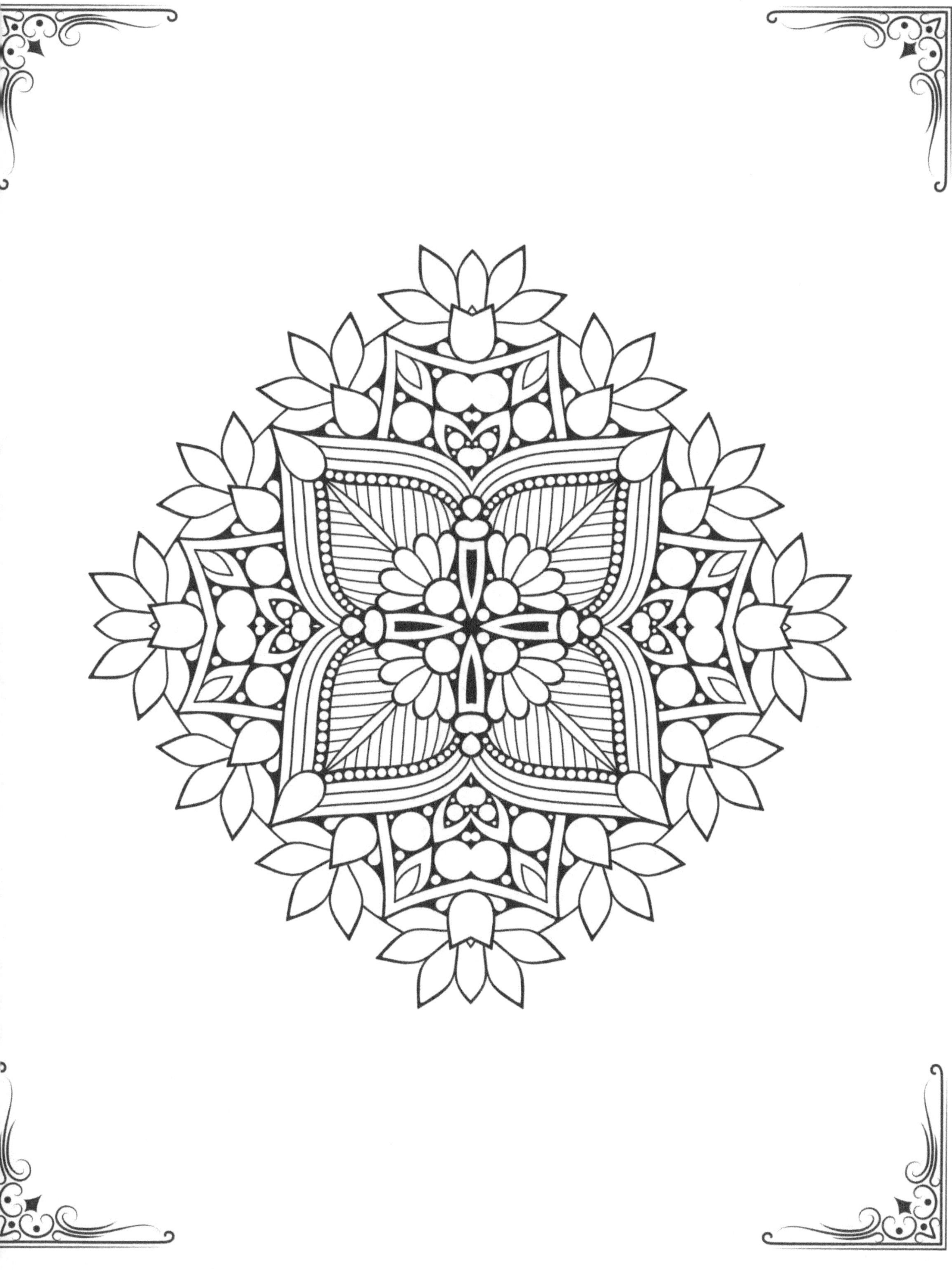

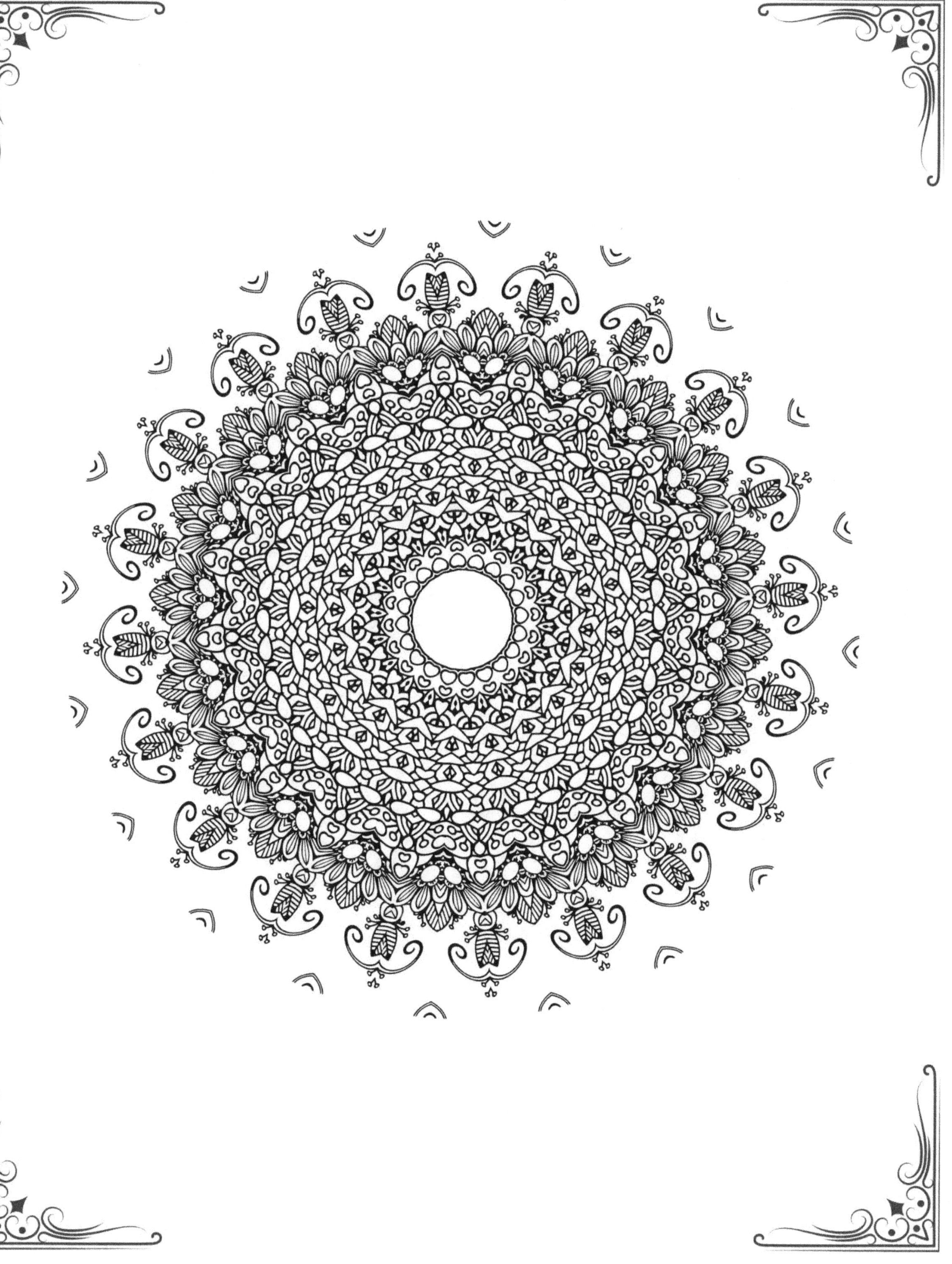

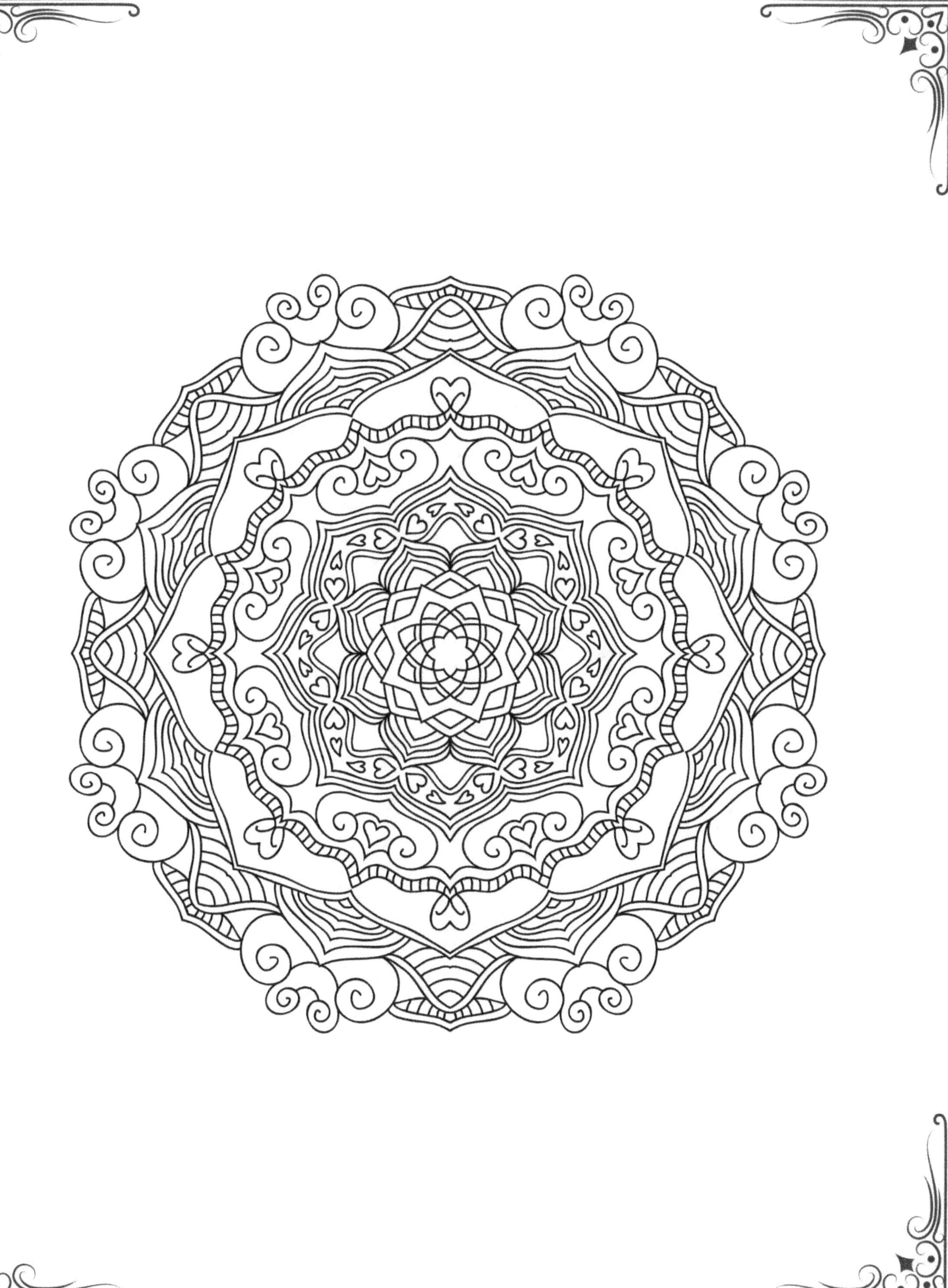

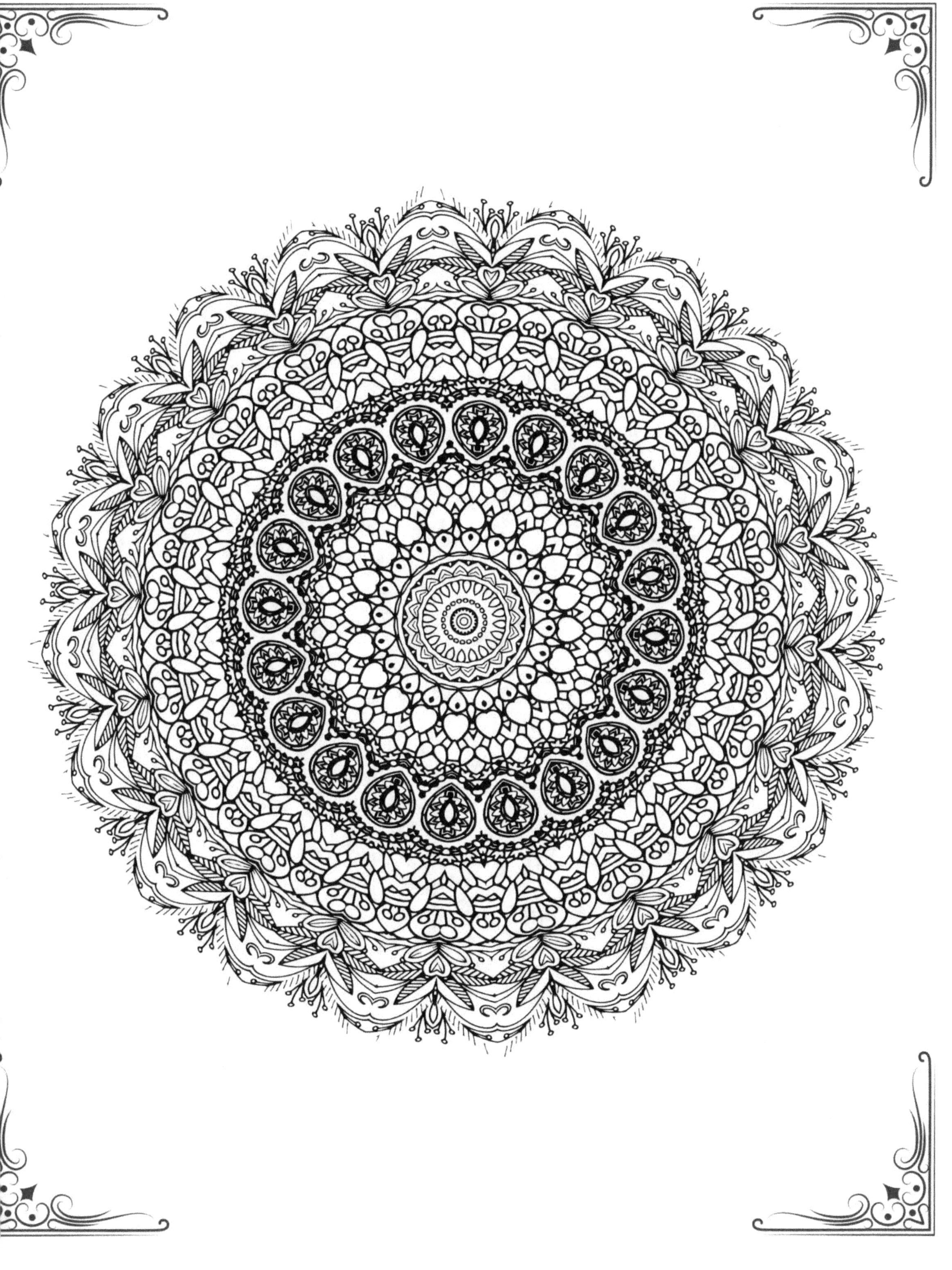

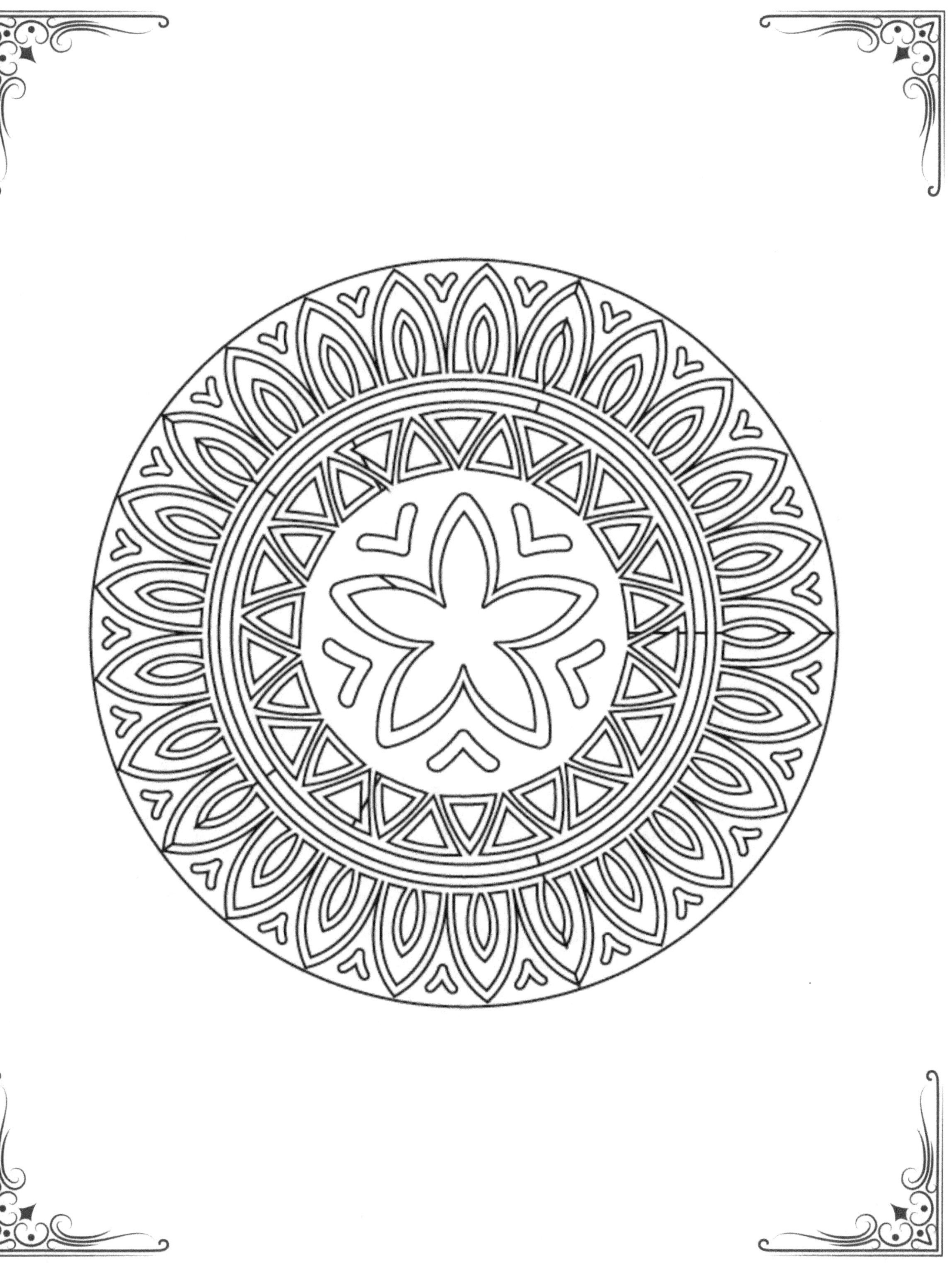

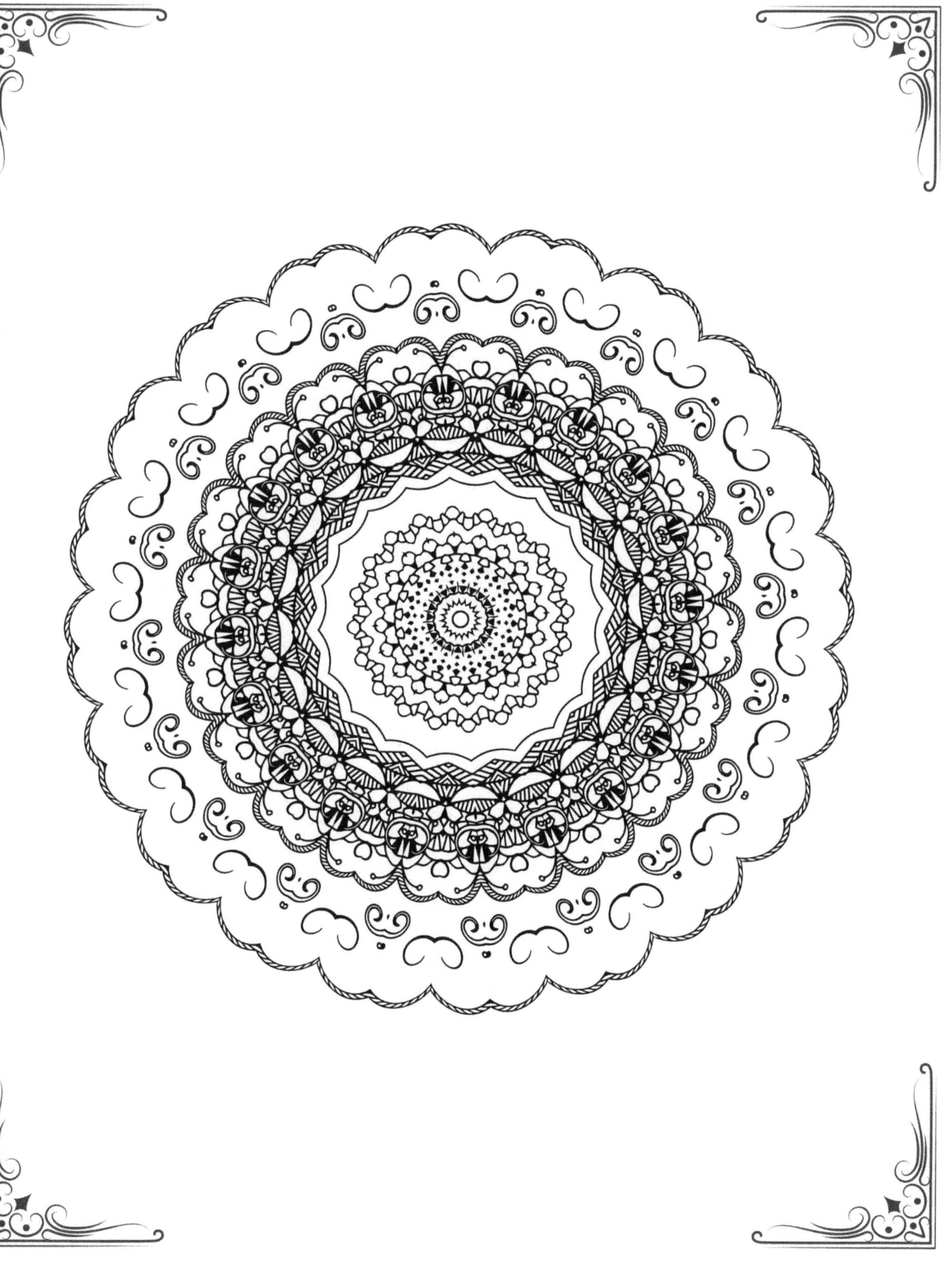

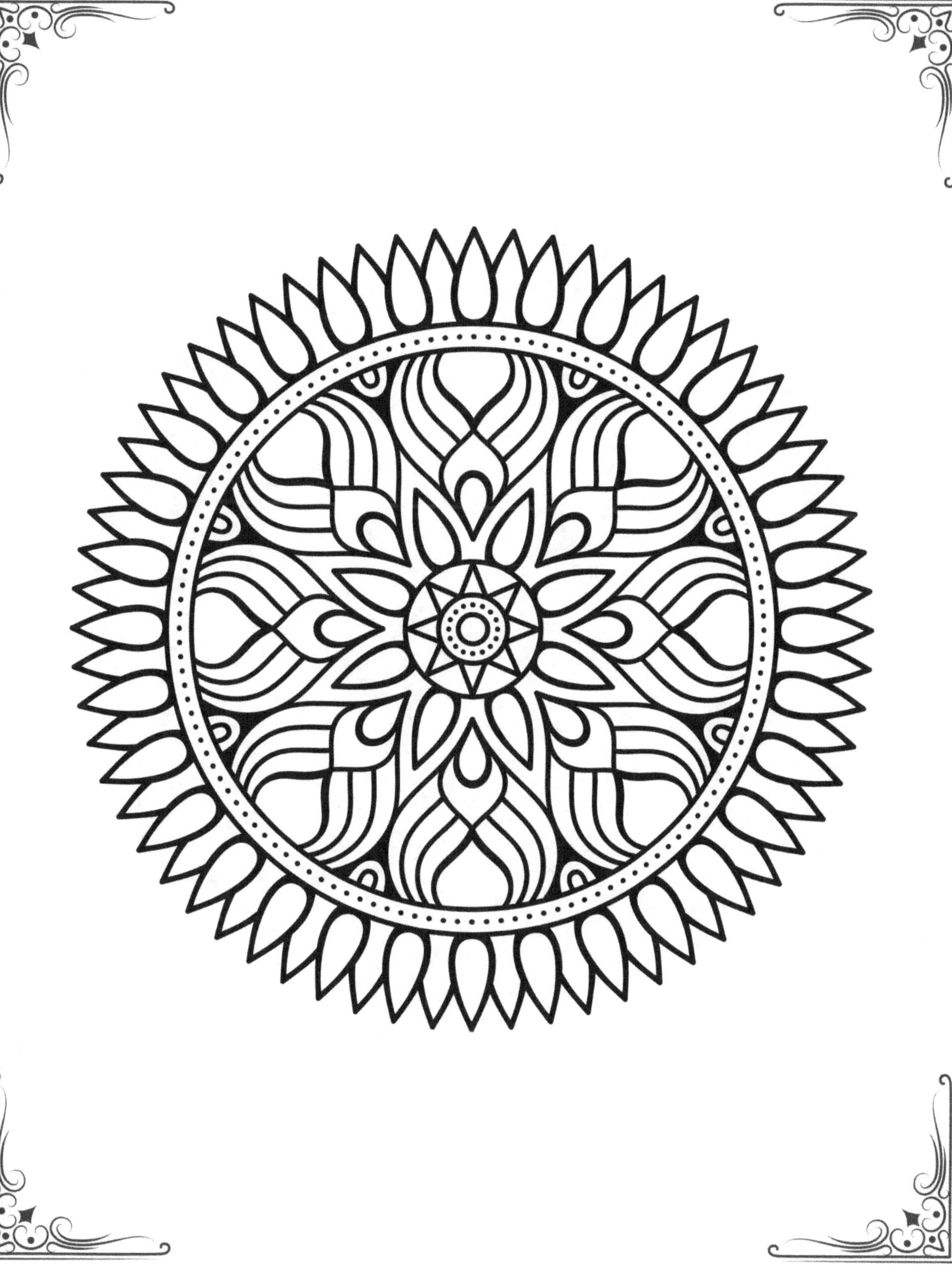

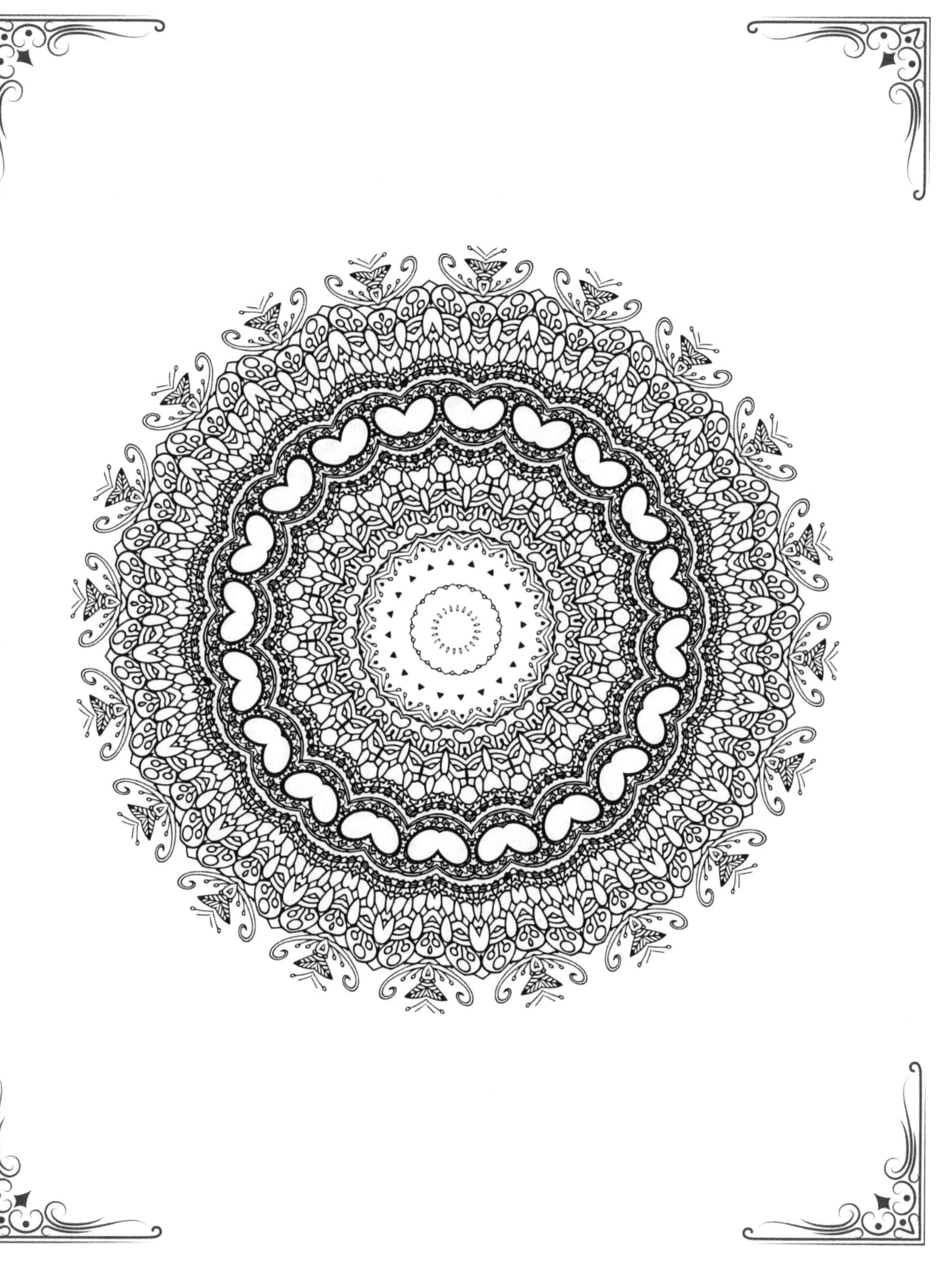

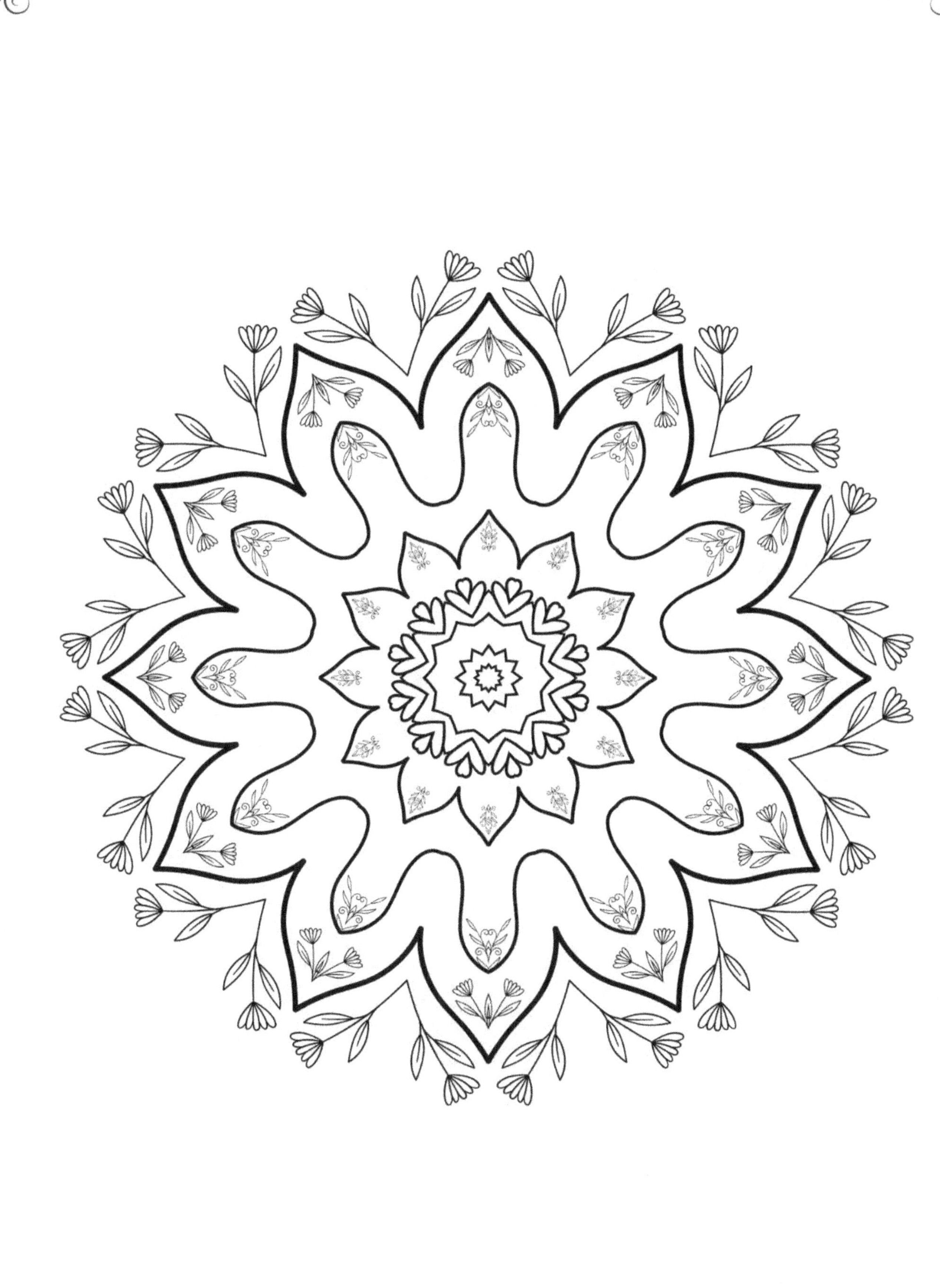

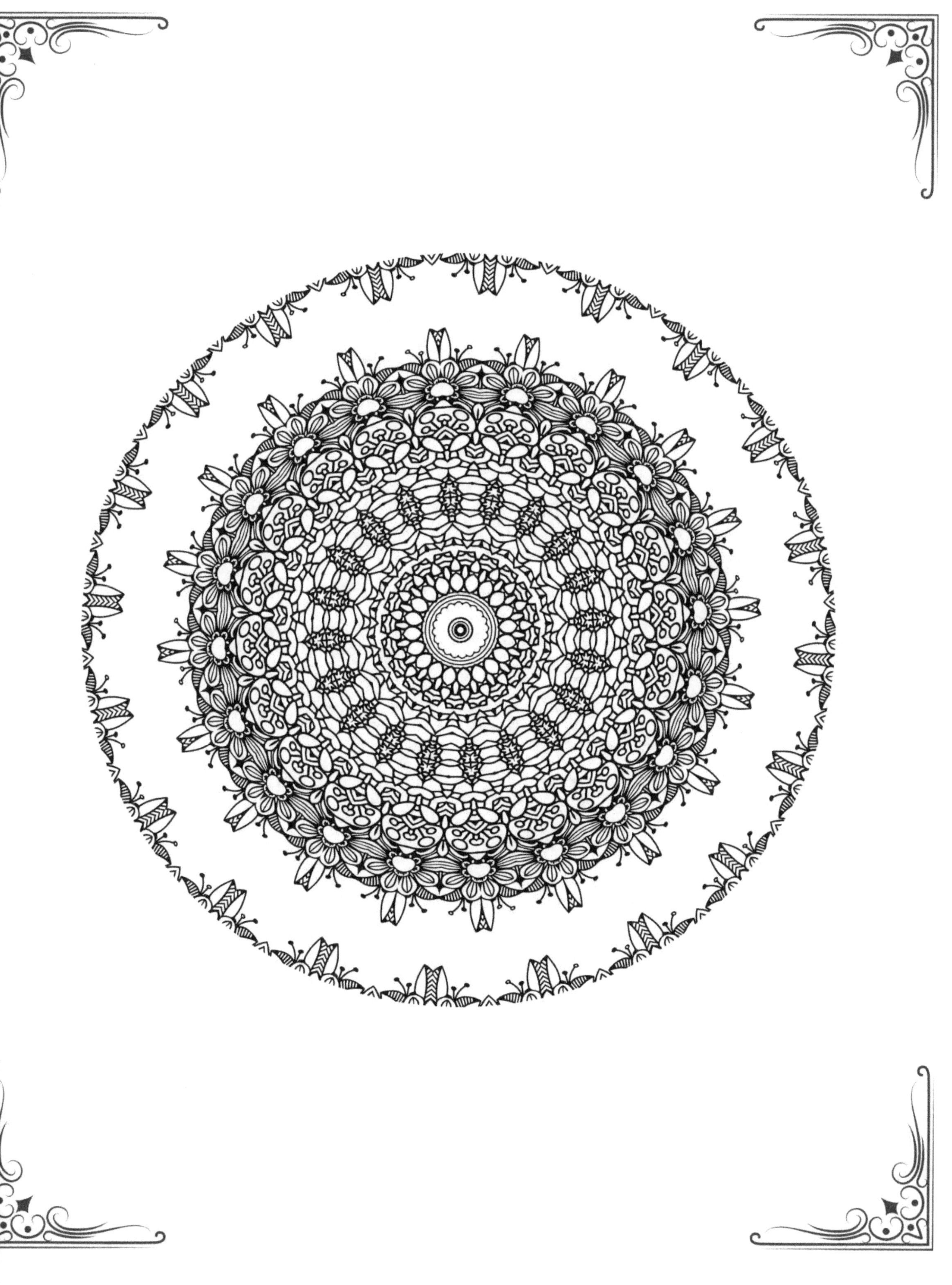

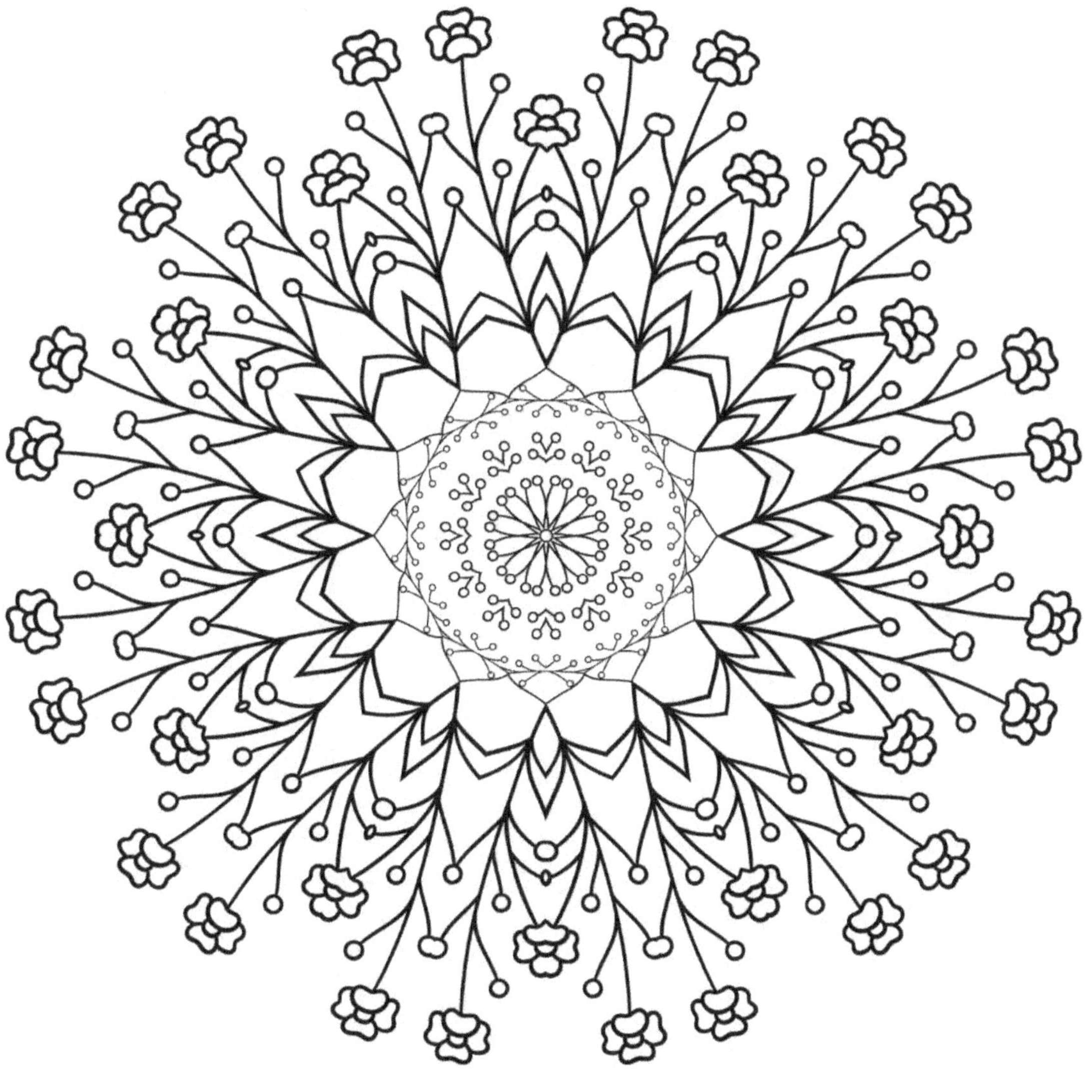

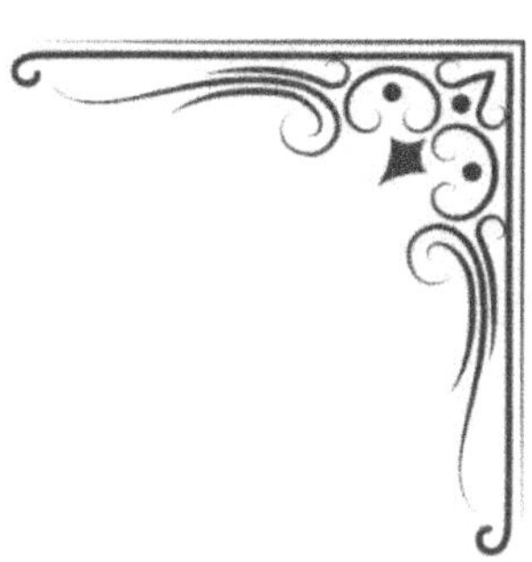
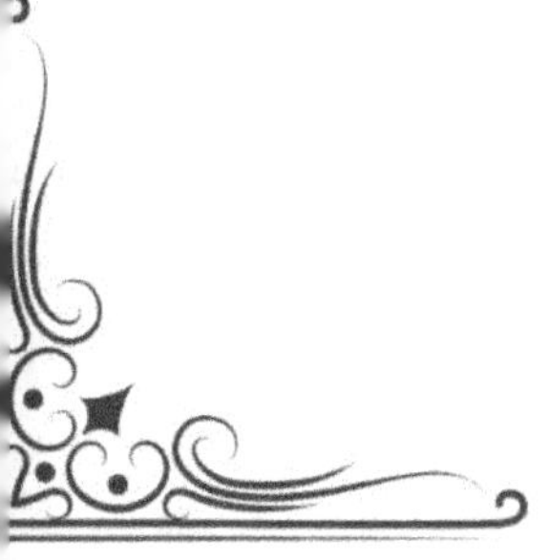
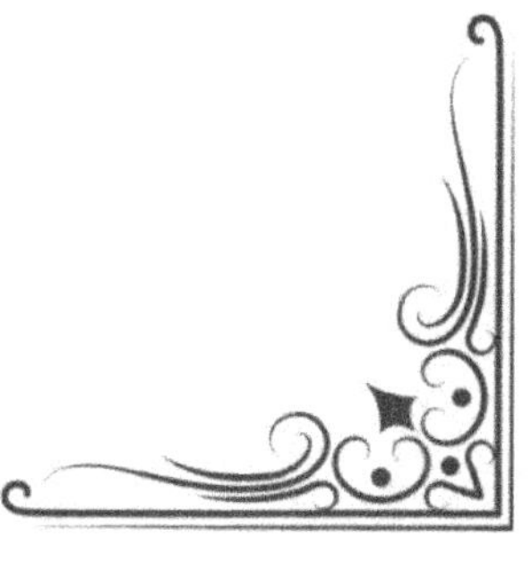

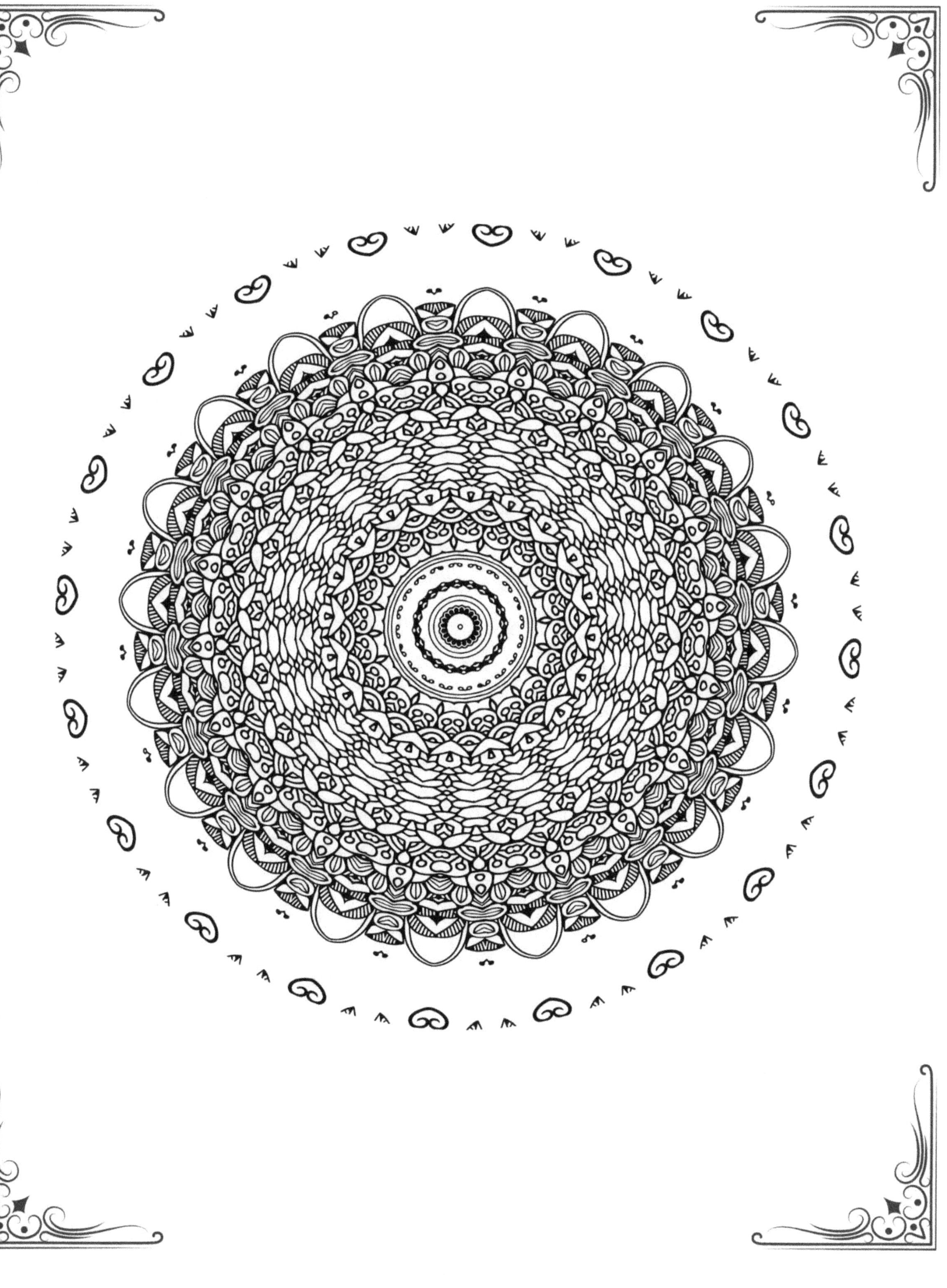

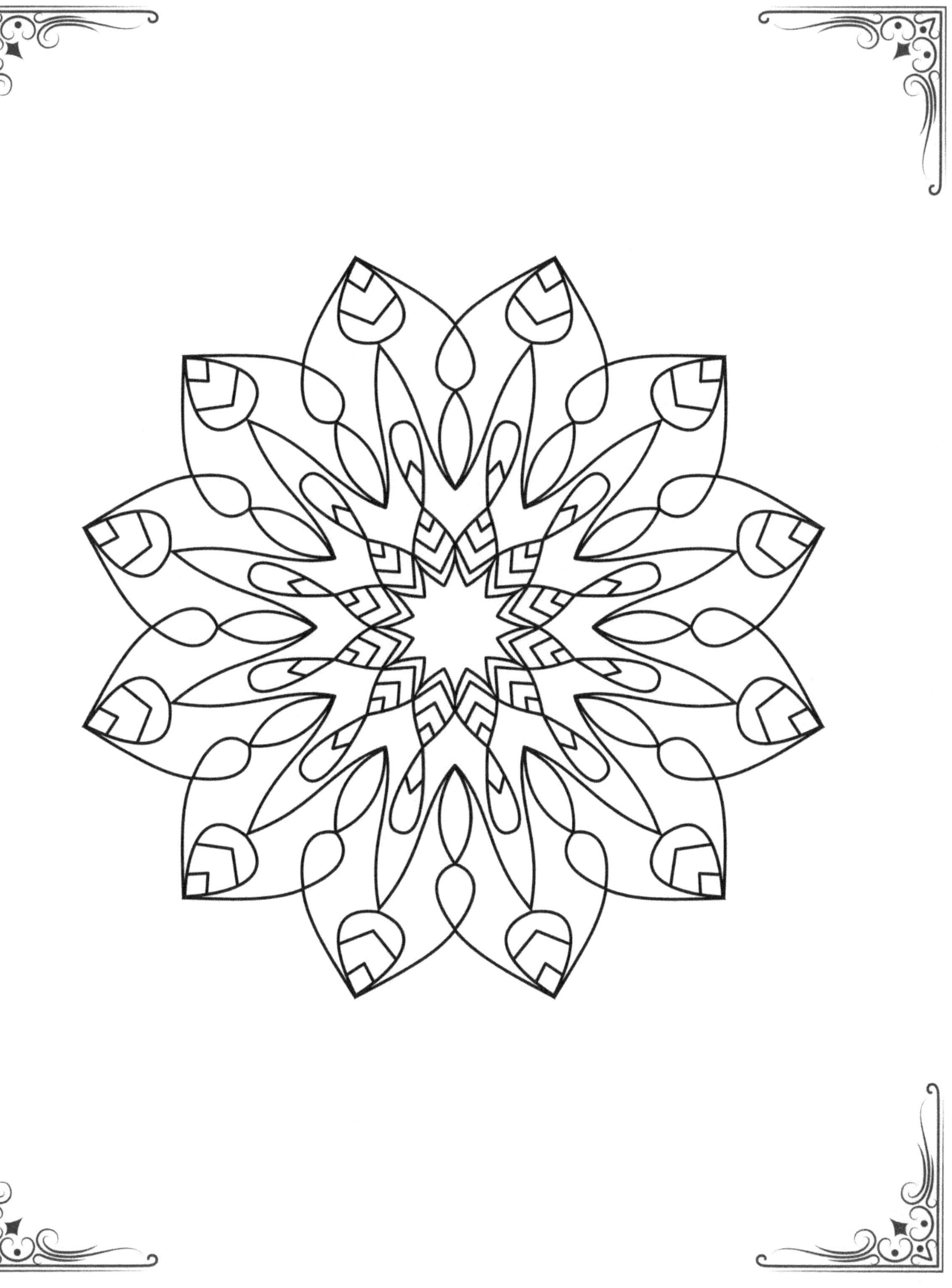

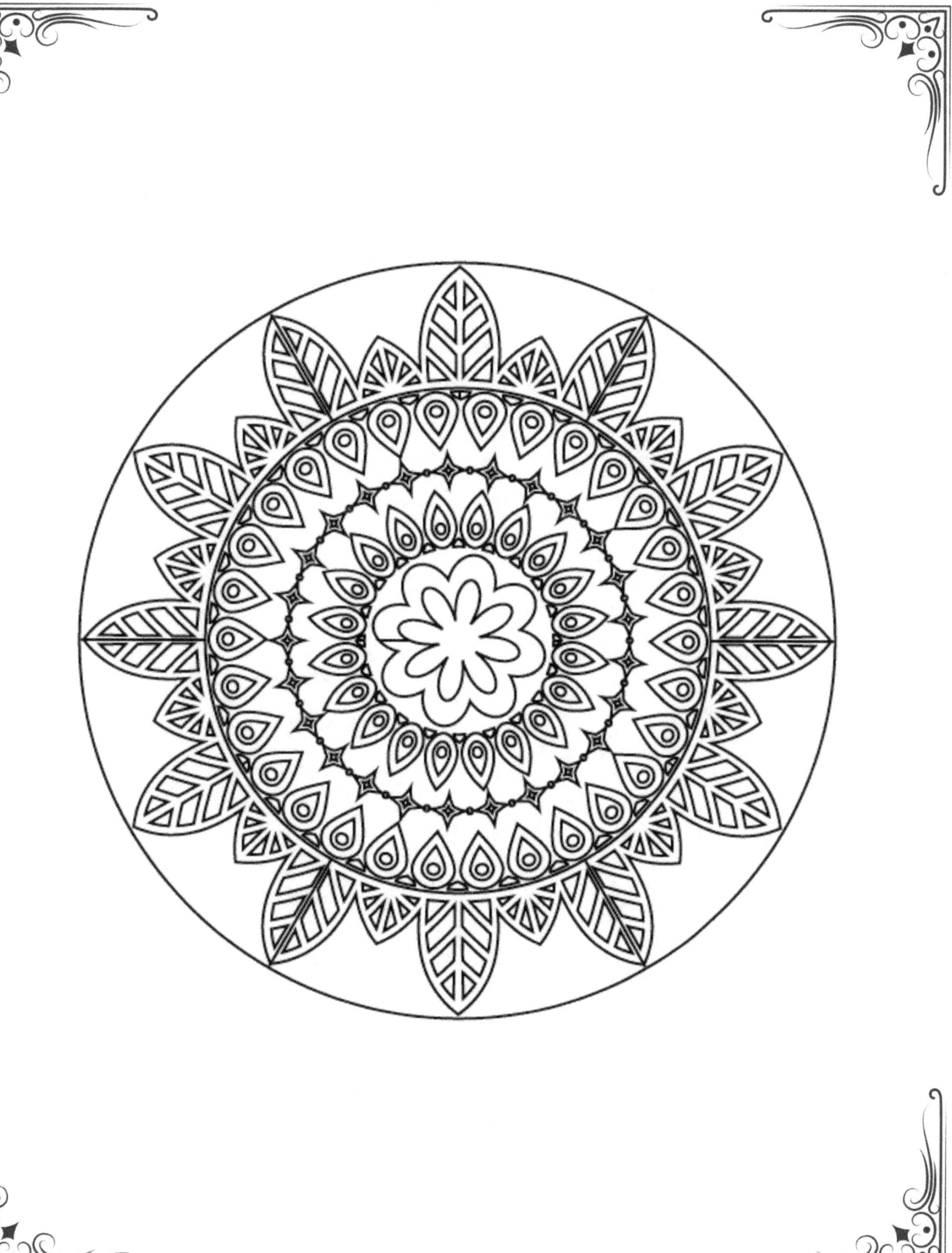

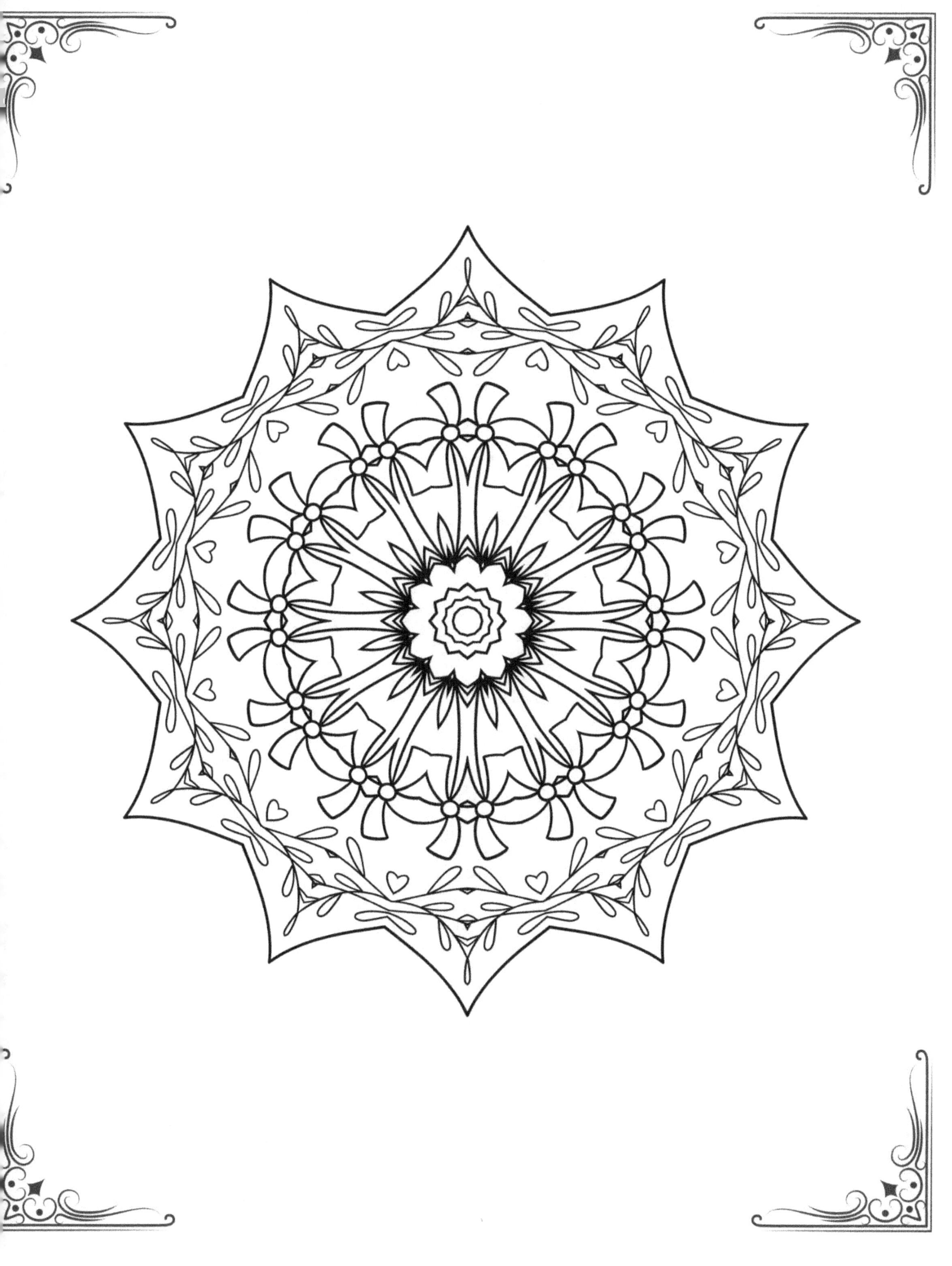

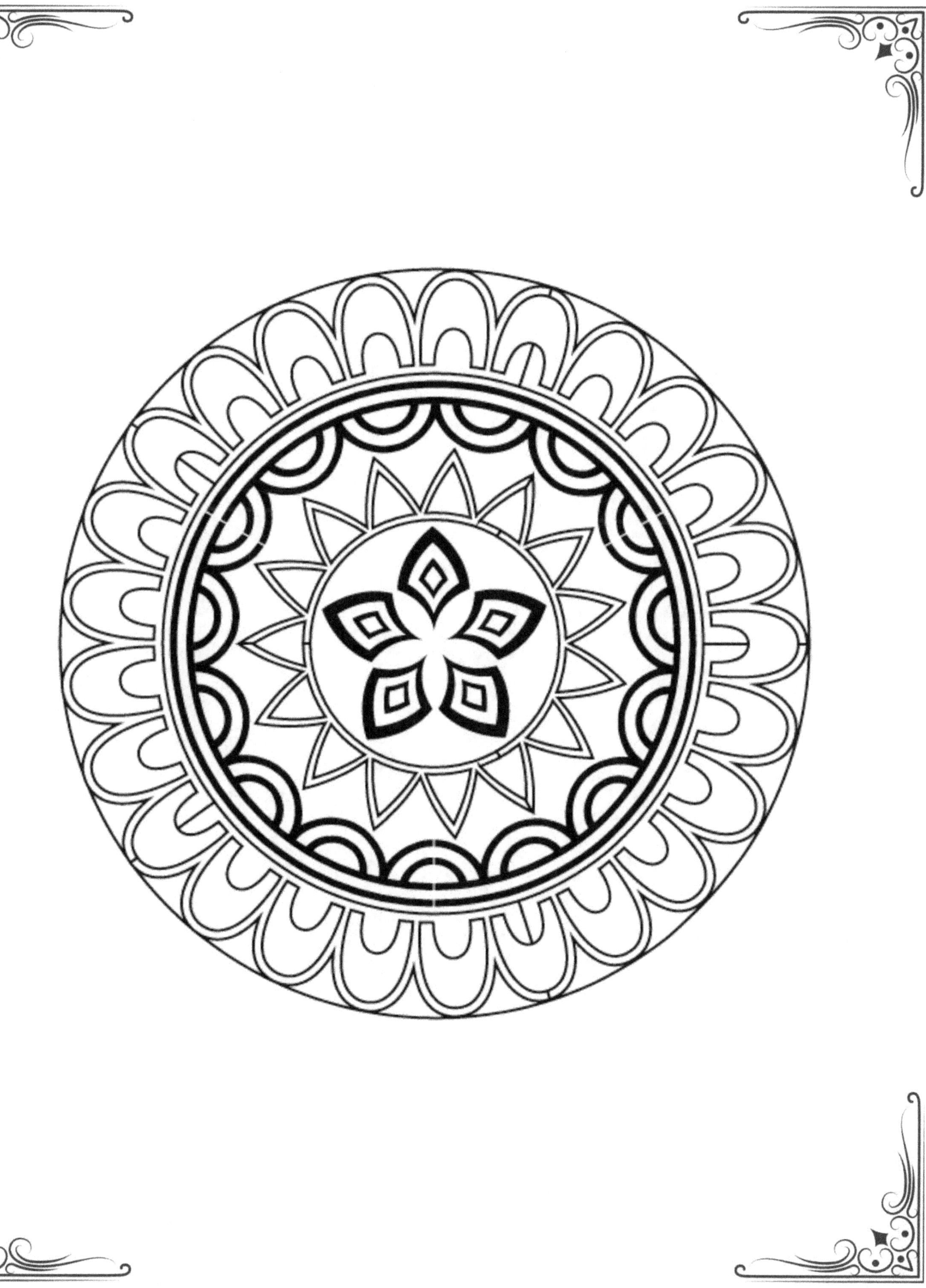

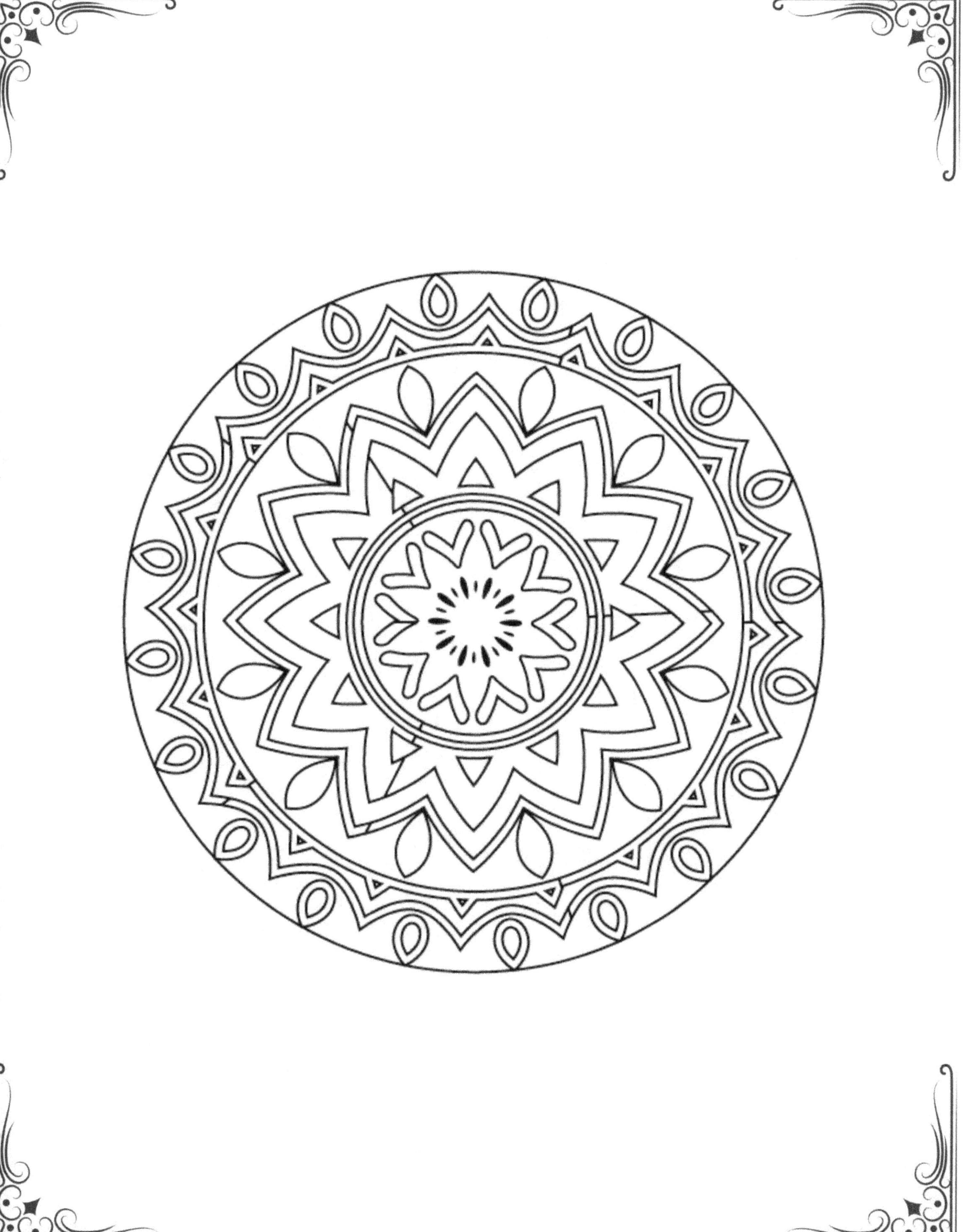

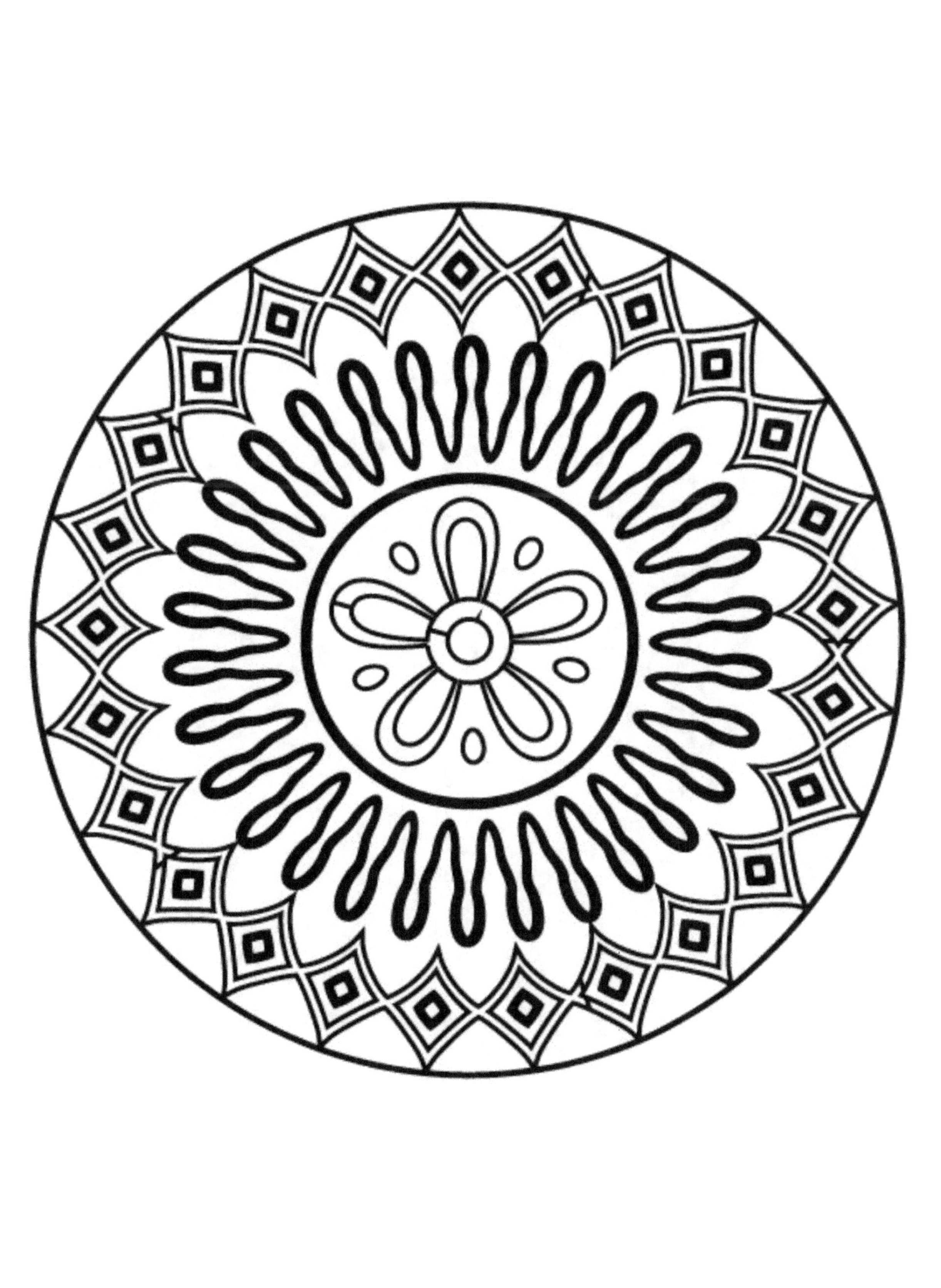

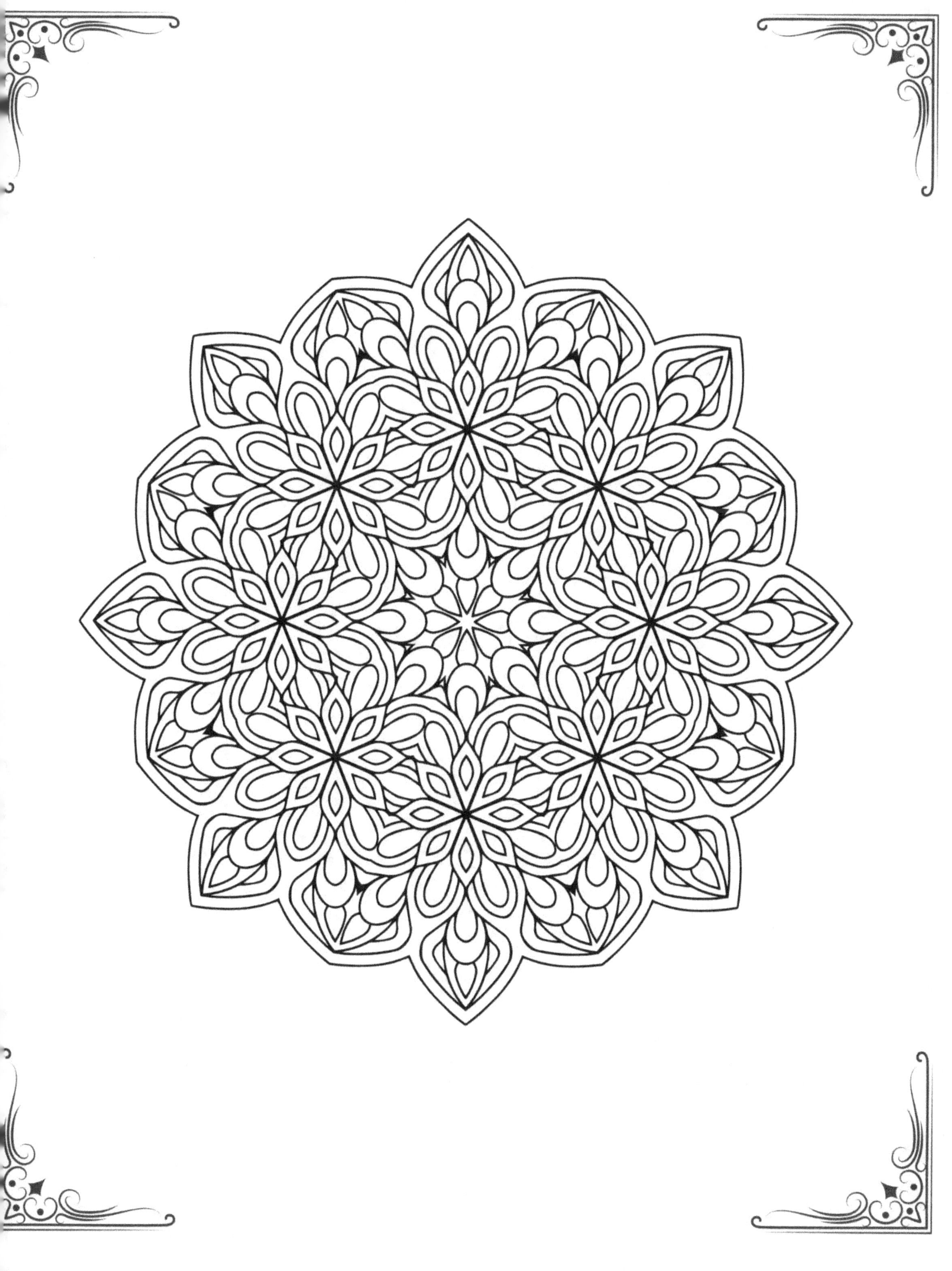

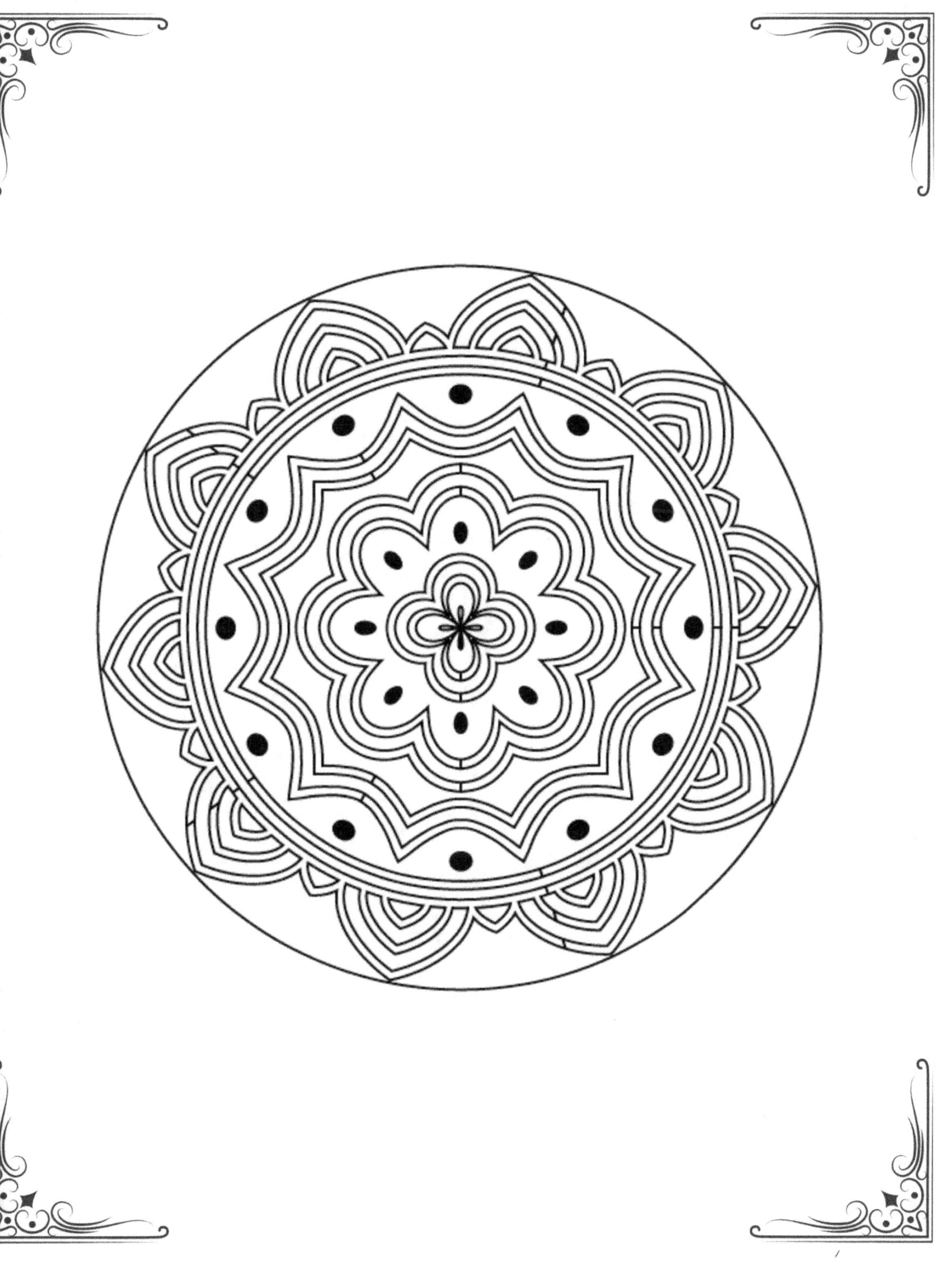

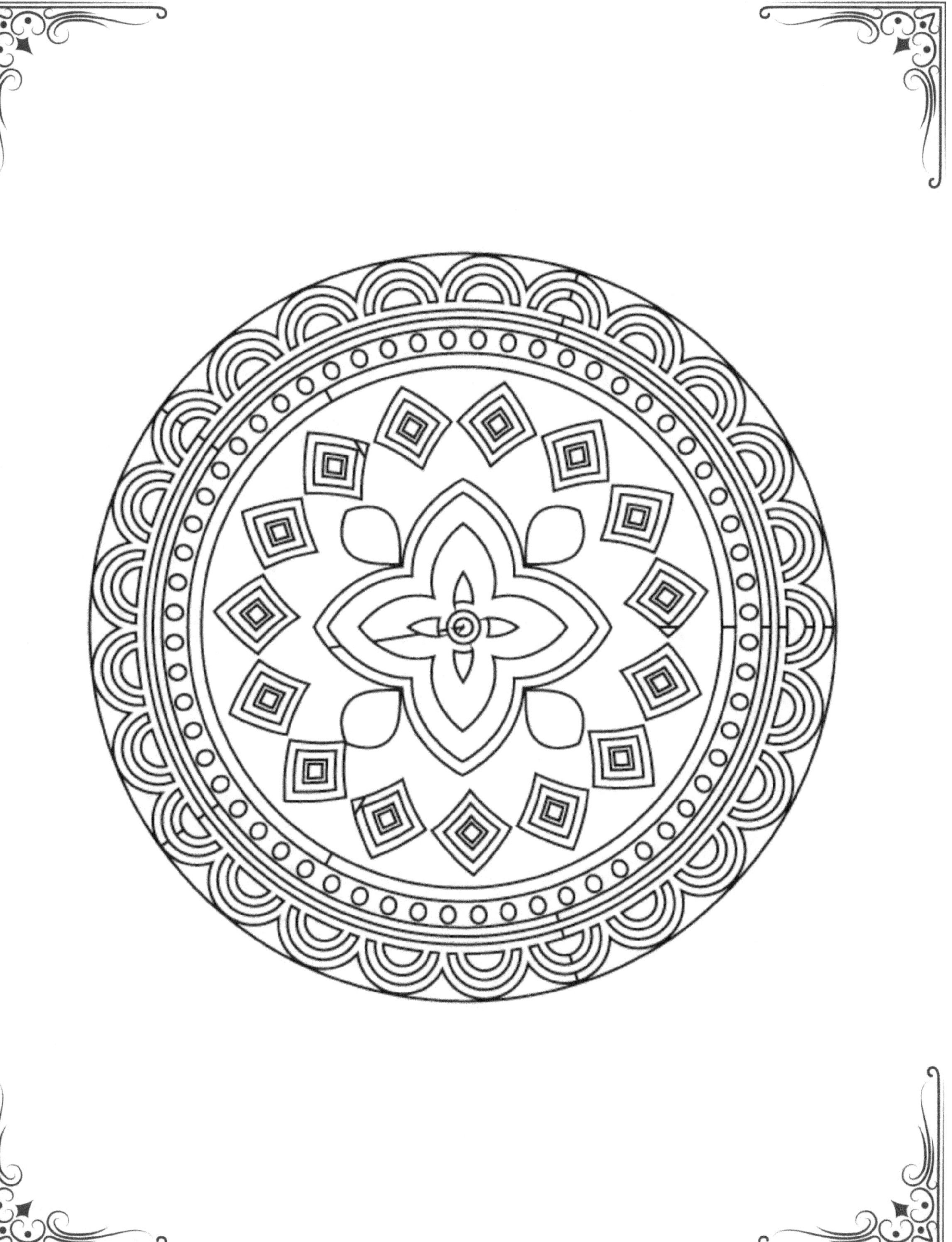

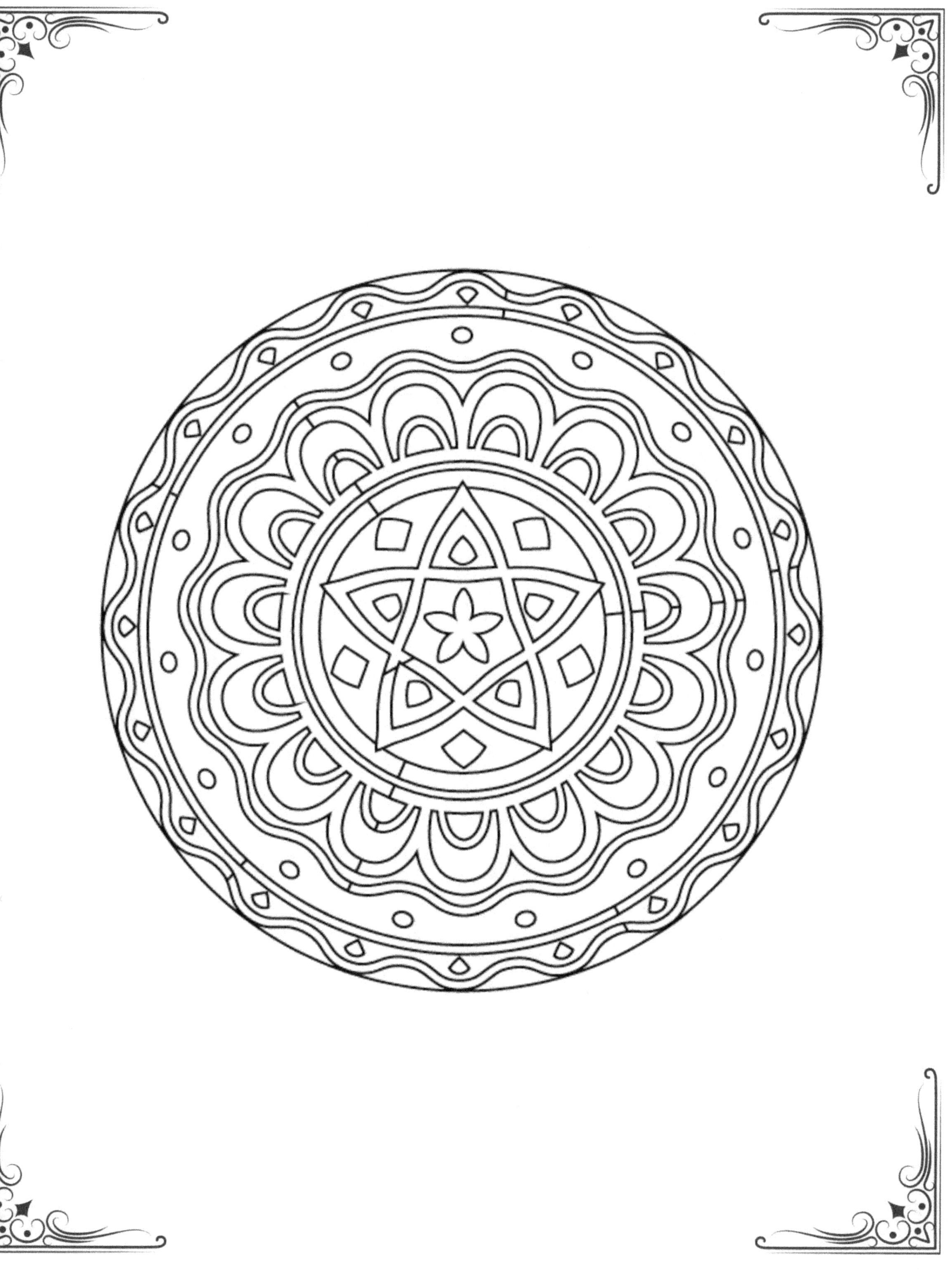

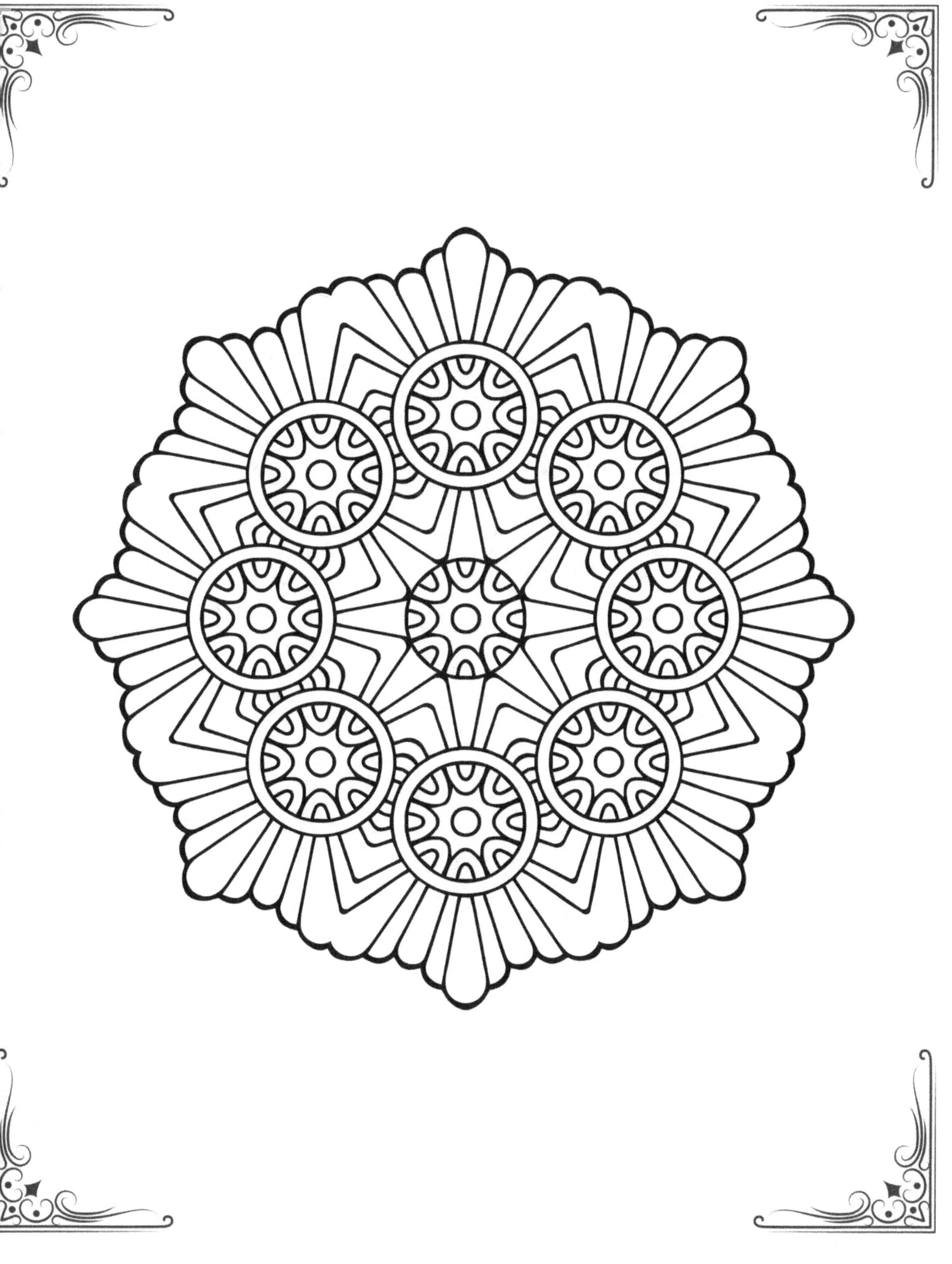

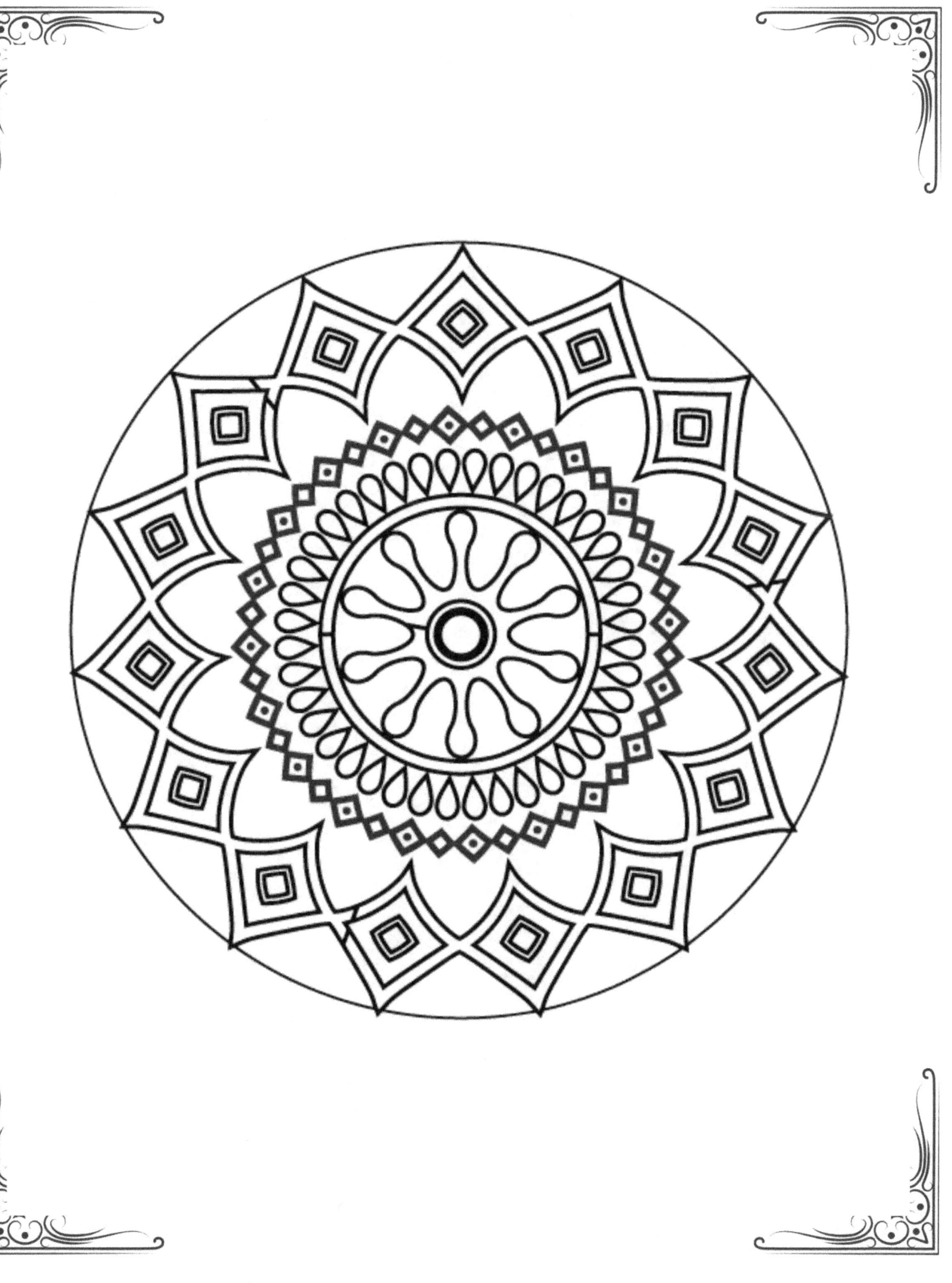

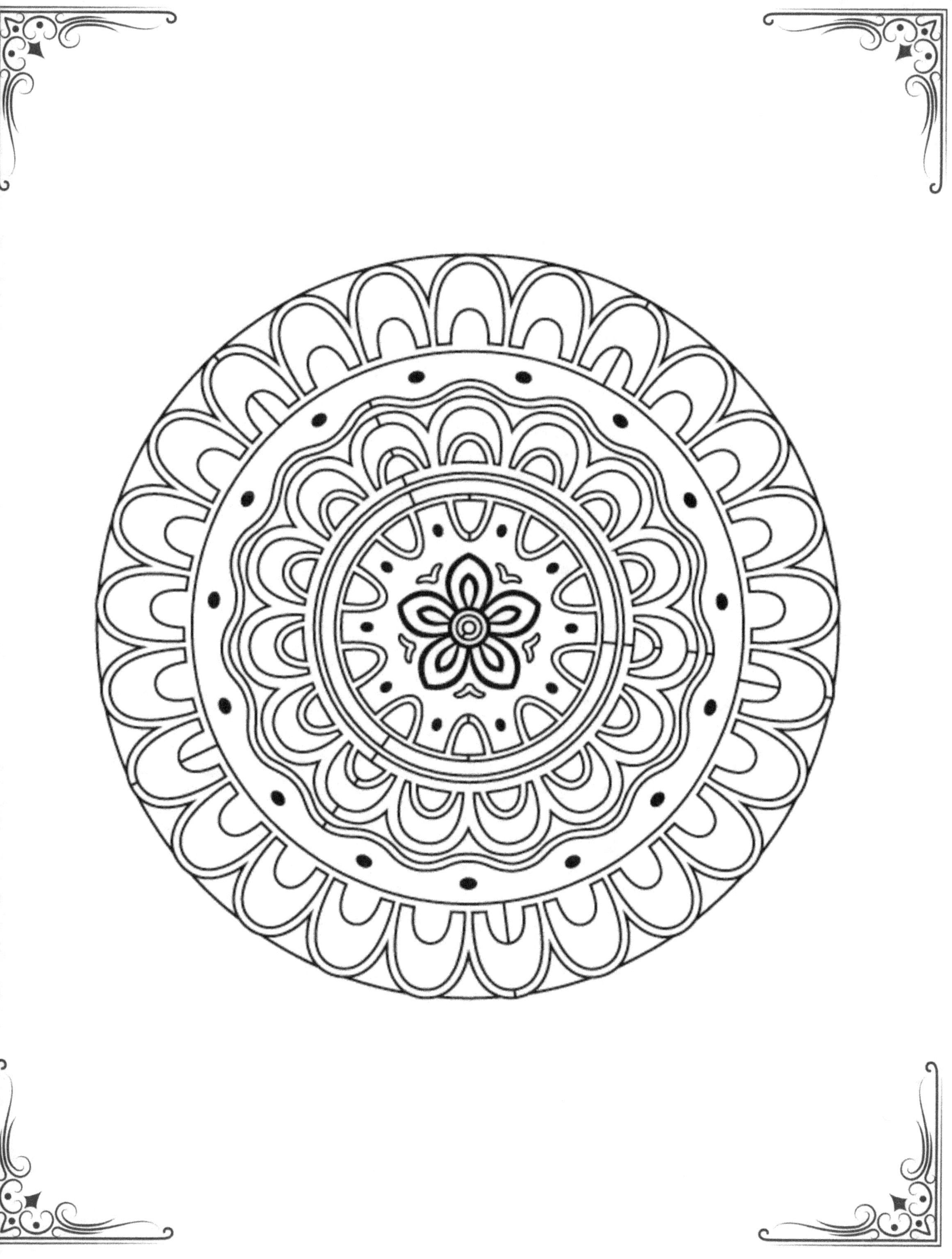

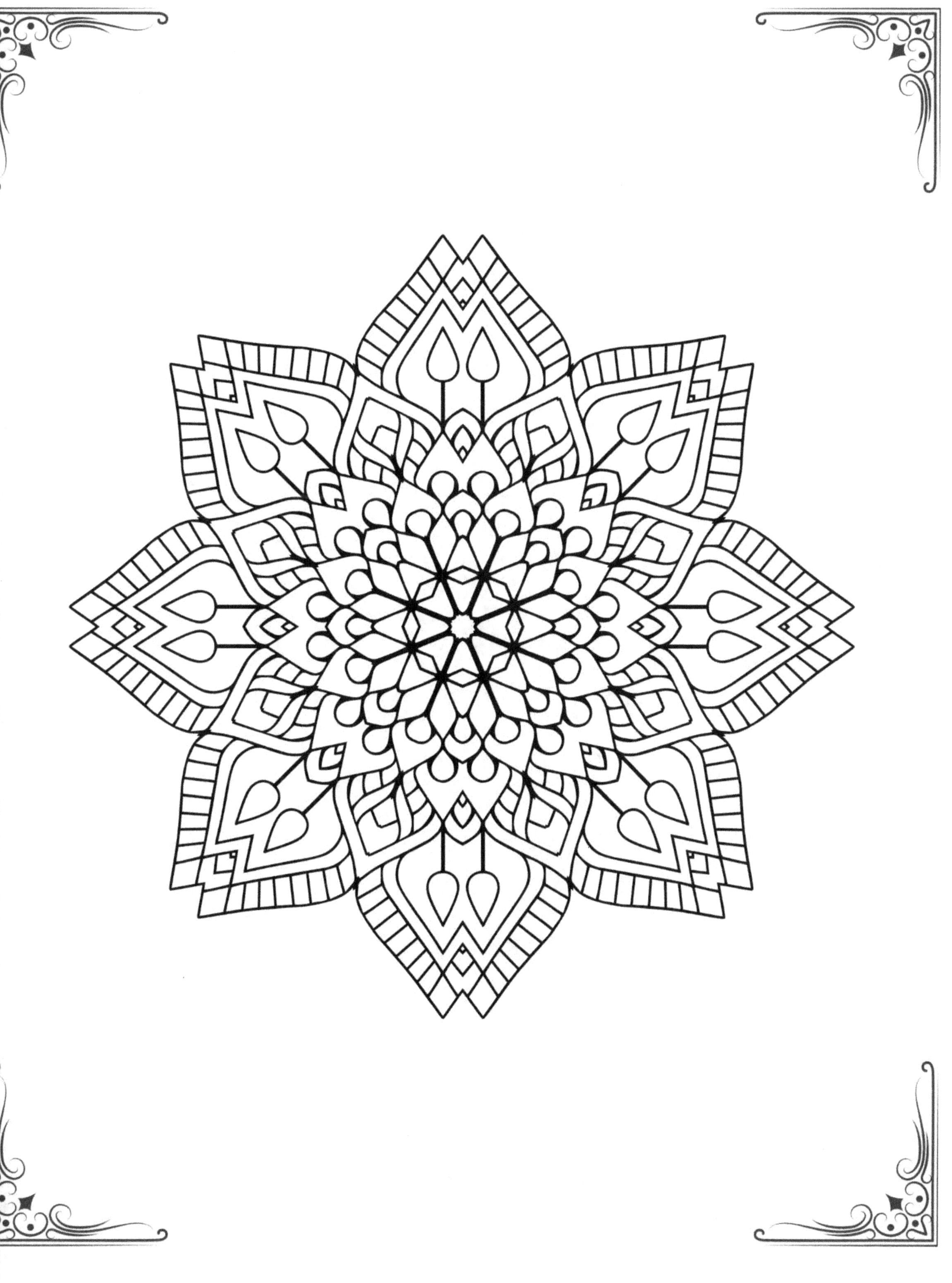

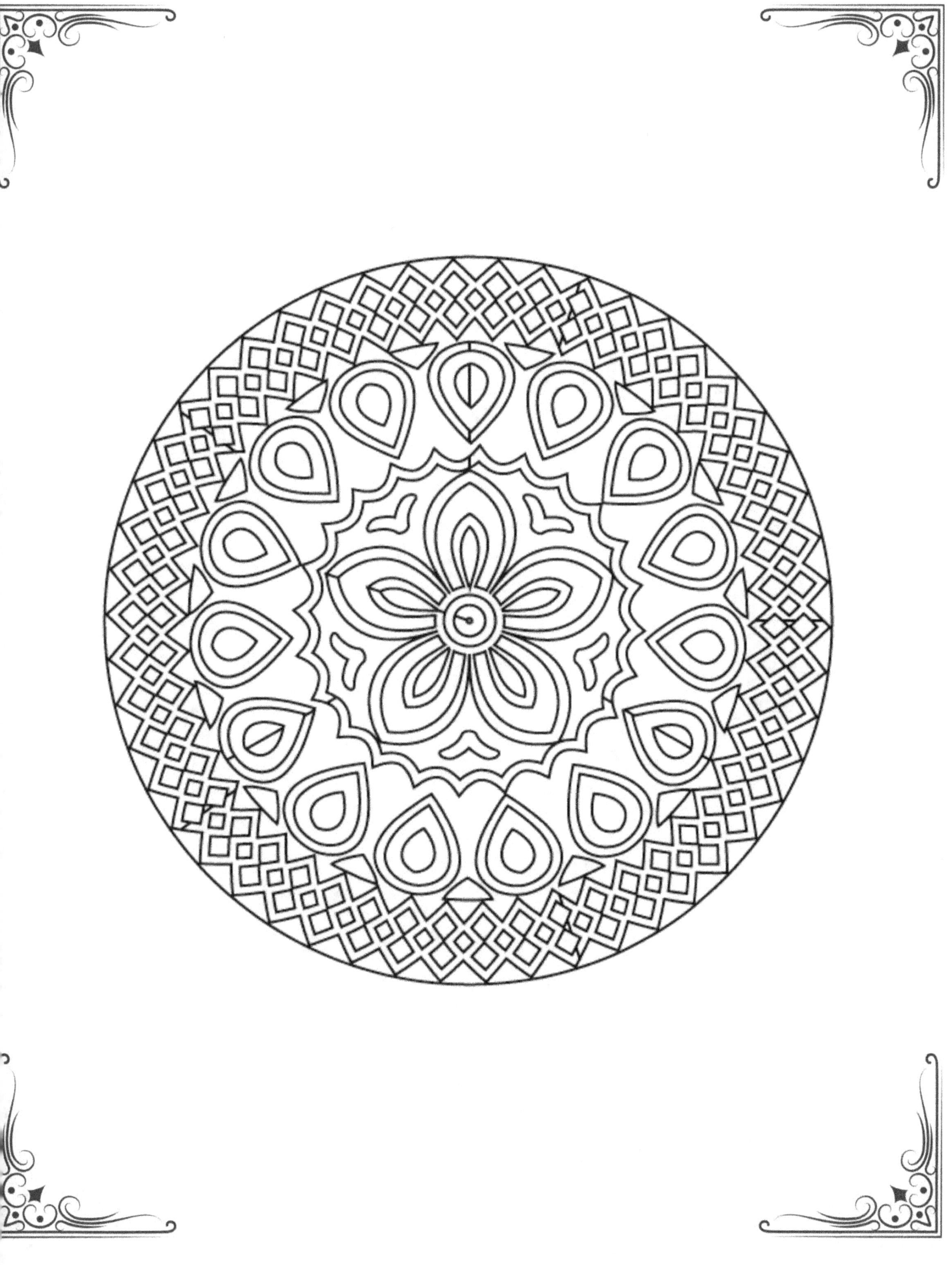

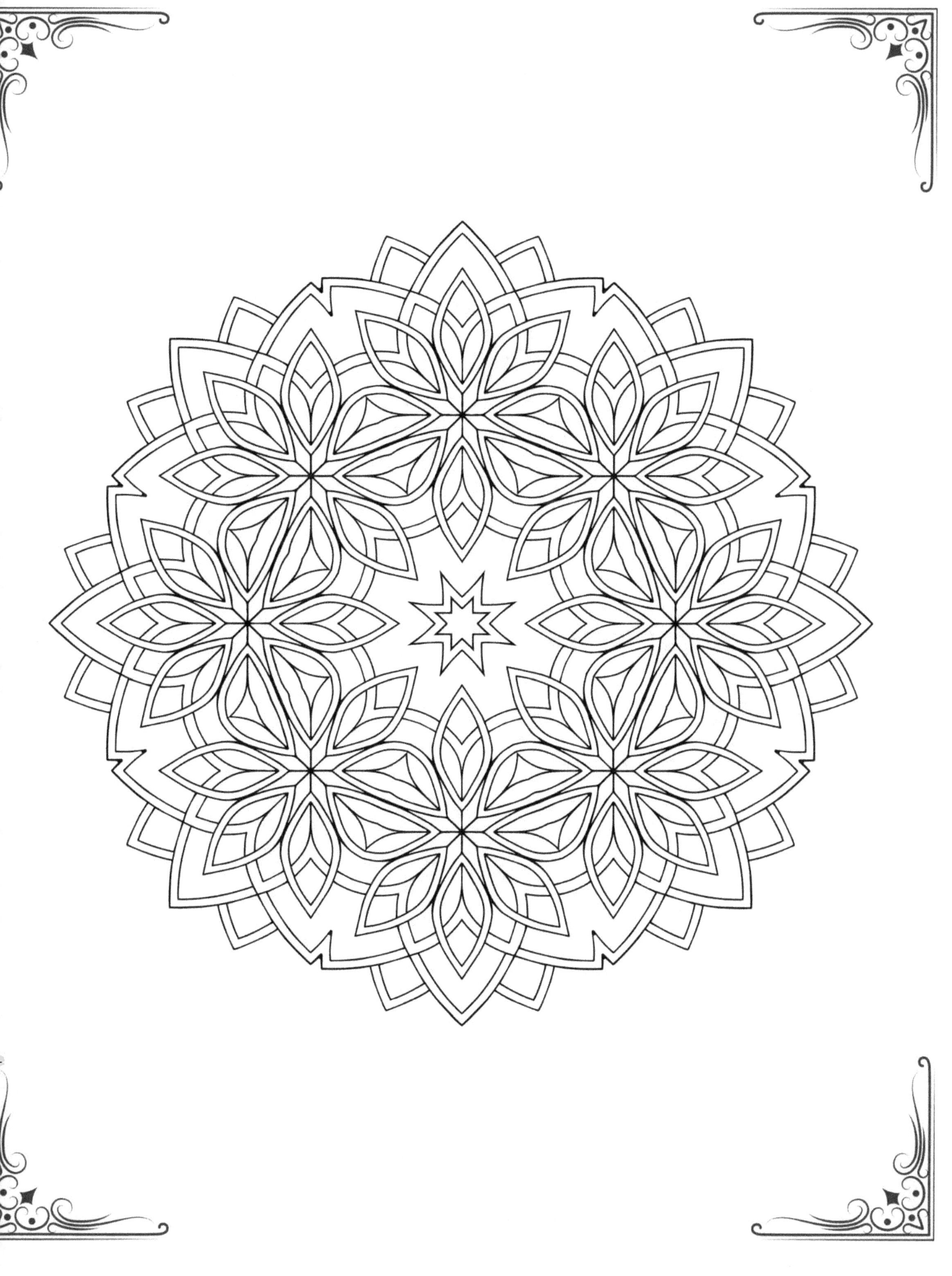

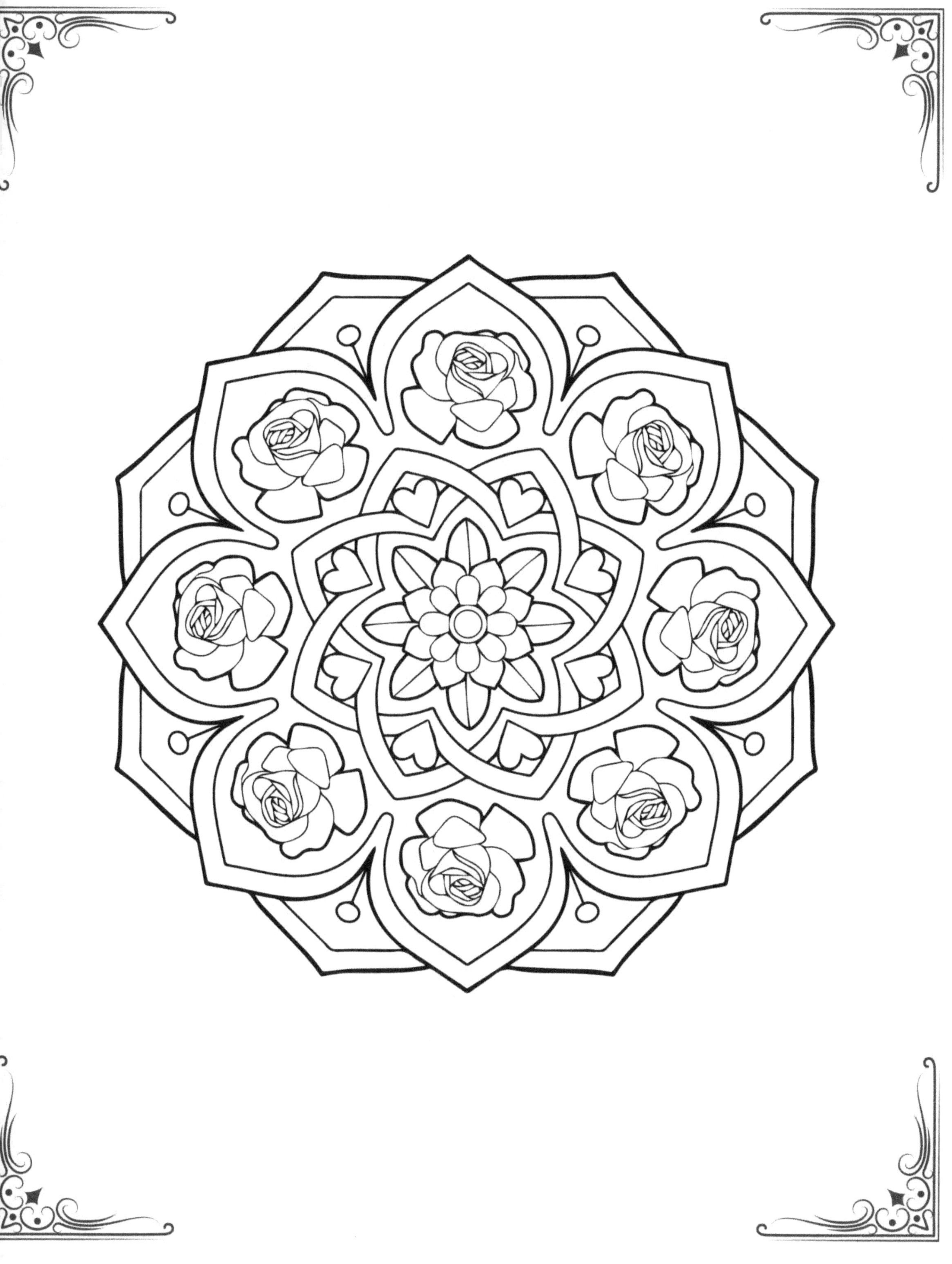

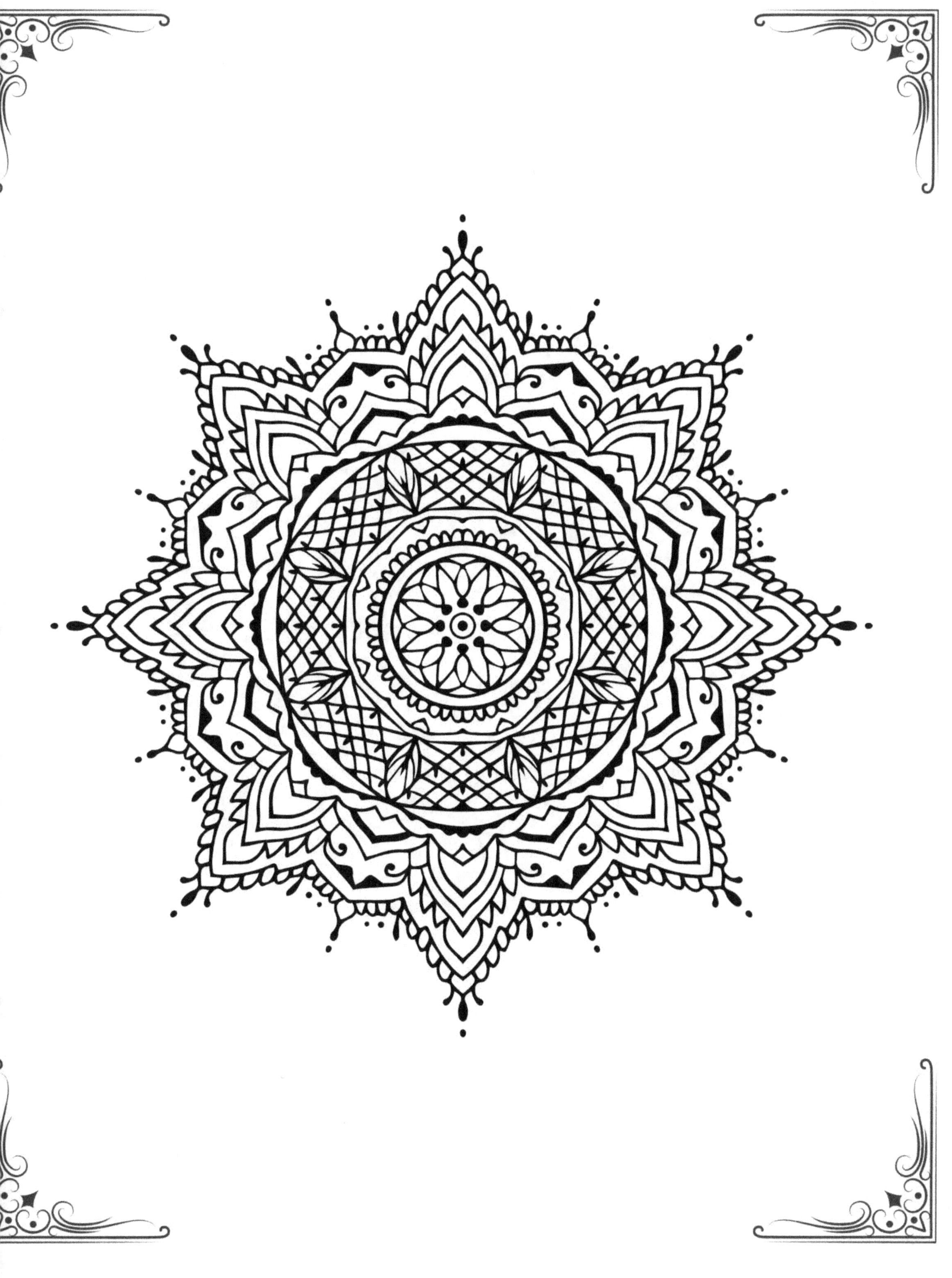

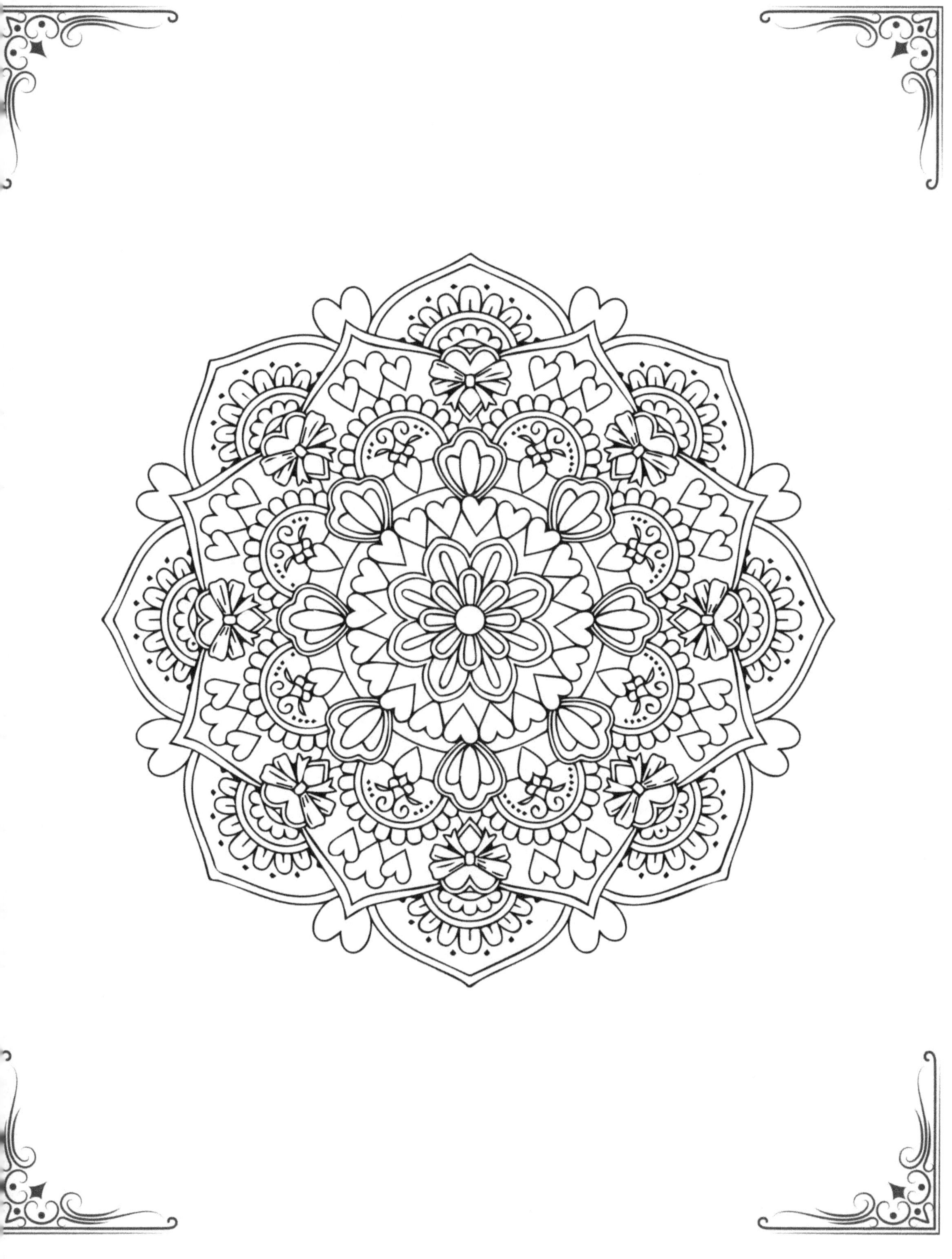

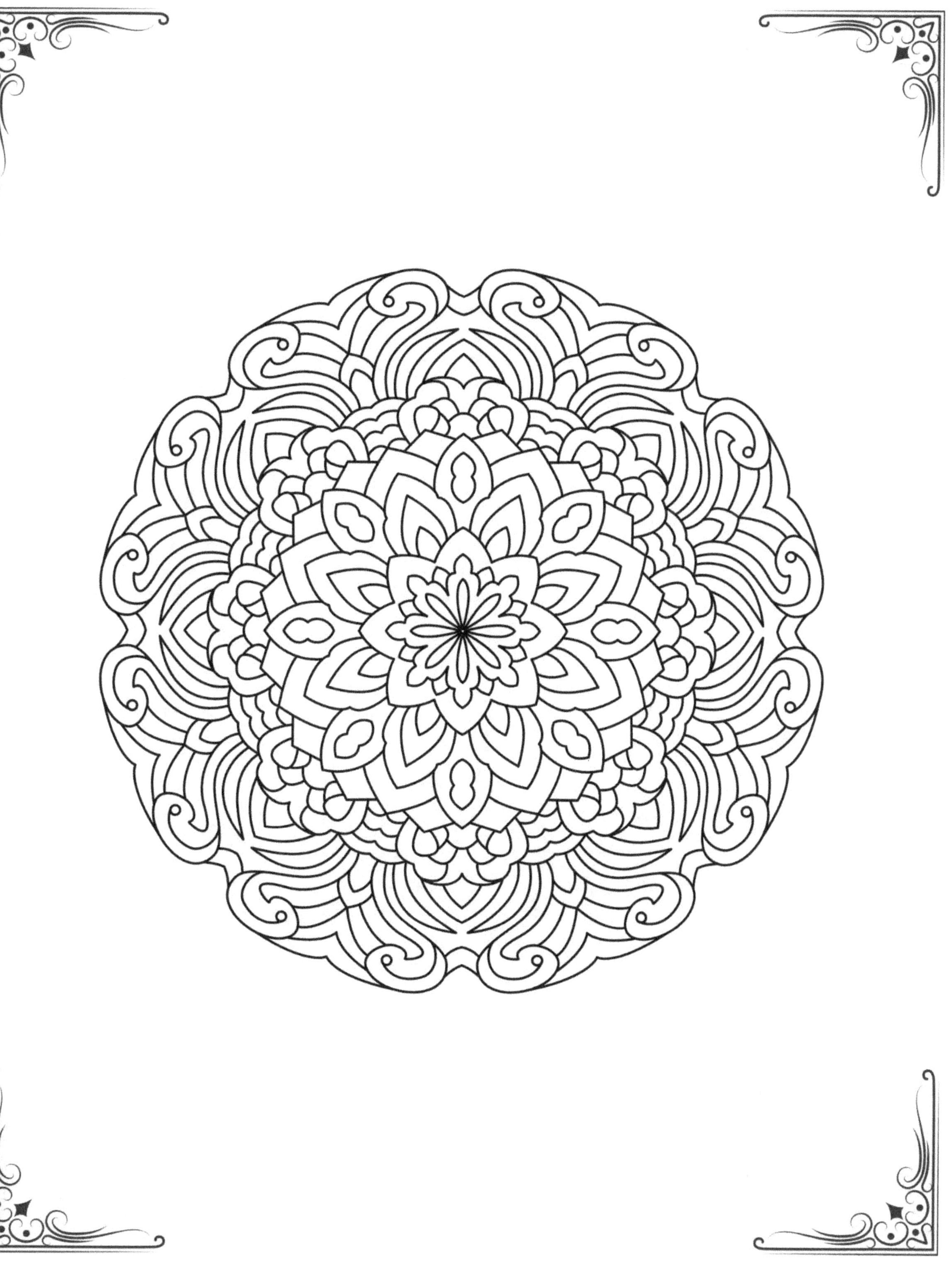